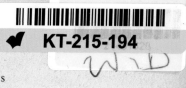

PENGUIN BOOKS

Not on the Label

Felicity Lawrence is an award-winning journalist and editor who has been writing on food-related issues for over twenty years. She is consumer affairs correspondent for the *Guardian* and lives in London.

Not on the Label

*What Really Goes into the
Food on Your Plate*

FELICITY LAWRENCE

PENGUIN BOOKS

For Matt, Anna, Cecy and Ellie

PENGUIN BOOKS

Published by the Penguin Group
Penguin Books Ltd, 80 Strand, London WC2R ORL, England
Penguin Group (USA) Inc., 375 Hudson Street, New York, New York 10014, USA
Penguin Books Australia Ltd, 250 Camberwell Road,
Camberwell, Victoria 3124, Australia
Penguin Books Canada Ltd, 10 Alcorn Avenue, Toronto, Ontario, Canada M4V 3B2
Penguin Books India (P) Ltd, 11 Community Centre,
Panchsheel Park, New Delhi – 110 017, India
Penguin Group (NZ), Cnr Airborne and Rosedale Roads, Albany,
Auckland 1310, New Zealand
Penguin Books (South Africa) (Pty) Ltd, 24 Sturdee Avenue,
Rosebank 2196, South Africa

Penguin Books Ltd, Registered Offices: 80 Strand, London WC2R ORL, England

www.penguin.com

Published in Penguin Books 2004
8

Copyright © Felicity Lawrence, 2004
All rights reserved

The moral right of the author has been asserted

Set in 11/13 pt PostScript Monotype Bembo
Typeset by Rowland Phototypesetting Ltd, Bury St Edmunds, Suffolk
Printed in England by Clays Ltd, St Ives plc

Contents

Acknowledgements

Much of my recent research into the food and farming industry has been carried out in my role as consumer affairs correspondent for the *Guardian*, and I am grateful to many colleagues at the newspaper who have encouraged me or shared their knowledge. In particular I should like to thank my editors Alan Rusbridger, Georgina Henry, Ian Katz, Harriet Sherwood and David Leigh, and my fellow correspondents John Vidal, Matthew Fort, Paul Brown and James Meikle. Stuart Millar and Leslie Plommer worked with me on The Way We Eat Now series, in which some of my pieces were first published.

My interest in the politics of food was sparked over twenty years ago by Caroline Walker and her husband Geoffrey Cannon, who first taught me how to investigate. Professors Tim Lang and Aubrey Sheiham have explained the system to me over many years. Tim Lang read large parts of the manuscript. Tim Lobstein and Kath Dalmeny at the Food Commission have been a constant source of information and inspiration. I am also grateful to Ed Mayo and the New Economics Foundation.

Don Pollard has worked for over ten years to bring to public notice the terrible conditions suffered by migrant workers in the food industry. Nuno Guerreiro has tirelessly supported Portuguese workers in the UK. Both gave generously of their time.

Patrick Holden and Craig Sams of the Soil Association helped me understand the power structures of the current farming system. Caroline Lucas, MEP, has shared her detailed knowledge on trade and the environment.

Alex von Tunzelmann provided research on soya and corn; Bibi van der Zee helped with Spanish translations.

For expert editing I am most grateful to Kate Barker, who

transformed the manuscript. At Penguin I am also grateful to Juliet Annan, Helen Campbell, Keith Taylor and Helena Peacock. Bill Hamilton, my agent, provided endless encouragement and was an invaluable sounding-board. Kate Parkin gave lots of moral support.

My husband, Matthew Bullard, opened my eyes to the developing world, and managed to keep cooking throughout the book's gestation.

I should also say a word of thanks to all those press officers at the major supermarkets and the Food Standards Agency who have answered my questions with such forbearance.

Finally, I should like to thank all those who gave me information who cannot be identified, but without whom much of this book could not have been written.

Introduction

In 1991 I came back to London after two years living in the Pakistani border town of Peshawar, working with refugees from Afghanistan's endless wars. My return to Western civilization came via the supermarket, since in order to celebrate my home-coming friends were preparing a special dinner. Shopping for it, as for most meals in industrialized countries these days, began and ended with a drive to the nearest big retailer.

I remember that shopping trip clearly because it was both exciting and, in some way I couldn't put my finger on at the time, vaguely troubling. I had been isolated from British culture for two years and I was experiencing the peculiar sense of dislocation that comes with seeing everything that was once so familiar as if for the first time. I was briefly glimpsing our food system from the outside.

Food from home is one of the things you most look forward to when you're abroad. I was almost drooling with anticipated pleasure as we drove past the boarded-up shops and cheap fast-food outlets in our high street. I had dreamed of sizzling bacon, soft smelly cheeses, fine wine and English chocolate. I chatted with my friend about the astonishing number of good foods you could find in supermarkets now, everything imaginable available in a one-stop motorized shop. As we queued for what seemed an age to get into the car park, we talked about how convenient it all was compared with life in a war-zone. Then, as our turn to go through the barrier came, my friend accelerated into a parking space, narrowly beating another car approaching it from the opposite direction. In Pakistan parking to shop had merely entailed swinging a pick-up truck in at right angles to a market stall, so I was momentarily startled by this uncharacteristic display of traffic-induced aggression. But there was no time to think about it.

We charged through the sliding doors, grabbing a wonky trolley on the way, and got going in the fresh fruit and vegetable section. It was full of produce from all round the world, things I had not only not seen while I was away, but couldn't remember being there before I left either: wonderful fresh herbs, different varieties of potatoes, summer asparagus alongside winter roots, the quintessentially English next to the temptingly tropical. 'Don't suppose you got much of this while you were out there,' my friend said. It was true that in the refugee camps there had been hunger, and malnutrition remains a semi-permanent spectre in some parts of Afghanistan. But in the relative safety of the border areas the problem was not lack of food but lack of money for it and lack of clean water. In fact we had been surrounded by plenty.

The Afghans are great traders and the bazaars were always full of fresh goods from the surrounding region. But people lived by the seasons, things came and went. The cool hills of the Swat valley produced mouth-watering strawberries for just two weeks a year. Grapes from the glacier-fed vineyards were sweeter than any I'd ever tasted, but they disappeared at the end of autumn. Mangoes, dripping with juice, lasted longer. There were tedious in-between weeks when the excitement of the first of the season's oranges had worn off and there was nothing much else in prospect.

Back in Britain, permanent global summertime had arrived. It looked awesome: row upon row of identically shaped, identically sized and identically coloured fruits; stack upon stack of blemish-free vegetables. I wondered if a genius in a white lab coat had invented it while I was away. But there was something missing. Under the glare of fluorescent light and against the hum of chiller cabinets, it took a while to work it out. Then I realized – there was no smell. No point in picking up the fruit here and feeling it or sniffing it to see how good it would taste. It was all hard, unripe and odourless. It was also heavily packaged. Wandering round the narrow lanes of Peshawar's old city had by contrast been an intense sensory and social experience. The pungent smells of spices and meat cooking over charcoal were irresistible; the air was always heady with the perfume of ripe melons, plums or cherries, overlaid with a faint whiff of human ordure. And despite the well-aimed jabs from men affronted by the presence of a Western woman, however well covered, there would be endless cups of green tea proffered by traders you visited regularly.

Where I had been living, suffering from V and D as it was cheerfully called (vomiting and diarrhoea) was as common as catching a cold. At least the supermarket food in its sterile packages could be counted on not to make you sick – yet oddly, people in Britain seemed to be worrying about food poisoning too. There were more and more cases of it, apparently. It wasn't just eggs; factory meat too was a bit of a worry now, according to my friend. Dressed in cling-filmed trays, like samples from an operating theatre, it looked fine to me: what was all the fuss about? I was impatient to get to the cheese aisle, where I could have agonized for hours over the enormous choice, though it seemed a shame that these too were not yet ripe. I was dispatched instead to fetch breakfast from the cereal aisle. How to choose here between the dozens and dozens of different packages on offer? Their labels were all variations on the same theme: wheat/maize, sugar and salt. I had forgotten there were twenty ways to process and market near-identical ingredients.

There were, it seemed, just two mental states possible on these shopping expeditions: everyone was either in an inexplicable rush, trolley primed in front like a weapon, or in a slow-motion daze, trolley drifting to the side in a defensive arc. That evening we were in the former state of inexplicable rush. Heads down, got to get it all done in an hour after work. The main thing was to avoid eye-contact, since it might trigger all those minor social obligations that would slow you down. Where have they moved the eggs to this week? Why do they keep moving things anyway?

Which is the shortest queue? Damn, the other one. Damn again, forgotten something. Too late now. The girl on the till was shovelling everything along the belt without glancing at us, and a line of people was huffing and puffing behind. There, all done in fifty-five minutes. We had a delicious dinner.

The sense of weirdness soon wore off. Since then, I have spent several years writing about food, and in the early 1990s I worked with Delia Smith and her husband, Michael Wynn Jones, as they launched *Sainsbury's Magazine*. Delia showed a whole new audience how to enjoy the global products now on offer. Part of her genius was to bring things which had previously been the preserve of exclusive delis – and sometimes, frankly, food snobs – within ordinary people's reach for the first time. I would rush home from work to try out the recipes myself. And once a week I would drive to the supermarket and fling everything into my trolley with the best of them.

But gradually, as a mother at home with small children, I began to look on the supermarket raid with dread. I knew I'd probably emerge hassled, with a bawling baby to manage. When my second child arrived, I knew I couldn't face loading two children into the car each time I needed something. Besides, we wanted somewhere to walk to pass the day, so I started shopping locally on foot again. Our high street had become run down, but there was still a good butcher, a hippy organic baker with odd hours, an ironmonger and a greengrocer. I found I got to know people this way, not just people whose circumstances were similar to ours, but people we would never have met before, from different generations. It was slower, more relaxed. I felt part of a neighbourhood for the first time.

On holidays in France, we went to the markets that still thrive in small towns. We'd be amazed at how much more successful the French were at hanging on to their culinary culture – at their pride in local produce and at the time they were prepared to devote to it. We stayed in places where shopkeepers still say 'Bon appetit!' as they close at noon for three hours and go home for long lunches. How many women must be chained to the kitchen sink preparing them, I always remembered to say as we flew home.

For all the sophistication of food production in the UK, a sense of loss lingered. The ritual that surrounds cooking and eating in countries where food cannot be taken for granted is often glaringly absent where it is available in excess. In our rush to remove the labour from feeding ourselves, we have lost the cultural significance of meals. Occasionally as I gobbled a sandwich at my desk, wolfed fast food on the run or threw together a meal of pre-cut chicken and ready chopped vegetables, I remembered the simple meals from communal bowls set on a Baluch carpet in a refugee's mud house, where the business of eating was serious. It wasn't just about fuel, it was the focus of human interaction. Sitting together over food was where adults exchanged news and views, where children learned to communicate. To eat alone was to be sad, uncivilized.

Paradoxically, as we have become more affluent as a nation, we have also become more anxious about our food and how it is produced. Although few of us in developed countries have to worry about hunger, food scares have come in rapid succession. First, salmonella in eggs, then BSE, then foot and mouth disease, then banned antibiotics in meat and honey, and chemical contaminants in fresh fish. We have learned that governments and their experts cannot necessarily be trusted to tell us the truth about what we eat. We have also learned that there are many things about the rapidly changing methods of food production that they either do not understand or cannot control.

There have been dozens of scares since. Although in some cases the risks might have turned out to be small, our anger and mistrust have grown as we realize that it is we who bear the risk while the benefit goes to the food and farming industry.

I have spent the last three years investigating the global food system for the *Guardian*. The ironies that struck me on my return to the West over ten years ago are more apparent now, the problems much deeper than I understood then. As I travelled around learning about food in Europe – meeting pig farmers in Suffolk, migrant workers in Spain, or chicken processors from Holland – or further afield – talking to prawn farmers in Vietnam, vegetable packers in Kenya, coffee farmers in Uganda, or migrating smallholders in Thailand – I began to see a pattern.

The damage to the landscape, the collapse of commodity prices, the exploitation of labour, the epidemics of disease and obesity, the concentrations of power we all worry about, are not the work of random or separate forces. The anxiety that has manifested itself in a succession of food scares is justified. I believe we are in the middle of one of the most significant revolutions since settled agriculture began 10,000 years ago. It is a revolution on a scale with the upheavals of our Industrial Revolution, both in its human and environmental impact. But this time it is global, not just national. It is a revolution whose social and ecological consequences we have so far failed to address.

Many of the ills of the current food system are ones foreseen by the anti-globalists and the anti-capitalists. But I am not anti-globalization: I do not believe we can resist its tidal wave any more than weavers could resist the Industrial Revolution. Nor am I anti-capitalist: you can hardly look to the achievements of Soviet collectivization of farms for alternatives to the free market. In fact, when you look at the structure of the food system, it becomes clear that many of the problems arise because food markets are not free markets, as I hope some of my journeys will show.

But nor do I think we can reduce everything to mere monetary value in the name of the free market. Farming has shaped our landscape over centuries. Millions of people around the world depend on food production for their living. We all eat; we all need good food. To imagine these are matters that can be confined to pure economics, with no reference to broader social policy, is lunacy. Food is, and always has been, about politics.

By any standard, our current system needs urgent reform. Just how urgent hit me recently in a field in East Anglia, when I found myself surrounded by young Iraqi men in a Portakabin filled with cigarette smoke and loud talking. With characteristic Kurdish hospitality, they insisted on sharing with me the only food they had – a packet of Rich Tea biscuits – while we got to grips with what they were doing wearing hairnets on a farm in the middle of the Fens.

I was investigating the use of migrant labour in the food industry and had come to watch the vegetable harvest at the invitation of a large-scale producer who grows and packs for the supermarkets. We had had a long and honest telephone conversation about the extent to which the food and farming industry in this country is dependent on foreign labour and how difficult it can be to make sure that it is supplied on the right side of the law, even when you check the papers. This particular farmer was expecting to bring in seventy-odd Lithuanians to pick and pack his harvest. 'They are good workers. We couldn't do without them.' But between our first talk and my arrival, a supermarket PR had become involved and the workers I had met the previous day on my guided tour of the fields and packhouses were somehow all local.

In the village pub that evening, the young farmers from neighbouring horticultural companies had gathered to let off steam. The jokes were all about the Bulgarian who drove the tractor straight at the barn. 'There I was waving my arms like a lunatic shouting, "Building, building!" but he just didn't get it.' And about the Lithuanian heavy who complained that the weather was too bad, the soil too wet, the packhouse too cold, and 'Can you believe it, he wanted to lie down!' I ended up staying the night.

Next morning I returned to the vegetable farm to say goodbye. Straying into a Portakabin loo, I was suddenly caught up in a surge of twenty-eight Iraqi Kurds pouring out of the huge packing shed next door for a brief break. There had been a brief moment of panic on both sides; then I tried a salaam and they produced the biscuits. It was a small gesture that created a bond between us – what food is about – and the antithesis of the system they were engaged in. They had been arranging root vegetables on plastic trays all morning for a supermarket order. Khaled, a charming, well-educated law student from Kirkuk, acted as their spokesman. We moved to one of the white minivans used to transport him and his friends on the hour-long drive to and from Peterborough each morning and evening, where he told me he had left Saddam's Iraq over eighteen months ago, paying smugglers to get him on to lorries, most of them food trucks, across Europe and into Britain. Some of the Afghans we had worked with in Peshawar had turned up in Britain by a similar route.

Khaled and his compatriots were living four to a small room, all in flats owned by his gangmaster. The gangmaster found them work. He deducted £25 a week rent from each of their pay packets, as well as tax and insurance, even though under the National Asylum Support Scheme they were not allowed to work, so the deductions had nowhere legitimate to go. They were doing twelve-hour shifts, from 6 a.m. to 6 p.m., for £3.50 an hour, and travelling made it a fourteen-hour day, often seven days a week. It was tough, boring and a little puzzling. 'We do not do this with our vegetables,' Khaled said.

Khaled explained how they had met hostility, sometimes open abuse, in Peterborough. 'People think we are ignorant. We are not ignorant, but we don't always understand your customs. There are different relationships between the individual and the community here, so we make mistakes. You will be my friend in London and we will share a proper meal together. Good Kurdish dishes, rice and nuts and pomegranate seeds and chicken.'

Well, perhaps not the chicken, Khaled, because that is where my investigations all started.

1. Chicken

It was the scald tank that got me in the end. I had expected trouble in the slaughter room, but we'd moved through there without incident. We'd already passed the electrocution bath and I'd slipped easily enough round the neck cutters slicing through carotid arteries. There wasn't as much blood as I'd feared.

I had been smuggled into a large chicken factory by a meat hygiene inspector who was worried about standards in the poultry industry. We were gazing into a hot-water tank into which the dead birds were being dipped at the rate of 180 a minute, to scald the skin and loosen the feathers before they went into the plucking machine.

It was 3 p.m. and as at many factories the water was only changed once a day. It was a brown soup of faeces and feather fragments and at 52°C 'the perfect temperature for salmonella and campylobacter organisms to survive and cross-contaminate the birds', the hygiene inspector pointed out. We moved on to the whirring rubber fingers which remove the feathers. 'Plucking machines exert considerable pressure on the carcass which tends to squeeze faecal matter out on to the production line. It only takes one bird colonized with campylobacter to infect the rest. The bacteria count goes up tenfold after this point,' he continued. I found myself wondering who had done the counting.

'But free-range and organic birds . . .' I started to ask without wanting to know the answer.

'. . . nearly all come through the same plants, yes. There's no difference except that in plants which process organic birds you can tell the organic ones. They are used to being allowed to run about a bit and so they try to escape when they are shackled.'

We went outside. There, towering stacks of birds in crates,

delivered earlier in the day by a procession of juggernauts, were being given a chance to calm down before being shunted into the slaughter room. They need to settle for the men to be able to pick them up by their feet and hang them upside down on the moving belt on which they begin their journey through the factory process.

The crates are made of plastic mesh with holes. The birds, which have typically been kept indoors all their lives, in twenty-three-hour-a-day low light for maximum productivity, tend to panic when they are caught and taken into the fresh air and daylight for the first time. As they open their bowels, the faeces fall from the crates at the top down through the tower on to those below.

'Pretty daft, isn't it?' the inspector said.

Half of the chicken on sale in UK supermarkets is contaminated with campylobacter. Campylobacter causes a nasty kind of food poisoning with severe, often bloody, diarrhoea. Although some worrying new strains of salmonella have been appearing recently, salmonella incidence generally has been falling, largely thanks to the vaccination of flocks, but food poisoning is still rising inexorably in this country, and chicken is the most common source of infection. Campylobacter can be killed by thorough cooking. Nevertheless the rise in the incidence of campylobacter infection in people mirrors the rise in chicken consumption.

'There isn't a great deal they can do when birds arrive at the factory with campylobacter in their gut. There are so many opportunities for cross-contamination,' Janet Corry, research fellow in food microbiology at the University of Bristol, told me. She had been generous with her time but sounded impatient with journalists writing exposés about chicken. 'Look, if you are going to process poultry at that price, there's not much you can do. The important thing is that they are killed humanely. The factories are designed to get them through fast. People want cheap food.'

Wander down the meat aisles of any supermarket and sure enough you will find mountains of chicken being sold at unbelievable prices. They're always there now, on 365-day 'special' offer. Chicken breasts: buy one, get one free . . . Chicken thighs: three for the price of two . . . Whole birds: half price.

We spend a much lower proportion of our income on feeding ourselves than previous generations. In the 1930s the average proportion of income spent on food was 35 per cent; today it is less than 10 per cent, although for the poorest fifth of the population the figure is still around one third. It is certainly true that we expect meat to be an affordable, everyday food in a way that our grandparents would never have done. Few of us have time or inclination to spend the hours needed to turn the offcuts that were traditionally the source of cheap meat into delicious meals. We want prime cuts we can cook fast.

Thanks to intensive factory farming, the industry has been able to deliver. Chicken is cheaper than it was twenty years ago, and we're buying five times more of it, spending £2.5 billion a year. Supermarkets have played their part in the deflationary process too, as chicken has become one of the weapons in retailers' price wars. But being able to buy a whole chicken for not much more than the price of a Starbucks cup of coffee comes at a cost.

The story of meat reflects the revolution that has taken place in our food system since the war. Chickens, like other animals, have become industrialized and globalized. We no longer know where they are produced or how they are processed. By the time we buy them in aseptic little packages, or processed into convenience meals, we have lost any sense of their origin. Until I worked in a chicken factory, I had no idea how the links in the chain fitted together. I am an enthusiastic cook, yet the extent to which processing has been transformed even in my lifetime had passed me by. It was an undercover stint in November 2001 with one of Britain's leading chicken processors in the West Country that first introduced me to the impact of that industrialization. What I needed to know was not on the label.

I had joined the twilight shift, at £4.50 an hour, reporting secretly for the *Guardian* newspaper, because I had been tipped off that the poultry being packed there as fresh British chicken breast for a supermarket was not what the retailer thought it was. The Devon women who packed poultry day in day out jokingly called it the Chicken Run. First you passed the guard in his sentry box on the unlit footbridge over the main railway line. The night trucks rumbled along the tracks below you as you crossed into the searchlights on the other side, where vast, windowless sheds loomed out of the mist. The darkness rang with the clanking of forklifts and the air was heavy with the smell of burning fat.

The Devon factory is owned by Lloyd Maunder, a family firm and leading supplier to Sainsbury's for over 100 years. It produces not just fresh chicken but West Country and organic poultry for the supermarket as well. Inside it is what is called a state-of-the-art fully integrated plant.

The vast majority of the 820 million UK chickens we eat each year are now processed in huge factories like this which combine an abattoir with cutting, packing and labelling the meat before it is transported directly to supermarket distribution centres. Over half the chicken farms in the UK are directly contracted to the factories too, rearing chicks delivered to them from the factory hatcheries, although British poultry farmers are increasingly struggling to stay in business in the face of cheap imports, particularly from Thailand and Brazil. The wholesale meat markets, supplied by independent farmers, around which a network of traditional butchers was built, now represent only a fraction of the trade.

The Lloyd Maunder website boasts 'total control and traceability', but I had been told by a worker at the factory that the 'traceability' claimed for the chicken had broken down – chicken breasts from Dutch crates were being repacked with new use-by dates and sent out with British red tractor logos for a Sainsbury's special offer.

Each EU-approved factory has its own health mark with which to stamp any meat it handles. Batches are also given barcodes. These marks are designed to make sure all meat can be traced as it moves through the system. It's a complicated paper trail but making sure the system of health marking works is vital to protect the public.

In the last few years environmental health officers have uncovered large-scale frauds where unfit chicken, condemned either for rendering or pet food, has instead been recycled back into the human food chain in vast quantities. Inspectors employed in the factories by the government's Meat Hygiene Service are supposed to reject any meat which is not properly health-marked. If the traceability had broken down, it would be a serious matter.

Before we started our evening's work, we had to be trained in hygiene and safety. There were a dozen or so of us: a farmer who could no longer make enough money from his farm and was taking a night job so that his family could stay on the land; an English teacher and a couple of other men who were there to earn extra money after their day jobs to pay for their children's Christmas presents; and a handful of Devon mothers made redundant from another chicken factory which had succumbed to global competition the previous week. They had trussing and cutting skills and came to work each evening once their children were home from school, 'to pay for the playstations and gameboys and bikes the kids need to keep up with their peers', as Linda, their supervisor from the old factory, put it with a roll of her eyes.

Our trainers seemed to have a pretty clear grasp of the economics of the industry. 'Competition is what it's all about these days.' The big chicken manufacturers want to become bigger. 'They seem to be after a monopoly. But maybe that's not such a bad thing, if we're going to stand up to the power of the supermarkets. Perhaps you don't know, but when a supermarket wants to do a BOGOF [buy one, get one free offer, pronounced bog off] it's not just them that pays for the extra, it's us,' she told us conspiratorially, as she showed us some slides about not picking your nose and the importance of washing your hands. We then had to watch a Sainsbury's quality assurance video that included

an earnest woman in a white lab coat measuring the length of a
carrot with a ruler. At the end we had to sign a statement that we
had watched it. 'That covers Sainsbury's for due diligence if
anything goes wrong,' the trainer explained. As the food chain
has become longer, protecting themselves from being sued if
safety breaks down at any point is of prime importance to the big
retailers.

'The biggest complaint we get from customers these days is
about product going off. Perhaps that's to do with the way we
all shop in our cars. Or perhaps it's the way we keep pushing
sell-by dates,' the trainer joked.

This is a reputable company and we were run through benefits,
career prospects and equal opportunities. We were warned
against discrimination on racial or religious grounds. 'We've got
Afghanistans [sic], Yemenis, Kurds, Kosovans, Croats, Serbs,
Lithuanians, Africans, you name it. And we take into account
their religious needs. Oooh yes, it's all Rama-dama-ding-dong
round here,' she said.

A final warning from the trainer. Don't pilfer. Someone had
been sacked not long before for taking bin bags. And don't trade
in illegal substances on the factory floor. Someone had been
caught for that too, and Customs and Excise were planning to
come back, possibly undercover. 'It could be one of you here
now,' she grinned as she scanned the room. I smiled inanely.

Then we were off to be kitted out with green boots, white coats,
hairnets and helmets – blue helmets are managers; white, regular
workers; green, rookies. We passed the staff noticeboard displaying the excellent official score given to the factory for hygiene
that month, and a warning that a customer had complained of
finding a whole Marigold glove in a portion of chicken drumsticks.

Then we went through the washing and disinfectant lobby to
scrub our hands and drag our boots through the foot wash, passed
down a narrow white-walled corridor, through the heavy doors
and into the main packing and cutting area.

The plucked and chilled chickens come in here upside down,

thousands of them swinging by their feet from the continuous, spiralling belts of metal shackles that start in the abattoir and wind around the ceiling of the huge cutting hall, where production lines stretch into the distance. Disco music blared out above the noise of machinery, and the decapitated birds jerked and dived above our heads in macabre syncopation. Some were dropped off whole on to the trussing line, others bobbed along to have their wings sliced off. Legs and torsos danced on, all limbs, no tops, until they too were chopped off by the machines and dropped on to a packing line. This is where the labour-intensive bit starts, since for supermarket orders the pieces have to be arranged by hand on plastic trays before going back into machines which wrap them and label them with prices and barcodes. The carcasses come on to a different track, with a metal fist through their innards.

Breasts have to be cut off by hand. A chain of Central Asian-looking workers were first tearing off the skin, then quickly flicking their sharp knives through to the bone and slicing the breasts away.

The Devon ladies, who were warm and raucous, had taken me with them to truss chickens on plastic trays because you get more money for that skilled job and they were trying to cover for me. I was no good at it. My hands were freezing. I was too slow off the mark changing and by the time I reached the glove dispenser the handwarmers had run out. An old hand from another section eventually took pity on me. 'Psst, what size are you?' She had a quick look over her shoulder, then reached down her leg and found me a pair from the stash in her wellies.

The packing lines displayed orders from the supermarket, crossed out and changed several times during the day. Processors risk losing their orders if they fall short of the supermarkets' requirements, which can fluctuate considerably, but in general the supermarkets are under no reciprocal obligation to pay if they want to cut back at short notice. An alert to supervisors on the labelling machine explained Sainsbury's new policy on barcodes and gave a clear indication of the balance of power between retailers and suppliers. If the barcode cannot be scanned at the till first time, the processor will be warned. Second offence: £500 fine; third offence: £1,000; fourth offence: £3,000; thereafter a Kafkaesque-sounding 'possible volume restructure'.

The night shift, when we moved into it, was a hardcore of foreign workers, many of whom spoke no English. The Devon mothers had returned to their homes and I had moved over to sliding breasts into trays, rough side down, good side up, curled over so those stringy bits couldn't be seen.

Then there was an unexpected pause. The chickens from the factory's own slaughterhouse had stopped winding through. The supervisor in charge of the line climbed up the huge ladder to the glass eyrie in the roof from where the managers can watch the workers below. We were given an early break. When we got back, a couple of dozen Belgian and blue Dutch crates filled with vacuum-packed breast fillets had been pulled in. We were set to packing those instead.

The crates were labelled GMB Meats, 'use by 25 November'; the vacuum packs said the same, 'use by 25 November' and carried the GMB Meats name. GMB Meats is a cutting plant in Wolverhampton which does not slaughter its own birds but buys them in from other British processors and imports from Belgium, Holland and other countries. The old health marks had been torn off but clean traces, saying Platte Kip (the Flemish and Dutch for chicken fillet), remained on the crates. The new health marks did not have batch numbers, making it difficult to trace their origin.

The vacuum packs were cut open and tipped on to the conveyor belts. Several chicken fillets fell down through the gaps and stayed at our feet while we packed into Sainsbury's trays for the next couple of hours.

There was a bit of aggro on the line by then. The clingfilm wrapper kept jamming and the Lithuanian next to me was indicating fairly forcefully that my elbows were taking up too much space. Further down the line workers were sticking a Buy One, Get One Free label on each pack as it emerged from the wrapper, before it trundled on to get its British red tractor logo and a new Sainsbury's label with a 'sell by 27 November' and 'use by 27 November' date stamp.

Sainsbury's had told me the previous week that all its fresh meat was 'completely traceable' to inspected and approved slaughterhouses which did not use subcontractors. When we confronted the company with our evidence it said that it was 'shocked' that a supplier had broken their agreement and used another company to cut its chicken without its knowledge. 'We pride ourselves on the integrity and traceability of our food, and take this extremely seriously.' It added that the chicken had undergone the usual tests and posed no health risk to customers. The company said it would completely review its meat-buying and introduce changes. Senior sources say this has since happened.

The tangle that is UK food and labelling law also became apparent. It would not actually be illegal to label foreign meat with the British red tractor logo, which in law means 'British farm standard', not necessarily produced in Britain, although of course most customers would be surprised to discover that. The use-by date on the giant vacuum packs I had helped to repack would have legal status and could not be changed if they had been intended for a caterer (as GMB Meats told us they were) but not if they were for an industrial customer repacking them. Putting the fillets in new packs with different dates might mean that the 'fresh chicken' was eight days old, but it would still meet Sainsbury's specification. Lloyd Maunder, having been asked by us to check, said at first that chicken from GMB was only ever packed for catering customers who did not specify a required country of origin. GMB did not seek to claim the meat was British, saying only that it came from EU-approved sources. Lloyd Maunder subsequently said that it had packed GMB chicken for Sainsbury's, explaining that it did very occasionally use other processors to cut its own birds for Sainsbury's, and that that was what had happened in this case. Officially, it could only do this with advance notice, yet Sainsbury's did not know what had happened. Lloyd Maunder's representative said that the company employed the highest standards of care in the operation of its business with its customers. When it had completed an audit of the factory after my investigation, Sainsbury's said it was satisfied that everything was in order. Trading standards officials said they had found nothing to investigate. Sources at the factory say that changes have also been made there since.

Sainsbury's subsequently informed me that they refuted any implied or stated suggestion that Sainsbury's sold chicken with altered use-by dates or that they or one of their suppliers extended the original specified use-by date of chicken. They also said that chicken at Lloyd Maunder was repacked into Sainsbury's packaging and that the date on the first packet referred to a 'repack-by' date, and that the date on their own packaging was the 'use-by' date for customers.

Those working on the frontline of enforcement in the meat trade fear that the system of health marking generally has broken down and is no longer sufficient to protect the public. Just how vital traceability is became clear when the pet-food scandal came to light. Sue Sonnex, a chief environmental health officer in Derbyshire, remembers clearly the day in December 2000 that recycled pet food entered her life. An anonymous caller had tipped off the council that a company on its patch, Denby Poultry, was taking condemned chicken – diseased and contaminated birds from big factories which should have been sent for rendering or to be turned into pet food – and trimming it, washing it with bleach, and cleaning it up before selling it back into the human food chain.

For the next two years the lives of Sue Sonnex and her colleagues were dominated by the attempt to unwind the complicated threads that linked Denby to over 1,000 other food manufacturers, wholesalers and retailers around the country. Sonnex wanted to know not just how far the chicken had gone but, more importantly, why the system allowed such abuses. Environmental health colleagues in Rotherham had discovered a similar scam to recycle pet food and achieved a conviction in 2000, but the tentacles of that operation reached far and wide and there had not been the money to pursue them. Other cases were coming up in other areas. It seemed to be the tip of an iceberg of meat laundering.

Sonnex quickly realized the weaknesses of the inspection system. Investigators found health marks belonging to one major factory and supposedly unique to it lying around in another cutting plant. The marks had been faked – easily done – in the Denby case. Denby Poultry Products was a pet-food-processing plant in Derbyshire registered to receive low-risk waste for use in pet foods. But it was laundering both low-risk waste and high-risk waste carrying hepatitis, Staphylococci and E. coli-septicaemia back into the human food chain. It sold cleaned-up waste to another company which applied illegitimate health marks to it before selling it on to other companies. The owner of Denby Poultry, Peter Roberts, known in the trade as Maggot Pete, was found guilty in his absence at Nottingham Crown Court in 2003. He is thought to have fled the country. Five other men pleaded guilty to conspiracy to defraud.

Official vets are employed at all meat factories to oversee inspection of poultry, including waste. But because there is a shortage of local vets, many of them are now young Spanish women. They can feel isolated and intimidated, and are often ignorant of British law. Many of the abuses take place at night after the inspectors have gone home.

Meat from the companies involved in the recycling had ended up, via major manufacturers Perkins and Shippams, in chicken products on the shelves of Tesco and Sainsbury's and in Kwik-save, and in schools and hospitals around the country, triggering food hazard warnings in April 2001. They had been unwitting victims of the scam. The retailers all have audit systems which are supposed to detect any abuses, but they had failed to pick up the problems.

Many environmental health officers remain unconvinced that measures taken by the Food Standards Agency (FSA) to control the illegal trade will be effective. They require factories to stain with blue dye all 'high-risk' poultry waste, that is, birds that are diseased. But they do not require the staining of 'low-risk' waste, in other words meat that is bruised, or has failed quality tests. The new system leaves the door open to abuse, according to Sonnex. It depends on poultry processors separating the different types of waste. Officially inspectors have only fifteen minutes a month allocated to supervising this part of the factory process, in plants that work twenty-four hours a day, seven days a week. The big pet food companies which use low-risk waste for cat and dog food lobbied hard against staining it and won the day. Commercial interests were also at work when it came to recalling products from companies caught up with the supplies of recycled meat. Two leading manufacturers initially refused to recall their products even when they were told they had been buying from a company which was laundering pet food. Only when threatened with naming and shaming did they cooperate.

But it is the economics of the globalized poultry industry that are at the root of the problem, according to Sonnex. When she interviewed the big processors who had failed to comply with regulations on disposing of their waste, they complained that they were being squeezed so hard on price by the retailers and operating on such tight margins that paying to get rid of the waste was often the final straw. The pressure applied by the major supermarkets to fund special offers and price cuts was often cited as the factor that had pushed them into cutting corners.

'Five major poultry houses were offloading their waste – these are big-name companies – to save on disposal costs. The meat was laundered through an unlicensed cutting plant and sold for about 40p a kilo to a licensed plant which gave it a health mark. It sold it on for £1.50 a kilo. Then it went through brokers selling it at a bit more and on to food manufacturers who are selling chicken products at £15 a kilo. The raw material is worth so little it makes economic sense to ship it hundreds of miles. It's more profitable than drugs. Everyone can take a piece. We'll pay a fortune for processed junk but we won't pay anything for high-quality raw ingredients,' Sonnex explained.

If we are ignorant of how our fresh meat reaches us, we are even further removed from understanding which bits of animals go into the processed meats that have become ubiquitous. I, like many a harassed working parent, have fed my children their favourite chicken nuggets, thinking that the white meat they contained must be healthier than the fattier red meats in hamburgers. It was Sue Sonnex who first enlightened me on the true origins of the chicken nugget. During her investigation she had been shocked to find a manufacturer making nuggets almost entirely out of chicken skin. The label is not likely to tell you, but of course what the factory I worked at and all the others like it are involved in is a division of parts that transforms a cheap bird into profitable 'added-value' goods. Our recently acquired habit of just buying chicken breasts leaves all the other parts to be disposed of. While Europe is big on breasts, the Japanese prefer thighs. The feet are a bit of a fetish in China, and gizzards often go to Russia. But that leaves the carcasses and mountains of skin. So the skin is shipped around the world to make chicken nuggets.

It was while following the trail of the chicken skin that I found the answer to another puzzle: why the mention of Dutch catering chicken makes the industry so twitchy. I went first to a reputable organic manufacturer to understand the process of making nuggets.

Gary Stiles has spent his life in the meat trade and now owns a small factory in Wiltshire. I watched with him as an army of small, perfectly formed nuggets marched along a conveyor belt. At one end of the factory line a pulp of half-frozen meat and skin goes into a giant stainless-steel hopper. Minced and mixed beyond recognition, it is then extruded through a small tube on to metal plates. These press it into pale pink nugget shapes which trundle on down the belt. Through a dust bath of flour and seasoning they go, before being lowered under a sheet of constantly pouring batter. Then they pass through a tray of scattered breadcrumbs and into a vast vat of boiling oil for thirty seconds. As they emerge, workers in white coats, blue hairnets and white boots catch them, bag them in plastic, and post them back for the last rites. The belt carries them into a nitrogen tunnel to take them down to freezing point and finally out into a cardboard box, labelled with Stiles's own-brand Pure Organics For Georgia's Sake or Tesco organic chicken nuggets, according to the orders of the day.

Stiles explained that you need some skin to keep the nuggets succulent. He reckons that 15 per cent is about right. Mixed in that proportion with breast and dark meat, it matches what you would get if you were eating a whole bird and he knows exactly where his skin comes from. Like the rest of his meat, it is bought from two organic farms he knows personally. Unlike some other manufacturers, he won't use more skin than that, and he won't use mechanically recovered meat (MRM) which is obtained by pushing the carcass through a giant teabag-like screen to produce a slurry of protein, which is then bound back together with polyphosphates and gums. He doesn't add large quantities of water, nor does he use other additives that some manufacturers use, such as soya proteins to restore the texture of meat, or emulsifying gums to stop the mix separating out again, or flavourings and sugars to make up for the lack of meat. But the trouble is, once you've minced bits of chicken to a pulp, that pulp could be anything from anywhere. With other manufacturers, sometimes it is.

When Leicester trading standards received a complaint from a member of the public about the quality of some nuggets, they decided to test twenty-one samples from seventeen different shops, including the major supermarkets.

In one third of the samples the label was misleading about the nuggets' content. One pack of nuggets contained only 16 per cent meat, 30 per cent less than it claimed. (And skin, of course, counts as meat.) The trading standards officials were unable to identify the brands involved for legal reasons – one company disputed their tests. Instead, they gave a warning to the worst offender. That was in 2002. Subsequent tests recently have shown that the manufacturer has not changed its ways.

That trading standards are not able to do more to stop the abuse is a reflection of the imbalance of power in the food business – small local authority enforcement departments with very few resources are pitted against panoplies of lawyers from the food industry.

But look elsewhere in the chain and it becomes clear that doctoring of our processed foods has not only become commonplace, it is also in many cases perfectly legal. Water is routinely added to catering chicken, together with additives to hold it in. If you've ever eaten a takeaway, a ready meal, or a sandwich containing chicken, the chances are that you will have consumed chicken adulterated like this.

The Netherlands is the centre of the tumbling industry, the process in which the bulking up of chicken takes place. Dutch processors import cheap frozen chicken from Thailand and Brazil through Holland's ports. The meat has often been salted, because salted meat attracts only a fraction of the EU tariff applied to fresh meat. The processors defrost the meat, and then inject a solution of additives into it with dozens of needles, or tumble it in giant cement-mixer-like machines, until the water has been absorbed. The tumbling helps dilute the salt to make the chicken palatable, so as well as avoiding substantial taxes, the processors can make huge profits by selling water. Once the chicken has been tumbled and/or injected, it is refrozen and shipped on for further processing by manufacturers or for use by caterers.

The story gets even less appetizing, as I discovered when I met John Sandford, leading trading standards officer in Hull City Council. He thought nothing could surprise him any more. Like many an unsung local authority hero, he has spent the last twenty years sustained not by a large pay packet, but by a Yorkshireman's sense of humour and dedication to honesty, as he has tried to keep up with the poultry trade. He was aware that they knew a trick or two, but when he saw some test results from the public analyst's laboratory in the autumn of 2001, he was nevertheless amazed. The chicken breasts he and his colleagues had collected for testing contained pork.

His investigations had begun in 1997 when trading standards officers were contacted by a restaurateur who couldn't get his chicken, bought from a wholesaler, to cook properly. It fell to Hull Council to test it and they found it contained 30 per cent added water. Sandford began puzzling over how the processors had managed to get so much water to stay in the chicken. Why didn't the water just flood out when it was turned into a takeaway or a ready meal or a chicken nugget? The chicken was from Holland. Some time later Sandford discovered that there was gossip among the producers in the UK that some Dutch companies had new methods of adulterating their meat. The FSA had been alerted to it. Now the authorities had to prove it. Sandford knew it would be a slog. 'When they realize you are on their trail, they just change their specification to disguise what they are doing in different ways. They are multi-million-pound companies with limitless money to spend on technology.' Sandford has a budget of £20,000 a year to spend on laboratory tests.

The breakthrough came when the laboratory he uses in Manchester was able to develop new DNA testing which could pinpoint protein from different species of animals. The first DNA tests on further samples of Dutch catering chicken – well-known brands which you can find used widely in takeaways, pubs, clubs, Indian, Chinese and other ethnic restaurants across the country – showed up the pork, and lots of water.

The FSA announced the results of the tests at a press conference in London in December 2001. Some of the samples of what were being sold as chicken breasts were in fact only 54 per cent chicken. Nearly half of the samples contained less meat than they claimed and were mislabelled. Most had originated in Thailand and Brazil. They had been exported to Holland where they had been pumped full of water, salts, sugars, gums, flavourings, aromas, and other additives which would hold the water in, even when the chicken was cooked. But instead of using the old trick of phosphates to hold the water in, the processors were using a new, little understood one, based on hydrolyzed proteins.

Hydrolyzed proteins are proteins extracted at high temperatures or by chemical hydrolysis from old animals or parts of animals which are no use for food, such as skin, hide, bone, ligaments and feathers. Rather like cosmetic collagen implants, they make the flesh swell up and retain liquid.

The FSA public line at this point was that adding water to chicken was not in itself illegal, so long as the meat and other ingredients that had gone into it were accurately labelled when sold by wholesalers. Adding proteins from other animals would not be illegal either. Their main concern was that the chicken was not being correctly labelled. 'The added water, protein and other ingredients do not have food safety implications,' it said. The fact that by the time you and I eat it in a restaurant or canteen, the chicken has no label on at all, and that we would have no idea that we were not eating real chicken, seemed not to count. On this occasion it was left to a colleague of John Sandford's from trading standards to condemn what he saw as an outrageous consumer fraud.

Shortly after this some documents came into my hands that suggested there was considerably more going on behind the scenes. What the FSA and the lab had been looking for was not just chicken adulterated with pork, but – much more troubling – chicken adulterated with beef waste. The possibility of BSE in chicken meat had raised its ugly head.

If the Dutch processors were injecting chicken with hydrolyzed proteins extracted from cow material, as these documents suggested, which bit of the cow were they coming from? If the processors were cheating and not declaring the presence of bovine proteins on the label, how could they be trusted to be following the regulations on removing certain high-risk cattle materials from the food chain? Would the process of hydrolysis kill off any infective BSE prions?

The baton had passed to Ireland where the Food Safety Authority in Dublin, tipped off by the English FSA, had started its own testing on chicken. Using a private lab with different and more sensitive DNA testing techniques, it found what it had been looking for: undeclared bovine proteins in chicken breasts from Holland, and lots more pork in chicken labelled 'halal'. Since much of the chicken was destined for ethnic restaurants where pork would be abhorrent to Muslims and beef to Hindus, it presented considerable moral dilemmas.

At this point, the authorities in England and Ireland were not really aware of what was going on. Until they knew the source of the bovine proteins, they could not rule out the theoretical risk of BSE. They hoped that the beef waste being used was collagen from hides, which would not present any safety risk – that was what the processors were saying. But the Dutch authorities, through whom the English and Irish were obliged to work, were being extraordinarily slow in checking the source of the proteins back down the chain. Sandford and the scientific experts at the FSA were becoming increasingly frustrated.

By now I knew from documents I had seen and conversations with expert sources that chicken adulterated with beef waste was also circulating widely in the UK and almost certainly being used in the manufacture of other chicken products, such as nuggets and ready meals. (The giveaway sign that your chicken has been adulterated is a slightly spongy texture.) We ran a piece in the *Guardian* saying so.

I had also been sent technical papers showing that the Brazilian poultry industry, working together with a Danish company, had developed the technology to extract hydrolyzed beef proteins from cattle blood and bone – BSE-risk materials in Europe –

and were marketing their new technique for turning water into money to companies in eastern Europe.

The English FSA's public response was that their tests had found no evidence that the adulterated meat was circulating in the UK, and that in any case hydrolyzed beef proteins being used by the Dutch were derived from hide. There was no safety risk. It was a labelling issue, since it would be legal so long as it was correctly labelled.

I was beginning to wonder if I would ever escape the subject of chicken, as were my *Guardian* colleagues, who had taken to clucking as they walked past my desk. The BBC's *Panorama* team were keen to take the investigation further and it made sense to join forces with them. I had traced the production of hydrolyzed proteins back to factories in Germany and Spain. *Panorama* began secret filming. Their evidence was shocking.

They caught a Dutch additive supplier and a German protein manufacturer on video boasting that they had developed unde-tectable methods of adulterating chicken with waste from cows. The cow proteins were mixed into additive powders which were then injected into the meat, mostly chicken breasts, by poultry processors so that it could take up as much as 50 per cent water. But they were able to break down the DNA of the cow proteins to such an extent that the authorities' tests would not find it. Proteins extracted from chicken waste could also be used, but the reason for choosing cows was that the raw material was even cheaper. The owner of the Dutch company which mixed the proteins into powders for the chicken processors to use told the undercover reporters that for more than ten years the industry had been extracting hydrolyzed beef proteins to inject not only into chicken but also into other meats such as ham. At least twelve companies in Holland were using the new undetectable hydrolyzed proteins. The owner of the German company said that the material for the beef proteins was cow hide from Brazil and that Brazil was BSE-free, but he declined to show the undercover reporters the process by which they were extracted.

At first the FSA maintained the line that it was a labelling issue, but then decided it was a major scandal and fraud. It is now pressing the European Commission to ban the use of proteins from other species in chicken and to limit the amount of water that may legally be added to 15 per cent. The industry says some added water is vital for technical reasons, to prevent the chicken from drying out. Despite a pioneering investigation by its own scientific experts, the FSA was hamstrung by the fact that in European law there was nothing illegal about what the Dutch were doing so long as they put it on an obscure label somewhere. A multi-million-pound hi-tech industry had been, and still is, able to import cheap frozen Thai and Brazilian chicken, doctor it with animal waste, and sell it to restaurants, institutions and manufacturers across Britain. It has run rings around the authorities for years. Eventually, no doubt, new regulations will grind their way through Brussels putting a limit on the amount of water you can add to chicken, and banning the use of foreign proteins, though how they will be enforced when processors already know how to beat the tests is not clear. Who knows how far the technology has spread? I have seen sales literature from additive companies offering protein mixes for all kinds of meats and for fish. It is worth remembering meanwhile that the good guys are those who only add, and presumably will continue to add, 15 per cent water to your chicken.

The more you ship food around, the easier it becomes to hide this sort of fraud. Most shoppers, when asked, say they prefer British meat because they want a short and accountable supply chain. But the structure of the globalized food industry is making it increasingly difficult for all but the largest British poultry farmers and processors to make a living. Farmers are going out of business in droves, and the processing side of the business is seeing rapid consolidation.

A chicken farmer, who may also have invested £1 million or more in chicken units with computerized feeding systems, may only make 1–2p profit per kilo for his birds. In the late 1980s chicken farmers received just over 30 per cent of the retail price of chicken, but today they are lucky to get 20 per cent. British chicken processors, whose factories require substantial capital investment and have high labour costs, are often working on margins of less than 1 per cent. If they cannot deliver the price the supermarket wants, retailers can also use the stick of sourcing abroad, from Europe where the high value of the pound to the euro favours continental farmers, or from developing countries where costs are lower and standards may not be so good.

It is only by keeping volumes high that conventional farmers and processors here can survive. Two thirds of chicken farms in the UK now consist of units of 100,000 birds or more. But that makes them dependent on the people who were squeezing their margins in the first place – the big retailers. They are the only people who buy in sufficient volume.

The story is not unique to chicken. Pig farmers and processors suffer similar problems. Ten years ago a British pig farmer made £9 profit per pig, in 2002 he lost an average of £3 per pig. Neither poultry nor pig farming receives subsidies. Only the biggest and most intense producers can compete. This is one of the consequences of our obsession with cheap meat. The constant drive to increase yields leads to ever-greater intensification. As the trade has globalized, the same trend is now being seen in developing countries. Small poultry farmers in Brazil and Thailand are being squeezed out by huge factory farms. It is a pattern that can be observed in most food sectors, from vegetable farming to confectionery manufacture. But where livestock is involved, the almost irresistible drive towards industrialization has particular consequences. The price is paid in animal welfare and vulnerability to disease.

The modern broiler chicken has been bred to fatten in the shortest time possible. (The name derives from a combination of the two traditional methods of cooking chicken: boiling and roasting.)

The broiler farms divide the year up into a series of eight-week cropping periods. Each 'crop' of chickens takes forty to forty-two days to grow from chick to 2-kg bird ready for slaughter. One week is taken to clean and disinfect the sheds before the next crop is begun – the units are not cleaned during cropping so that after two to three weeks the wood shavings on the floor of the sheds are completely covered with poultry manure and the air is acrid with ammonia. Everything is automated. Computers control not just the heating and ventilating systems but also the dispensing of feed and water. The feed and water are medicated with drugs to control parasites or with mass doses of antibiotics as necessary.

Sheds these days typically hold 30,000–50,000 birds. Space and heating cost money, so the more birds you can pack in, the greater the yield. The UK government guidelines currently advise that there should be a maximum stocking density of 34kg of bird per square metre of floor space. In fact a survey conducted by Compassion in World Farming in 2001 found that only Marks and Spencer stipulated this as a maximum. Most other supermarkets permitted stocking densities of up to 38kg per square metre. This allows each mature chicken an area smaller than an A4 sheet of paper. By the time the birds reach the end of their lives, the sheds are so crammed that they can hardly move. Animal welfare groups have regularly video-recorded signs of acute stress in birds including feather-pecking and cannibalism of dead chickens. Mortality rates are high, at 1 per cent a week seven times higher than in egg-laying hens. Once the shed is carpeted with chickens, it can be hard for the stockman to see all those that have died before the others start feeding on them.

Two companies – Ross Breeders and Cobb – supply 80 per cent of the breeding stock for commercial broilers around the world. Much research has been devoted to genetic selection to produce the most efficient bird. The RSPCA, which says that it sees the suffering of broiler chickens as one of the most pressing animal welfare issues in the UK today, produces a little pamphlet, called *Behind Closed Doors*, which shows the effect of that genetic selection. More eloquent than any description is a series of matching pairs of tiny photographs in the margin of each page. The top photograph shows a normal egg-laying hen taken at intervals of a few days, as it grows from chick to maturity. Underneath is a parallel picture of the broiler chicken taken at the same intervals. By day nine, the broiler chick's legs can barely keep its oversized breast off the ground. By day eleven, it is puffed up to double the size of its cousin. It looks like an obese nine-year-old standing on the legs of a five-year-old. By day thirty-five, it looks more like a weightlifter on steroids and dwarfs the egg-laying hen.

In 1957 the average growth period for an eating chicken was sixty-three days and just under 3kg of feed was required for each kilo of weight. By the 1990s the number of growth days had been reduced to forty-two to forty-three, and little over 1.5kg of feed was required. The industry is working to reduce the lifespan still further. By 2007 birds are expected to reach the required 2kg weight in thirty-three days.

But genetic selection to produce birds that work like factory units of production creates serious health problems – their bones, heart and lungs just cannot keep up. A large proportion of broilers suffer from leg problems: you can tell when you buy a chicken from the hock burns – dark red patches – on the leg around the knee joint. The industry disputes just how much of a problem lameness is. A study in 1992 by the University of Bristol found that 90 per cent of UK broilers had a detectable problem and over a quarter of birds had leg problems severe enough to affect their welfare. The industry has done its own survey and says that fewer than 4 per cent of birds have significant problems, but has not made the research available in the public domain.

Lameness is not just a welfare problem. Birds that sit in fouled litter and cannot stand up suffer more skin disease. Deaths from heart attacks or swollen hearts that cannot supply enough oxygen to the birds' oversized breast muscles are also common. If these diseased birds make it to the processing factory, inspectors are supposed to weed them out along with DOAs (dead on arrivals), but with chickens moving through at 180 or more a minute, some slip through. A 1996 *Which?* survey of chicken on sale in leading supermarkets found several birds with severe bruising, disease and skin infections.

Because broilers grow unnaturally fast, those which are kept for breeding – and are therefore not slaughtered at six weeks but allowed to reach sexual maturity at about fifteen to eighteen weeks – have to be starved, otherwise they would become too big to mate.

Factory farming in these sorts of conditions is heavily dependent on the use of drugs to prevent or treat disease. Pigs, chickens, laying hens, sheep, calves, dairy cows and farmed fish all receive routine dosages of antibiotics either through injection or in their food and water. By the end of the 1990s about 450 tonnes of antibiotics were being used on farm animals in the UK each year – about the same quantity as on humans. Many of the antibiotics given to farm animals are the same as, or related to, antibiotics used in human medicine.

Farmers were first allowed to feed livestock antibiotics as growth promoters fifty years ago, just ten years after this lifesaving class of drugs first became widely available to tackle human disease. By wiping out competing bacteria in the guts of chickens, the antibiotics speeded up the rate at which the birds absorbed food and grew. They also acted as a prophylaxis against the diseases common in factory-farmed chicken.

Scientists are still arguing about the impact of the use of antibiotics in animals on the effectiveness of these drugs for humans. Many are extremely alarmed by their overuse; others are less convinced of the dangers. But international bodies are agreed that at the very least it makes sense to be cautious. In 1999 the government's Advisory Committee on the Microbiological Safety of Food (ACMSF) said: 'Much of modern medicine depends on the control of infection with antibiotics and if this were to

become largely ineffective, it would have calamitous consequences . . . We believe that giving antibiotics to animals results
in the emergence of some resistant bacteria which infect humans.'

The EU banned an antibiotic called avoparcin for use in
animals in 1997 because of the likely development of resistance
in humans to the related antibiotic vancomycin. But its legacy
remains. Because it was given in low dosages to chickens in feed
or drinking water, it didn't kill bacteria completely but allowed
some to survive and develop resistance. Now we are facing
vancomycin-resistant enterococci – that is, superbugs in humans
which cannot be treated. Vancomycin is the most powerful
human antibiotic available, the last line of defence for patients
with the hospital superbug MRSA.

In 1998 the UK poultry industry said it would remove all
growth-promoting antibiotics from feed voluntarily, ahead of a
European ban which comes into force in 2006. But by 2003 it
had become clear that one in five producers had quietly slipped
back into the habit. Richard Young, an organic farmer and expert
adviser on antibiotic use to the Soil Association, worked out that
something fishy was going on. Overall antibiotic use actually
increased rather than decreased after the voluntary ban. Many
producers had found that their birds were falling ill without the
growth promoters and resumed administering them. Others had
switched to far greater use of therapeutic antibiotics prescribed
by vets. I have seen production sheets from a large chicken
factory, sent to me anonymously, which make clear that its
chicks, both free-range and indoor-reared, are still routinely
given antibiotics in their water.

The 2003 FSA survey of chicken found that half of the
salmonella and half of the campylobacter detected in retail samples
were resistant to at least one antimicrobial drug, and nearly a
quarter to several other drugs which are needed to treat humans
when they are infected by these food-poisoning bugs.

Ironically, while industrial farming has risked compromising
the effectiveness of antibiotics for humans, its heavy drugs use

has not prevented regular and catastrophic outbreaks of disease in intensively reared animals.

Some 2,000 British pig farmers went out of business between 1998 and 2002. For many, the beginning of the end was the arrival of swine fever. The disease spreads through intensive pig farms like wildfire, and devastated the UK industry in 2000. Mark Hayward, a pig farmer in Suffolk, was badly hit. His farm was not infected but nearby ones were and he was banned from moving his animals. 'It's very, very infectious and very nasty – you get vomiting, wasting, high fevers, sudden death. You go into a pen one morning and two or three of them are ill; by the end of the day the whole pen is ill. We worked like shit to keep the disease off our land. But we couldn't move our pigs for five months.'

They couldn't sell the pigs that were reaching their full weight, and they couldn't turn off the relentless production cycle of sows in pig giving birth. 'We were stacking up three hundred and fifty pigs a week with nowhere to put them. It was horrendous. Three hundred pigs in pens where there should have been a hundred. They were fighting. It was so distressing staff started to leave.'

Swine fever was an early warning that the regulations on importing illegal meat and treating animal feed were not being enforced. It cost Mark's farm, which never caught it, £100,000.

Nearly a quarter of a million pigs in his part of the world were destroyed. Just fifteen months later, the warning unheeded, foot and mouth struck. It was first spotted on pigs in an abattoir in Essex, but by then animals which had been trucked all around England had spread the disease. From the Welsh hills to the Lake District, from the weald of Essex to the moors of Devon, animals had to be slaughtered. The countryside was burning with the funeral pyres of sheep and cattle. The army had been called in and the government had been forced to postpone its chosen date for a general election.

It was the turn of the Dutch army to be called out in February 2003. Avian flu had broken out in the eastern province of Gelderland. It enforced a ban on movement in a desperate effort to stop the disease spreading through the intensive poultry units in the Netherlands. By April it had spread to Belgium. Exports of eggs and chickens were banned. By the time the Germans had caught it in May and started sealing their roads, over 30 million Dutch and Belgian chickens had been destroyed. A Dutch vet had also died, having caught the disease from an infected bird, briefly sparking fears that the virus could mutate and trigger a flu epidemic in humans.

It is not a coincidence that European farmers have lurched from crisis to crisis like this. Our methods of farming livestock intensively and of moving animals vast distances make them particularly vulnerable to epidemics of disease. For centuries traditional farms were mixed, partly to take advantage of the virtuous circle of plants feeding animals whose manure could then feed crops, but also as an insurance against the risk of disease. Farm diseases are usually quite specific, and attack one type of livestock or crop. The best way to prevent them is to avoid keeping too many of the same animals together in one place, and to rotate them so that the cycle of diseases and parasites is broken. Organic farmers know this. Once a disease does strike, just as isolation works with human illness, so keeping animals away from contact with other animals of their type is the best way of controlling it. Modern systems of monoculture do the opposite. Meat and livestock are not only regularly transported around the world but also kept together in great crowds in the same place year after year. By the time a disease has been noticed, it has often taken devastating grip.

The final cost of the foot and mouth outbreak of 2001 has been estimated at £8 billion, although the true financial cost to rural economies as large parts of the countryside were effectively shut down is incalculable. Some 4 million animals were slaughtered, although just 2,000 cases of foot and mouth were confirmed. The earlier BSE crisis, caused by feeding old cattle back to herbivore cattle in the pursuit of maximum yields, cost British farmers £1.6 billion in lost export markets alone. The UK poultry industry escaped the European epidemic of avian flu in 2003, but it was back on red alert in January 2004 as the disease struck again, this time cutting through flocks in south-east Asia and claiming lives as it spread to the human population. The World Health Organization warned that if the bird virus mutated and attached itself to human flu, the consequences would be devastating. Imports of meat from Thailand were banned by the EU when it emerged that the Thai government had been covering up the fact that its flocks were infected. The strain of flu was particularly virulent and the *Lancet* said that if it became contagious among people, the prospect of a worldwide pandemic was 'massively frightening'.

2. Salad

In an idle moment I decided to reconstruct the contents of a 99p bag of washed and ready-to-eat salad. Of course you are not meant to do this, the whole point of bagged salad being that we are too busy to wash our own lettuce leaves, let alone count them. But I wanted to know how many you get for your money. Erring well on the side of generosity, I reckoned that for roughly £1 I had bought two leaves of frisée, one leaf of red radicchio, and two leaves of a pale green crunchy variety of lettuce. This portion was livened up by eighteen tiny whole leaves and seven torn pieces of dark green leaves about the size of a 2p coin.

Bagged salads did not exist before 1992. Now two thirds of households buy them regularly. The value of the UK salad vegetable market had in fact grown by 90 per cent between 1992 and 2002. By 2002 it was worth £1.25 billion – more than the total value of the sliced bread market, or the breakfast cereal market.

This does not mean we are eating 90 per cent more salad – volumes have grown only by 18 per cent over the same period – just that the food industry has found ways to make much more money out of salad.

Time was when we ate lettuces in summer and, following our northern European seasons, switched to root vegetables and brassicas in winter. But now, thanks to global sourcing and advances in packaging technology, we have got used to the idea of eating a variety of salads all year round.

Modified-atmosphere packaging (MAP) can now increase the shelf life of prepared salad by over 50 per cent, making it possible for supermarkets to sell us washed and bagged salad from around the world. Lettuce and salad leaves are harvested from fields in

the UK, southern Europe or the USA one day and reach a
packing house either the same day or a day or two later if
imported. The salad is cut or separated out into individual leaves
by gangs of workers, then washed in chlorine, dried and sorted
before being packaged in pillows of plastic in which the normal
levels of oxygen and carbon dioxide have been altered. Typically,
in MAP, the oxygen is reduced from 21 per cent to 3 per cent
and the CO_2 levels correspondingly raised. This slows any visible
deterioration or discolouring. The salad is then trucked to a
supermarket's distribution centre where it will be dispatched for
delivery to the stores. The MAP keeps it looking fresh for up to
ten days. Some lettuces imported from the USA are kept fresh
in MAP for up to a month.

Unfortunately, some research published in 2003 in the *British
Journal of Nutrition* suggested that this new invention to prolong
shelf life and provide us with convenience while multiplying
profits might actually destroy many of the vital nutrients in salad.

A team of researchers and volunteers at the Rome Institute of
Food and Nutrition had conducted an experiment. They took
lettuce grown by a cooperative and gave it to volunteers to eat
on the day it was harvested; lettuce from the same source was
then given to volunteers to eat after it had been packed in MAP
straight after harvesting and stored for three days. Blood samples
of the two groups were analysed after they had eaten the salad.
The researchers noted that several antioxidant nutrients – which
protect against ageing, degenerative disease and cancer – such as
vitamin C, vitamin E, polyphenols and other micronutrients –
seemed to be lost in the MAP process. The volunteers who had
eaten the fresh lettuce showed an increase in antioxidant levels
in their blood, but those who had eaten lettuce stored for three
days in MAP showed no increase in antioxidant levels. The
researchers noted that nutrient levels fell at a similar rate in lettuce
stored in normal atmospheric conditions, the difference being
that a lettuce stored normally showed signs of limpness after a
few days whereas with MAP, the illusion of freshness is preserved.

When the results of this trial were published, they provoked a defensive debate among packers in the UK. Jon Fielder, director of a company called Waterwise, which sells ozone-based disinfecting systems to salad packers, wrote to the trade magazine the *Grocer* saying that it couldn't be the MAP that was to blame for destroying nutrients.

It is commonly acknowledged that MAP does have an effect on the depletion of nutritional value of salad, however it is the chlorine used by most UK packaged salad producers in the washing process which has a far worse effect on consumer health. In most cases, the salad leaves are immersed in water with chlorine which is an oxidizing disinfectant. The chlorine level is usually maintained at a minimum of 50mg per litre – twenty times higher than in the average swimming pool.

In fact the Italian researchers had not used chlorine, so the MAP must have been responsible for the nutrient loss, but it was a helpful addition to public knowledge to have the industry view on chlorine washes.

Chlorine washes leave surface residues of chlorinated compounds on lettuce, and because of this the process is banned in organic production. Some chlorinated compounds are known to be cancer-causing, but there appears to be little research on those left on foods treated with high doses of chlorine, the process having evolved in an ad hoc way.

'As well as disinfecting out the bugs, they disinfect out the taste of fresh leaves, as anyone who has eaten salad straight from the garden knows,' Fielder points out. But it is controlling bugs rather than preserving taste or nutrients that wins most attention. As Fielder says, 'In a litigious society, and with the prospect of damage from bad publicity, no supermarket dare risk having E. coli food-poisoning bugs on the salad they sell.'

There appears to be good reason for supermarkets selling prewashed salads to worry. Between 1992 and 2000, the period in which bagged salads took off, nearly 6 per cent of food-poisoning outbreaks were associated with ready-to-eat salads and prepared fruit and vegetables. In 2000 two serious outbreaks of salmonella poisoning in the UK were traced back to lettuce. One person died as a result.

Once the market started growing so rapidly, the government's Public Health Laboratory Service (PHLS) decided to monitor bacteria levels in salads. A study of refrigerated ready-to-eat salads sold at retail stores in the UK in 1995 found that 6.5 per cent contained listeria, and 13 per cent E. coli bacteria. The most recent PHLS survey in 2001 found salmonella in five samples and high levels of listeria in one sample of ready-to-eat salad from three major supermarkets. One of the samples containing salmonella also contained E. coli bacteria. Fuller investigation subsequently uncovered an outbreak of salmonella poisoning in different parts of England and Wales caused by the salad. The majority of the samples were fine but, as the authors of the study pointed out, the new methods of packing raised new dangers.

Effective decontamination of ready-to-eat vegetables is difficult . . . the decontamination efficiency of the washing system in terms of pathogen removal is generally unknown, and there is increasing concern regarding the microbiological safety of such products and the effectiveness of current methods.

E. coli bugs are usually spread from human or animal faeces, either from the unwashed hands of farm or packhouse labourers, from manure that has not been properly composted, or from contaminated water. Good hygiene practices are essential to controlling them. But Jon Fielder, even as someone who sells disinfecting technology, says, 'The longer the factory chain the harder it is to control contamination. I always feel I should wash the lettuce I buy even if it is bagged and ready-to-eat.'

It might seem obvious that ensuring that those who work with fresh prepared foods are healthy, have access to proper sanitation at all times, and are well trained in good hygiene is vital. Standards of hygiene in factories and packhouses themselves are generally high and meticulously monitored. But in almost every other respect the system of employment that prevails in the food industry today militates against decent conditions.

The preparation and packing of fresh foods such as salad are now dependent on cheap, casual labour. That cheap labour has been largely provided by migrant workers. The labour-intensive business of sorting, washing, cutting and packing leaves by hand could not be done without them. Many of them, however, are now living in this country in appalling squalor.

Casual and frequently itinerant labour has gone together with agriculture for as long as anyone can remember. In Britain, from the early nineteenth century, gangmasters were contracted to collect labour from the villages around farms to bring in the annual harvest. The 1867 Agricultural Gangs Act defined a gangmaster as a person 'who hires Children, Young Persons or Women with a view to their being employed in Agricultural Labour on Lands not in his own Occupation'. Until twenty years ago, the work was often done by women in rural communities to earn a bit of extra money while looking after the family, or by students taking temporary summer jobs on farms. But in the last two decades the whole nature of the industry has changed.

Advances in agricultural science have helped extend the British season well beyond the old holiday times. Many farms are no longer simply places where food is grown, but sophisticated industrial complexes built around packing sheds and lorry parks. When they are not harvesting and packing their own produce, the big farms today are trucking or flying in supplies from abroad and packing them. The majority of the fresh food we buy is now wrapped in plastic. The need to pack fresh produce has been driven not so much by consumer demand as by the supermarkets' requirements, for barcode scanning at the till or for the food to be protected while it is moved around centralized distribution systems, for example.

Supermarkets are now open long hours, seven days a week. Packhouses operate twenty-four hours, seven days a week, partly because farmers wanting to supply the supermarkets have had to make substantial investment in packing and labelling machinery to meet their specifications and need to work the capital as hard as they can, and partly because supermarket ordering systems demand complete flexibility from suppliers.

At the same time, long working hours, and greater numbers of women going out to work, have led to an increased demand for convenience from time-pressed shoppers. The combined effect has been an explosion in this new form of economic activity. Other industries with such year-round demand do not depend on a casual and shifting workforce, but the food industry has stuck to the old nineteenth-century systems.

Labourers are often needed at very short notice and for long and unsocial hours. A recent report by the House of Commons select committee for Environment, food and rural affairs (Efra) describes the system. A supermarket might, for example, find that during hot weather its sales of salad have increased dramatically and will place an order with a supplier to provide extra washed lettuce later that day. The packhouse suddenly finds it needs an extra thirty or forty staff for the day and asks its gangmasters to provide them. The gangmaster may subcontract the order for workers if he doesn't have enough people on tap. The risks of meeting changing demand are thus transferred from the retailers to the workers.

Supermarkets rarely have written contracts with farmers or packhouses promising to buying certain quantities, although farmers are obliged to commit to supplying certain amounts to them. The farmers are both required to take the loss on any surplus and to meet any shortfall at their own expense by importing if their own harvest does not meet demand. This is what happened in the summer of 2003. The exceptionally hot weather caused much of the UK lettuce crop to mature at once, leaving major producers with a shortfall on their commitments to supply supermarkets in subsequent weeks. They had to make up quantities by airfreighting in lettuce from the USA and selling it at a considerable loss. The market price for a head of lettuce went from roughly 30p to 80p. Some supermarkets continued paying farmers the lower price agreed at the beginning of the year, but were able to hike their own prices in the shops because of high demand and shortages. When the farmer's profits are under such intense pressure, one of the few things he or she can still control is the cost of labour. The prices paid to farmers are nowhere near the cost of carrying a permanent workforce large enough to cope with fluctuations in demand.

The work is hard, as agricultural labour has always been, often in freezing conditions in refrigerated plants. Industrial injuries are common. The pay is unattractive and never guaranteed. Small wonder that the need for labour is no longer met by the indigenous population. Instead, large numbers of migrants have filled the gap.

I first became involved in the issue of migrant labour when the *Guardian* published my description of the Devon chicken factory where I worked packing chicken for Sainsbury's (see Chapter 1). Its staff included eighteen or so different nationalities. There was no suggestion that any of these were illegal workers, but shortly after the piece, I began to get phone calls. Did I know about the fifty Russians in the Portakabin on a meat factory site in Derbyshire? Or the dozens of Russians also in Portakabins packing salad leaves in Hampshire? Could I look into the streams of untaxed minivans full of foreigners going to farms and pack-houses in the Vale of Evesham? Most of the calls were anonymous tip-offs, some of them clearly motivated by xenophobia, but others not. Some were from people disturbed about the conditions they could see migrants were being housed in. Others were from people worried that their own jobs and pay were being undercut by exploited illegal labourers being paid less than the minimum wage. One was from a farmer who said he couldn't pay people properly any more: he was being undercut by rivals who, he felt, were only able to accept the supermarkets' demands for constant price reductions because they were using illegal labour; he faced the choice of doing the same himself or going out of business.

Since then I have visited factories, farms and packhouses in many areas, or simply talked to local people who can see what is really going on; to local Immigration officers, who are not officially allowed to talk to the press but who fear that casual employment has been handed over wholesale to criminal gangs calling themselves employment agencies; to farmers who fear they will lose their contracts if they say publicly what they are prepared to admit privately, that it is almost impossible to recruit sufficient casual labour legally to meet supermarkets' endlessly fluctuating demands; to packhouse managers who will talk about the frequent Immigration raids on illegal workers in their *last* jobs; to trade union organizers in food companies who witness it all happening, including in one case a police helicopter buzzing around a chicken factory while illegal migrants, who appeared to have been tipped off, legged it through the fields. I have also talked to many migrants and visited them where they live.

What has become clear is that the scale of migrant labour in the food industry is much larger than anyone is prepared to acknowledge, and that a very substantial proportion of that labour is being employed illegally. The Efra committee said it was appalled that no attempt had been made to assess the extent of illegal activity in this area. Doug Henderson, chief executive of the Fresh Produce Consortium, who appeared before the committee representing the producers, admitted that it was 'a very large black economy . . . a dreadful situation' and that the problem was deteriorating. He also said that VAT, tax and insurance scams provided 'a huge opportunity for very substantial fraud . . . that has encouraged the criminalization of the activity'. Don Pollard, who did extensive research for the T&G union on exploitation of workers in agriculture and food processing in the latter half of the 1990s, estimated then that at least 50 per cent of workers were controlled by gangmasters, with perhaps as many as 100,000 people being involved.

But the numbers now look much higher. Operation Shark, a pilot investigation into illegal labour carried out by government departments in 2002, covered the whole of the fish-processing industry in Scotland. It targeted the big labour agencies supplying thousands of workers to gut, fillet, cut and pack fish, much of it salmon for the major retailers. It sent a counter-fraud unit to raid a large fish company with half a dozen factories supplying supermarkets. It found that over 50 per cent of the workforce of 100 people at one factory were foreign. Of those more than one third were in the UK illegally. Of the local workforce, 10 per cent were claiming benefits they were not entitled to. The factory was working three shifts, and the foreign workers were doing either twelve hours or double shifts of sixteen hours a day, seven days a week. They were being paid less than the minimum wage, though exactly how much was hard to tell, since the gangmaster was deducting accommodation charges as well as tax and insurance. The result of Shark was that two health and safety orders were put on fish companies to curb excessive hours. Two gangmasters had their contracts worth £8 million and £1 million a year terminated. But at the time of writing no other charges have been brought.

David Jackson, the former police officer in charge at the time of the government's Operation Gangmaster, the overall programme of which Shark was a part, said that these figures were representative of conditions they had found throughout the fish-processing industry. Another senior investigating officer, who is both instinctively cautious and trained in number-crunching, has extrapolated figures from the numbers of factories and packhouses, and from the typical finding of Immigration raids. He told me that given that about half the workforce in food, catering and construction appears to be employed illegally in some way (workers switch in and out of these sectors), the figure for illegal workers in the UK is probably nearly 2 million.

By definition, it is impossible to know how many people work illegally. But what is not in any doubt is that exploitation of these labourers is not the exception but the norm.

Authorities investigating the illegal use of labour in the food and agricultural industries can see a pattern emerging right across the country and fear that it bears the hallmarks of a series of mafia operations. 'The MO [modus operandi or method of operation] of the gangmasters is so similar across the country, from the south of England to the north of Scotland, making use of the same sophisticated techniques to exploit loopholes in UK law, that we suspect there is some dominant controlling mafia, with mafias from different countries having carved out particular areas,' one senior official explained to me. The only ones who appear to operate differently are the Chinese gangs, who have descended in large numbers in the last couple of years on King's Lynn and seem to have cut out the middle men.

The mafia-style system works like this: gangmasters set themselves up as 'employment agencies' in the form of one or more limited companies. They are usually small companies with two to three owners but often with turnovers of £8–10 million a year. They recruit workers from abroad, sometimes being involved either directly or indirectly in smuggling them in and providing them with false documents. The migrants will often have been charged huge sums to be brought here and some are in debt to the gangmasters when they arrive. The gangmasters may use a core of legal workers from EU countries or students from eastern Europe and the former Soviet bloc given permission to come under government schemes for agricultural employment as a cover. So, for instance, Portuguese workers are used as cover to bring in Brazilians on fake Portuguese IDs. The gangmasters then provide workers with housing and transport, which not only ensures that the workers remain completely dependent on them but also provides a way of disguising the fact that they are paying less than the minimum wage. Rents deducted are often extortionate. They charge the packhouses, factories and farmers the going rate of £6–7 for an hour's labour plus VAT, and deduct tax and insurance from the workers' pay packets, even when it has nowhere legitimate to go because the workers are on fake IDs. This ensures that the books of the companies they are supplying with labour are kept clean. The gangmasters then go bankrupt before paying tax and insurance or VAT, which are collected retrospectively. It is quite common for them to declare themselves bankrupt owing between £1 million and £3 million in unpaid tax and insurance and VAT, much of which will have been moved offshore and thus be inaccessible to UK authorities. Once they have gone into liquidation they frequently reappear as phoenix companies, with the same directors supplying workers to the same sites just days afterwards but trading as a new employment agency under a different name. Clone companies are also created which provide subcontracted labour to the mother company, partly as a way of disguising the frauds further but also to get round restrictions which prevent bankrupts being directors of other companies.

Violence and crime of other sorts to hand in hand with these illegal employment activities. Intelligence briefings on gangmasters have included details of the Azerbaijani Stanley signature – the slash of the knife that goes up from the back of the shoulder and down across the chest – and Kalashnikovs on farms, used to keep workers in order. Intimidation and punishments are meted out to both legal and illegal workers. Sometimes intimidation turns into murder. At least two murder investigations currently underway appear to involve the murder of one migrant worker by another. Some gangmasters are known to be involved in running prostitution and drug smuggling rings. Protection rackets have also grown up around this activity. Workers have described these to me. At one house in southern England, for example, new arrivals are befriended by an eastern European runner for a gangmaster. After a few weeks he returns to the house with thugs armed with knives to collect any cash from wages that has been hidden under mattresses. Few migrant workers are able to open bank accounts. No one complains for fear of being shopped to the Immigration authorities.

Not all gangmasters are criminal. In response to growing concern, the supermarkets have for example agreed to nominate a handful of suppliers whose gangmasters will take part in a trial to address some of the issues under the auspices of the Ethical Trading Initiative. But it is becoming very difficult for honest ones to compete. When I have asked experts working in the territory to name a good gangmaster I might interview, they only ever come up with one person – Zad Padda. He's a second-generation Asian gangmaster based in Birmingham. He says that failure to grasp the nettle is making it harder and harder for people like him who want to operate within the law to survive. He supplies mainly Pakistani and Yemeni workers to horticul-tural companies in the Vale of Evesham, paying £1 million a year into government coffers in tax and insurance. He is advising the government on systems to check labourers' documentation and has introduced language courses and training for migrant workers. But he says that unscrupulous operators can always undercut him. According to one source, the unofficial going rate for labour was about £2.50–3 a hour in his area at a time when the minimum wage was £4.20. 'It all comes down to price. If that's the only basis on which you buy your food, you'll end up with illegal labour.'

While there has been much trumpeting recently by the Home Office and other government departments of raids which have caught illegal workers, actually arresting and successfully prosec-uting those who run the system has proved more difficult. The workers not only bear the brunt of the appalling conditions but suffer the punishment too.

An enforcement officer in East Anglia expressed the frustration many working in the area feel. (We spoke before Lithuania's accession to the EU in May 2004 when it was still illegal for most Lithuanians to come to the UK to work.) 'A local gangmaster has been to Lithuania to recruit directly. We know that. We also know there is plenty of violence – there have been court cases to deal with attacks by illegal migrants on other migrants, people being burned with hot irons, blackmail and extortion, that sort of thing. Individuals get deported – you'd be amazed how many pay slips have names like Marilyn Monroe on them. But no one seems to be able to get the big fish. The law's incredibly weak. Because the employment is devolved to a gangmaster, it's also the gangmaster's legal responsibility to check the papers. But all the employer has to do is show that he checked the papers and "believed" they were genuine. They are very easy to fake. It all comes down to money at the end of the day. I go to the supermarket and I want the cheapest price. That's where the chain starts, with all the competition to cut prices.'

Most of the workers involved are too frightened to speak out. But I have spoken to many, just by approaching them in the workplace, who have described this system exactly. Most will not give their names for fear of being deported or of violent retribution.

Even those who are in the UK legally are often too afraid to complain or are unaware of their rights. But many Portuguese workers, who as members of the EU are entitled to work here, have been able to give a clear picture of the prevailing conditions in the food industry. If the government is hoping that the accession of ten new countries to the EU giving their nationals the right to work here will solve the problems, the experience of the Portuguese should disabuse it. Although they could in theory be employed directly by the packhouses and factories, in practice they rarely are. They are dependent on the gangmasters for housing as well as jobs, since few local people are prepared to rent direct to them. Moreover, without the gangmasters' transport they cannot get to the jobs which are in remote rural areas, with shifts often starting at night or very early in the morning.

Both supermarkets' representatives and the farmers' union deny that they have benefited from the low wages paid to illegal workers. The suppliers argue that since they pay the gangmaster

the going rate, not an illegal cut-price one, the system does not
enable them to cut down on labour costs. But what it does enable
them to do is turn the supply of workers on and off like a tap,
and keep the tap running when they need to, well beyond any
legal limit on maximum hours. The supermarkets have driven
down prices and transferred the risk to suppliers; they in turn
save money by not carrying the spare capacity that flexibility
really demands.

The UK supermarkets are of course working in a global market
these days. The drive to lower prices comes from international
competition as much as anything. If you want evidence of the
impact of supermarkets' price wars on wages, none could be
clearer than that from the USA. Even the pro-business magazine
Business Week was moved to question in a recent cover story
whether Wal-Mart, which owns Asda in the UK, had become
too powerful. Wal-Mart, it said, has relentlessly wrung tens of
billions of dollars in cost efficiencies out of the retail supply chain,
passing savings on to shoppers as bargain prices.

With a global workforce of 1.4 million, it plays a huge role in wages and
working conditions worldwide . . . However, Wal-Mart's seemingly
virtuous business model is fraught with perverse consequences. On
average, in this staunchly anti-union company, America's largest private
employer . . . sales clerks pulled in $13,861 a year in 2001. At the time,
the federal poverty line for a family of three was $14,630.

In the autumn of 2003, 70,000 grocery workers in southern
California went on strike as supermarkets tried to freeze or lower
wages in order to compete with forty Wal-Mart supercentres due
to open in the state. A *New York Times* editorial on 15 November
2003 summarized why this apparently distant industrial relations
problem affects us all.

The supermarkets say they are forced to lower their labour costs to
compete with Wal-Mart, a non-union, low-wage employer aggress-

ively moving into the grocery business. Everyone should be concerned about this fight. It is at bottom about the ability of retail workers to earn wages that keep their families out of poverty. Wal-Mart's prices are about 14 per cent lower than other groceries' because the company is aggressive about squeezing costs, including labour costs. Wal-Mart uses hardball tactics to ward off unions . . . workers are already only a step – or a second family income – from poverty. Wal-Mart may also be driving down costs by using undocumented immigrants. Last month, federal agents raided Wal-Marts in twenty-one states [and now the company] is facing a grand jury investigation.

The undocumented workers were employed through an agency, and Wal-Mart denies knowingly using illegal labour.

In the UK, with its much stronger employment legislation, the impact of price wars has been passed further down the line. It is not the regular workforce employed by the supermarkets themselves that has felt the squeeze, but the casual labour that works for the suppliers to whom so much of the business risk has been devolved.

I am often asked where all this goes on, as if it were confined to small pockets of the country. It suits sections of the media to characterize these workers as 'bogus' or 'failed asylum seekers'. In fact the labour is constantly moved around and fits no easy categorizing. Workers move in and out of different sectors, and in and out of legality. They may be students allowed to work only twenty hours who work longer, or seasonal workers who overstay their visas, or asylum seekers not allowed to work, or economic migrants who have entered the country illegally and have no intention of claiming asylum. As David Jackson of Operation Gangmaster put it: 'It might be south-west for mushrooms one week, flowers in Lincolnshire the next, then greenhouse produce in Lancashire, then fruit in Evesham, salad in Sussex, cockles in Scotland, and so on.' Packhouses and food-processing factories are everywhere and the conditions are the same right across the UK.

I spent some time last summer and autumn in Sussex near Chichester, an area where several large packhouses have been built to supply supermarkets with salad and flowers. Immigration officers were conducting a series of raids on the minivans run by gangmasters to take migrants to their jobs at different companies. There were also raids on houses and caravans owned or rented by the employment agencies. On at least one occasion, according to witnesses, police took the precaution of being armed and in large numbers before descending on a caravan site. They came at night and caught several Brazilians who had been working illegally on farms. They were deported, but according to sources many more escaped detection because they were out working the night shift at the time.

A few miles up the road from there and around the time I was making one of my visits to Sussex, Southern Glass Produce, the large nursery which packs imported cut flowers for Sainsbury's, was raided by Immigration officials as part of a crackdown on an alleged multi-million-pound illegal labour ring. Forty-five illegal workers were arrested here and at four houses where they were being accommodated by a gangmaster in Littlehampton. Among them were Mongolians and Lithuanians. Most will be deported. The ringleaders were arrested. Two men have been charged with possession of forged documents. Inquiries are continuing, according to the Home Office.

A couple of weeks earlier, in October 2003, Immigration officials raided a large salad and vegetable producer in the Vale of Evesham. Bomfords is one of the main suppliers to the leading UK food processors and retailers, having Tesco, Asda, Sainsbury's, Safeway and Somerfield among its customers. It not only grows its own produce on 5,000 acres of farmland but imports large volumes of salads and vegetables for packing in its pack-houses. It has been growing rapidly and in 2003 acquired the substantial Gerber Fresh Produce business. After the raid on Bomfords, twenty-two Polish workers were taken away for further investigation. Sixteen were released and returned to work;

five were found to have very good forged work permits; and one was found to have a work permit that had run out. The raid was carried out with the full co-operation of Bomfords, who make sure that any gangmasters they use are registered for VAT and complete tax returns. The company also checks with workers what they are being paid. Workers' documents are checked and forwarded to the Immigration office if there is any doubt.

Over in Lincolnshire, raids by Immigration officers had been on hold for five months because of a dispute with the local police about budgets. Their return to active operations came shortly after these other raids, when they were invited in by a company called Greencell, which packs exotics for the supermarkets and has supplied many of the main retailers at various points. The raid revealed 22 illegal workers – Brazilians, Poles, Lithuanians, Latvians, one Czech and one Albanian, all of whom were detained. The gangmaster has not been named while Immigration investigates what efforts he had made to check the workers' documentation. 'He may have a defence if they had forged documents and he believed them to be genuine,' it said. Greencell stated it had asked Immigration officials to visit because it wanted to make sure it was using only legitimate labour.

The pattern of employment is the same right round the country. Sometimes the scale of it is hidden within larger conurbations – the labourers of Evesham, for instance, are mostly transported from Birmingham; those in the south-east may be brought out to work from London. It is in East Anglia that the impact of today's system of food production on migrants and the communities in which they find themselves is most clearly seen. The flatlands of the Fens are among the most productive agricultural areas in England, and the network of small towns around them have become the packhouse capital of the UK. Far from any large city which might provide labour or housing, the scale of economic migration here is highly visible.

Thetford is typical: a small town in the middle of Norfolk, surrounded by lowland heaths and wetlands. Its prosperous market square reflects its past glory as Anglo-Saxon capital of East Anglia and more recently as home of Thomas Paine, the eighteenth-century radical and champion of the abolition of slavery.

The Red Lion, the old coaching inn in the main square, is 'the Portuguese pub' now, where the migrants who provide the labour to many of the food factories, packhouses and farms in the region congregate in their brief moments of leisure. It was here that I met Joaquim. He has been employed by a gangmaster packing vegetables and salads in the Norfolk factories for a few years. He's Portuguese and here legally but he was nervous. Some of the people he has worked for have used violence on others. There were things he didn't want to talk about.

The first factory he worked at – a big company supplying supermarkets – was staffed by a mix of legal Portuguese workers and illegal Russians and Ukrainians. The supervisor would always give more work to the illegals – and they in turn would give him backhanders to make sure they could get work or the best positions on the production line. There was a lot of corruption, so if work was slack, as it often was when supermarket orders were suddenly cancelled, you wouldn't get any. It was piecework and if you worked really hard, you could earn £400 a week. That was when they decided to change the system so the maximum you could get was £200 a week. 'I was on a carrot line, sorting them by appearance. You could get good at it. You couldn't stop when you had done your eight hours though, you had to carry on till the order was finished. After that I worked in a salad factory. It was a good company but the hours were unpredictable, and then a gangmaster offered me a bit more money for driving a minivan, taking workers to the packhouses, so I did that. The vehicle had no tax or insurance and was supposed to take twelve but we'd drive eighteen. It had no MOT and the steering was dodgy, which was a problem because we had to turn right on a roundabout into the packhouse. There weren't any windows, so that people couldn't see who was inside.

Sometimes you would get a warning that Immigration were coming, so then you would make sure there were no Russians or Brazilians that day, only Portuguese people.

'I would be charged thirty-five pounds a week to share a tiny room and in some jobs after all the deductions I only got sixty pounds in my pocket a week even though I worked long hours.

'One of the gangmasters would boast that he could take any woman to bed. He'd say the women had no choice because they were illegal. There was an attempted rape in one house – there's lots of sexual harassment, but this was serious assault. One of the women in the house who was legal rang the gangmaster and threatened to go to the police. So he told her she was sacked over the phone and then came round to evict her.

'The orders would come suddenly and you would be taken to the factory. But then if there was no work you would be taken back to the house after just a couple of hours. You might work for one factory packing from six a.m. till one p.m. and then get taken to another factory for a four p.m. to ten p.m. shift. There was a lot of violence to enforce the regime. In the first three months I saved nothing. It was easy to blow your money at the weekend on drink. Then I decided I had to get out of the trap and be very disciplined. I worked sixteen hours a day and saved everything to escape.'

The Red Lion was one of Fatima's haunts. Fatima is fiftyish with dyed dark hair and bright red lipstick. Her plucked eyebrows have been redrawn half an inch higher on her forehead so that her expression is one of constant amused astonishment at her predicament. She had been trying to organize Portuguese workers locally into a union to fight for their rights, but when her gangmaster found out, she was evicted without warning from her accommodation in Thetford. She managed to get herself a caravan in a field to live in and was happy to have escaped the tied housing which made her so dependent on the gangmaster. He had put her in a house with ten South African men he used as his enforcers and she didn't feel safe. There was lots of sexual harassment by the Portuguese supervisors at work. The gang-master was then arrested and charged with not paying tax and insurance, she says, and the business and workers were handed over to another gangmaster, but one of the managers is the same as before. When I met Fatima she was working through the new gangmaster doing twelve-hour night shifts, six days a week, with no overtime payments, for a printer who prints the labels for supermarket ready meals. When she complained that it was too cold to work in the factory, she was threatened with a beating. She had decided to go home. 'There is a lot of racism,' she said. 'It's horrible here.'

There are 4,000 Portuguese workers living in Thetford and the surrounding areas and an unknown number of Brazilians. Fatima is friendly with many of them and took me on a tour to meet them. In one small house in a 1970s estate in nearby Brandon, a town serving more food factories, she introduced me to Agostinha. Agostinha is a survivor, a big Portuguese woman in her mid-thirties with lots of bleached blonde hair, a deep voice and a ready laugh. She and Jose, her Brazilian husband, younger by several years, were sharing one small bedroom in the house with her ten-year-old son Pedro, who goes to the local school. There had been eight living in the house the week before, but three of the Brazilians, a couple and their little girl, also at a local school, had just been deported. The bailiffs had called to collect debts left by previous tenants, South Africans. The land-lord had threatened to evict Agostinha, but the police had intervened.

They each pay £100 a week for their one bedroom, and the landlord's usual terms are pasted up by the front door: £7 per bed per night. He keeps a key and comes in whenever he feels like it, sometimes at night, to check up on them. Agostinha showed me her room, rushing round with air-freshener spray before I went in, apologizing for the mess. The room was jammed with their possessions – suitcases, piles of clothes and shoes, a bowl of fruit, cuddly toys, a homework folder, a few ornaments, a small double bed and a child's single bed in the corner. Everything was as neat and ordered as it could be in such a tiny space.

Over a communal Sunday lunch she had prepared for everyone in the house, Agostinha told me about her work experiences. She was first employed cutting and packing salads at the factory nearby. The lettuce would come along the line for them to cut, different ways for different clients, one way for Tesco, another way for McDonald's. Then they'd put it back on the belt to go for washing in a rolling carpet of water and chlorine. As it came out you picked out the bad leaves and packed the good ones. The chlorine burnt your eyes but everything was very clean. Then there was work for a while, trussing birds, at a chicken factory supplying the major retailers. Agostinha developed wrist pain but was told to carry on working and did so for three weeks while in pain. She says that the factory manager told her it wasn't a problem and that she must work faster. But then it got too bad to continue and they sent her home. The local doctor had diagnosed tendonitis and she is now on the waiting list for an operation on her hand at the NHS hospital. She was given no sick pay by the gangmaster despite having paid tax and insurance. She had been told by social security that she would be receiving state benefits soon.

She also told me about 'a guy at one of the gangmasters, Junior, everyone knows who he is, he's the one who fixes the Brazilians' papers. You pay three hundred pounds to a lawyer through him and everything is taken care of.' They charge the Brazilians to come to England – many of them have sold houses and cars at home to pay – and then they shop them after a few months when they owe them wages. It means they can make more money charging the next lot to come. This brutal practice was a recurring theme among the migrants I spoke to.

I wondered what it must be like for Agostinha's son Pedro, witnessing all the coming and going, and living in such cramped conditions. 'He cried nearly every day for the first year, there was such a lot of racism at school, kids would keep telling him he was the son of a bitch and should go home.' She'd actually like to go home, but her husband's papers are stuck with the Immigration office in Croydon. They were taken by Immigration officials who raided the house looking for a South African who wasn't there. Since Jose is now married to her, he is perfectly entitled to be in the country, but despite making the trek to London twice Agostinha has been waiting a year to get them back so they can travel. She laughed at the craziness of it all. 'Well, do you want us or want to get rid of us?'

Teresa, by contrast, was pale, thin and seven months pregnant. She and her husband Joao live slightly north of Thetford in Watton, another small Norfolk town, along with several other Portuguese workers. Joao's eyes were bloodshot with exhaustion, and he seemed to shrink into his fragile frame. Their tiny one-bedroomed flat was up a metal staircase, along a corridor with a filthy carpet and bare live electricity cables hanging from the ceiling. Teresa had been unable to work recently, having suffered from serious depression, which was being treated by the local GP. But she had done shifts in many of the food factories and packhouses in the area, always working through gangmasters because that was the only way she and her husband could get housing. She did a spell at a canning factory where they cut labels off supermarket cans that had been dented and put new labels on top to cover the dents. She'd work on the potato packing lines at weekends. The worst job her husband had was in the cat food factory where the gangmaster would have them picked up with Chinese workers for night shifts, dragging everyone in, just so that a supervisor could line them up and walk along pointing with his finger: 'You, you, you and you' and then send the rest home without work. During a period without work Joao had to sell his gold wedding ring to buy food.

A Portuguese friend in the town had had her car vandalized, and another Portuguese couple had been attacked in the street one night, so Teresa was fearful of going out. The flat was expensive – £80 a week – and after long hours in his current job in a duck-processing factory Joao was left with £60 a week after all the deductions. But at least they weren't living with rats any more. When they complained about conditions to one gangmaster they were evicted. They were told by the Citizens' Advice Bureau in King's Lynn to go to the council because they were homeless, but were too frightened to do so. If it's known that you cause trouble, you don't get the jobs. They are now however on the council's social housing register.

Citizens' Advice Bureaux (CABs) around the country have catalogued a huge number of cases similar to these. Since illegal workers rarely consult them, this catalogue probably represents a fraction of the true number of abuses. A CAB in Norfolk had to call in the police when it was trying to help a group of Portuguese workers because the gangmaster had brought along his own 'security people'. A CAB in Bristol reported Portuguese workers being housed twenty-seven to a house while packing mushrooms. Another client was living in a house with seven people but only two beds, while working fifty-five hours a week. He was paid £4.10 per hour and had £35 deducted for this accommodation. A CAB in Cambridgeshire helped a number of Portuguese nationals working on the land, where the employer had provided accommodation in partitioned containers with no water supply. Rent and transport costs were deducted from their pay. One client was paid £83.85 for a week's work and charged £80 rent. The workers were made to sign agreements in English which they didn't understand to repay recruitment costs of up to £100 if they left the job within six months. A CAB in Suffolk looked after 100 Portuguese workers who had had jobs in a food-processing factory. When they were sacked by the agency which employed them they were all immediately evicted. Ukrainians in the Midlands were being charged £600 for documentation they had never seen, and then being paid less than the minimum wage.

And so the list goes on, with problems of migrant labourers re-ported from Dorset, Bedfordshire, Cambridgeshire, the Midlands,

Norfolk, Suffolk, Bristol, Hampshire, Northern Ireland. The list of abuses includes the use of violence to enforce conditions, threats of eviction, extortionate rents, dangerous housing, breaches of health and safety regulations, wages below the legal minimum, tax deducted but no record of it at the Inland Revenue, instant dismissal for trivial or personal reasons.

Occasionally, when there are deaths, the news hits the headlines, as when three men were killed and five others were seriously injured when the minivan taking them to harvest spring onions collided with a high-speed train on an unmanned level crossing in Worcestershire. Police inquiries were complicated by the fact that the workers did not know one another, were of different nationalities, including Somali and Iraqi, and the driver spoke no English. The farmer had been warned several times that minivans transporting his workers were not using the crossing correctly.

Although the housing conditions frequently and blatantly flout UK regulations, local authorities are reluctant to act. A group of local authority consultants, Cambridge Housing and Environmental Consultants, explains why. They cite a case where a redundant coaching hotel in a small village to the north of Spalding was found to be housing sixty-five workers in ten bedrooms, with no kitchen or heating. The fire escape was sealed and because there was an immediate danger to the residents the property was closed, at which point the residents presented themselves to the local authority as homeless. Other properties in the village were being used in the same way and the result was considerable tension with the local population 'which had required the police to devote many manhours to keeping the peace'. But the local authorities hesitate to intervene, knowing that if they do they are likely to have to provide alternative accommodation from their already overstretched housing stocks. 'Gangmasters know and exploit this,' the housing consultants say.

One of the local doctors in Thetford, Dr Giles Smith, wrote to the Efra select committee asking why no one could stop the gangmasters recruiting people. His practice has some 700 Portuguese on its lists, as well as Russians and Chinese. Dr Smith told me he had seen increasing evidence of migrant workers doing long hours and night shifts in vegetable factories becoming 'long-term sick'. 'They are being abused and overworked. Quite a few have industrial injuries and get dumped on the sick system. They then apply for housing from the local authority. I feel for them, but I feel for the services the NHS is trying to provide too. We're hanging on by our fingernails. There has been no extra funding to provide the care we should be giving. My colleagues and staff are spending vast amounts of time sorting the problems of non-English speaking patients. The strain on the infrastructure – medical, police, education, housing, sewage, roads – is intolerable. There is huge resentment in the town. I fear there is going to be tribal war.'

The Efra committee, after hearing at length evidence from retailers' organizations, farmers, unions and others, reached the damning conclusion that

the dominant position of the supermarkets in relation to their suppliers is a significant contributory factor in creating an environment where illegal activity by gangmasters can take root. Intense price competition and the short time-scales between orders from the supermarkets and deliveries to them put pressure on suppliers who have little opportunity or incentive to check the legality of the labour. Supermarkets go to great lengths to ensure that the labels on their products are accurate. We believe they should pay equal attention to the conditions under which their produce is harvested and packed . . . supermarkets cannot wash their hands of this matter.

MPs also said they were 'appalled by the lack of priority given to what is supposed to be the government's coordinated response to illegal activity by gangmasters'.

Nuno Guerreiro runs the Portuguese Workers' Association as a volunteer. He represents Portuguese workers who find themselves in difficulty. Files bulging with cases fill part of his small East London flat. We met there and talked about the dangers of our failure to debate the need for economic migration openly, while he pressed Portuguese delicacies on me – air-cured ham, sweet melon, stuffed olives and handmade bread. 'There's an old Portuguese saying: animals eat to survive, people eat to socialize. Please, eat . . .'

He, like most others I have spoken to, is convinced things are getting worse. 'Look, here's an example from Lowestoft. Forty Portuguese workers who were being housed in overcrowded caravans complained that they hadn't been paid. The agency sent in its heavies with bats and threatened them with violence. The police had to intervene. Here's another. Wisbech 2003. A group of young Portuguese men coming out of a bar were attacked by a large group of young Britons. One of the Portuguese men was kicked thirty times in the head while the aggressors shouted at them to go back home. Local police said it was one of the most vicious racist attacks they had seen. But no government will tackle it.' I asked him why he thought that was. Why, when the way the system works is so obvious to people labouring in it and to those living in rural areas, has there been such a conspiracy of silence about it? 'The government and the supermarkets want cheap food. But we'll all end up paying in the end.

'Look, never mind the questions of nationality and justice, let's say you don't care about social tension either, think about this at the most basic, selfish level. Treating people like this is not a good idea. We are forcing people to live in squalor, in bad housing with wages so low they cannot live. They are bound to be ill. Bad housing and bad diets – these are the sort of conditions that before the war sustained TB. These are the people who are cleaning your salad.'

When the English outdoor salad season comes to an end in late October, much of the production moves to Spain. Several large English producers have acquired farms there, mostly in the

Murcia and Andalucia regions, to enable them to guarantee year-round supplies of salads to supermarkets.

Spanish farms are also the source of many of the Mediterranean vegetables such as peppers and aubergines sold in British supermarkets, along with tomatoes, cucumbers, celery, out-of-season broccoli and organic produce. Quite apart from the climate, the costs are lower there, and the exchange rate favours euro countries when it comes to exports.

EU structural funds have helped create this new horticultural industry. They have paid for a motorway network to be driven right through Spain, so that refrigerated lorries scarcely have to leave the dual carriageway as they plough from Almeria in the south to the further reaches of northern Europe.

The land is arid, and the regional governments are proud of their 'miracles', saying that like the Israelis they have made the desert bloom. The dramatic economic growth has transformed an area that was until recently among the poorest in Europe. English literati travelling through it in the 1950s and 1960s never failed to mention the destitution they saw. Thanks to intensive farming, the Almeria area alone now produces nearly 3 million tonnes of fruit and vegetables annually, mostly for export to the UK, Germany, Holland and Belgium, earning £1 billion in export revenue a year. But the success story is already losing its varnish. There is talk of EU social funds being needed to pay for a planned abandonment of some of the lands where the soil or water is most polluted. Its critics say the 'miracle' is ravaging the area.

I arranged to meet Hector Gravina early one morning in a hotel favoured by British package tour companies on the Costa Blanca. The Spanish organic farmers' association was running a conference here and I had been told there would be a chance to meet the chief of agri-environment from Spain's Ministry of Agriculture, along with other leading academic experts. Everything had been done by email, with the timings left rather vague, so I wasn't quite sure who I was looking for. I was scanning the crowds of passing holidaymakers when a short, wiry man, with a dramatic scar slashed across his forehead to his beetling brows, official conference bag slung across his shoulder like a bandolier, enveloped me in a great bear hug and a swirl of roll-up cigarette smoke. '*Hola!*'

Standing back for air a few minutes later, I took in Hector Gravina, a veteran campaigner from Spain's Friends of the Earth: black leather jerkin, black trousers, long-sleeved red T-shirt, close-cropped black hair, left in a little mop on top, with a tiny pigtail curling down his neck behind, and the remnants of a goatee beard on his chin.

'You have chosen a good day. Our tour bus is going round one of the most beautiful nature reserves of Spain. I can show you the most intensive agricultural production in the country, the fields of plastic, and then you see organic lettuce being grown in the shadow of the farmhouse that inspired our great playwright, Garcia Lorca, to write *Blood Wedding*. But first we will have it from the horse's mouth, let's catch the man from the ministry . . .'

The chief of agri-environment, Manuel Ariza, a substantial, jowly man, had just arrived in the lobby. Hidden behind his black sunglasses, his eyes gave no clue to his sympathies when I asked what he saw as the main issues for Spanish agriculture, but traces of a good breakfast were just visible on his shirt, hinting at a man who enjoys his food. 'Agriculture is three per cent of our total GDP. Intensive farming represents fifty per cent of the total agricultural area. It is mainly concentrated in the Mediterranean arc. We are Europe's California,' he said as solemnly as a textbook, then his whole body heaved with laughter. 'So we have all their problems, problems with water – pollution of coastal waters, exhaustion of ground water, problems with soil degradation . . .' Then he disappeared into his official car while we piled on to our bus.

We drove along the coast, where any gaps in the line of hotels were filled with cranes and construction sites for new apartments and golf courses. Then we passed into a dramatic landscape of desert rock, blazing with light and stunning shadows. 'The Sahara is creeping up, you can see how intensive agriculture has accelerated the process and where the hills have lost any ground cover,' Hector pointed out.

At Nijar, the sea of plastic greenhouses began. The greenhouses did not look like greenhouses so much as old army tents, an invasion of plastic sheeting pitched over wooden or metal poles that stretched as far as the eye could see. The plastic was greying and drooping, opaque with dust and splashes of chemicals. There was no visible greenery. Agrochemical adverts appeared like milestones at regular intervals. All the big companies are here – Bayer, DuPont, Monsanto, Syngenta. Here and there diggers were at work excavating soil that had become saturated with chemicals or so exhausted by the cycle of three harvests a year that it was no longer economical to farm it and new soil had to be brought in.

This is the driest part of Europe and the water supply is indeed at crisis point here. Unlike the olives, almonds and other traditional crops of the region that used to be farmed on mixed holdings with sheep and goats, horticultural crops are thirsty, and salads the thirstiest of them all. Intensive agriculture has competed with the tourist industry to be the most extravagant user of water. The groundwater has become polluted with pesticides. The water table has been infiltrated by the sea as a result of over-extraction. Excessive use of chemical fertilizers has led to nitrate levels that are in some places ten times higher than World Health Organization safety limits.

The nitrate problem is not confined to Spain. Intensive farming in England has also polluted groundwater, damaging the ecology of streams, rivers and lakes and ruining coastal waters. Some 55 per cent of the country has recently been designated as 'nitrate vulnerable zones'.

Much of southern Spain has already run out of drinking water. The tourist and farming industries currently depend on aqueducts bringing water from rivers further north. But now those supplies are inadequate too. So the Spanish government hopes to get EU funding for a plan to divert part of the Ebro river to bring water from the north of the country to the south to feed the lettuce and other vegetables. It involves building over 100 dams, 1,000 kilometres of canals and pipes at a cost of 18 billion euros.

Hector was among the 1 million protestors who took to the streets in March 2002 to campaign against the plan. It was one of the greatest public displays of anti-government sentiment in Spain since the days of General Franco. The project would threaten the Ebro Delta, Europe's second largest wetland. The government still hopes to proceed, however. Meanwhile, many farms in the south have taken to extracting water illegally to get round government restrictions.

Our tour bus eventually emerged from the plastic wasteland into one of the last remaining nature reserves on the Cabo da Gata, and stopped in front of the romantic ruins of a farm, with old drystone walls marking out terraces of gnarled olive and wild fig trees. Much of the land here was abandoned in the 1960s, when the Spanish migrated in their thousands to escape the grinding poverty that went with living on its poor soil. No one wants to go back to the good old days.

I caught up with the man from the ministry again and asked him what he thought would happen in the next twenty years. 'Of course this intensive vegetable production is not sustainable. We will have to switch back to rotating crops. Olive production is sustainable here.' He bent down to admire a desert snail with beautiful markings, and invited me to join him in the official limousine. 'The chemical companies started to promote prod-ucts, the farmers started to misuse them, the plants grow in excess, they need more water, the farmers are thrilled, but you can't go on doing that, taking three or four crops a year from soil. Over time the exploitation of the land will shift. Mediterranean vegetables will move to the Magreb where the laws are less stringent – European countries have already invested there, it's cheaper and there is still beautiful land there. We'll grow more organic and farm more extensively. There'll be warranties against residues for produce from outside the EU – we'll test more and reject produce with pesticide residues, so it will be safe – but no warranties for the environment . . .'

I said that not many British government officials would be quite so outspoken. 'Ah well, I've survived a few governments. I'll take the risk. That is my personal opinion of course, not necessarily the view of my government. Now, where's lunch . . . ?'

We had stopped in the middle of the nature reserve, at a viewpoint over the scorched and rugged hills. The men had brought out a paella dish the size of a paddling pool and placed it over a camp fire and were emptying a 5-litre can of local organic olive oil into it. Ariza took a swig of chilled beer and continued the argument: 'Globalization of food is not the answer. It is a system designed by finance people and lawyers. Of course, individuals will have to change.' The prawns were going into the paella at this point – Ariza leaned over and inspected the label on the box. 'It says "Produce of South Africa",' he laughed. 'No, but I am optimistic for Europe. The environmental problems will be brought under control in the West and the USA. They will be passed on instead to poorer countries. The real problem will be with the petrochemical companies. They will have to find their money elsewhere.'

There is little sign of that at the moment. The by-products of the refining of crude oil – the plastics that have made the greenhouses, the toxic pesticides that are applied to the plants – are heavily promoted. It is still standard practice in Spain to rely heavily on chemical pest and disease control.

The pristine-looking leaves we have acquired an appetite for cannot achieve their cosmetic perfection without a little hi-tech help, particularly when they are grown outside their normal season. Intensive monoculture of salads with extended seasons of cropping allows the buildup of pests and diseases in the soil.

There has been a correspondingly rapid increase in pesticide usage. Salad leaves are particularly likely to contain pesticide residues. Lettuce appears on the 'persistent offenders list' for pesticide residues compiled by the Consumers' Association from government data, in the company of apples, celery, grapes, fresh salmon, pears, peaches and nectarines, strawberries and wholemeal flour.

Most large producers in the UK are fairly coy about what pesticides they use. So I spoke to an agricultural technical consultant who works with the agrochemical industry in Spain. He explained the system to me on the condition of anonymity.

'Lettuces have a two-and-a-half to three-month growing period here in Spain. They are sprayed every week with a mixture of fungicide and insecticide except for the last two weeks. There is lots of pesticide resistance, so the products we used last year were completely different to the ones we were using five or six years ago. Some of them are very toxic. For example, we treat the lettuces with dithiocarbamates as a preventive – the English seem to use a lot of these. They are very hazardous. But there's a fungus called sclerotinia that can suddenly flare up where you have had intense cropping of the same lettuces in the same place. This monoculture allows a lot of funguses and pests to flourish. It is devastating, you can lose half the crop. With the plastic hothouses it's bad too, they are all so close together, pests spread through those crops like wildfire. I also have to advise growers to use more pesticides than I would like because if there is just one tiny aphid, their whole crop can be rejected by the supermarkets. If you want something so perfect that you can't even see one tiny aphid on it, as though it came not from the soil but from a factory, of course you have to use much more pesticide.

'Many of the seed varieties the supermarkets want are patented. The seed companies have developed hybrids in consultation with the retailers. They cost a lot, so once you've invested in them as a farmer you can't afford to take risks. The seed companies give you a whole agrochemical recipe to go with them, so of course you follow it.★

'Because lettuces grow first from a few outer leaves, with the heart developing later, the outside leaves are where the nitrates and pesticides are most concentrated. By the end of a crop cycle they can have been treated with eleven or twelve doses of pesticide as well as several fertilizer applications. More and more lettuces are sold by the supermarkets as hearts only. This conveniently removes the contaminated outer leaves as well as allowing them to charge for a "premium product".'

Most supermarkets and producers will say that pesticide usage is being reduced as companies are encouraged to switch to 'integrated crop management' (ICM) in which instead of routinely spraying, farmers make more effort to diagnose and treat problems as they arise. However, ICM appears to have made little difference to residues. Growers in the UK have their problems too.

The government's Central Science Laboratory records the overall usage of pesticides in the UK. Its most up-to-date figures (1999) show that outdoor salad crops received on average four insecticide sprays, two fungicide applications and two herbicide doses. Soil sterilants were also heavily used to control weeds and the recurring problems of funguses. Lettuces grown indoors were treated with even more fungicides. While there had been some decline in the amount of pesticides used between 1995 and 1999, general usage of pesticides on these crops has increased

★ The agrochemical industry has seen rapid concentration in the last few years with a series of mergers and takeovers. Six top companies, Syngenta, Bayer, Monsanto, BASF, Dow and DuPont accounted for 70 per cent of the US $27 billion-worth of agrochemical sales worldwide in 2002. They have also moved heavily into the seed industry and now control about 30 per cent of it, in what for them is a virtuous business circle. Many seeds now come with a seed 'dressing' of pesticides already applied, which is a major contributor to the increase in pesticide use, according to Barbara Dinham, director of Pesticides Action Network UK.

dramatically since 1986 and is still several times greater than it was twenty years ago.

Government tests for residues in salads on sale in shops bear this out. The most recent Pesticide Residues Committee monitoring report found that half the lettuces bought from major super-markets, including both Spanish and English produce, contained residues and one third contained residues of more than one pesticide.

One sample contained residues above the statutory maximum residue level (MRL) of propamocarb, an insecticide which works on the nervous system in a similar way to organophosphates, and one contained residues of vinclozolin, a chemical not permitted for use in lettuces in the UK. It is one of a group of endocrine disrupters, that is, a class of chemicals which interfere with hormones that are sometimes popularly called gender-benders.

The UK government testing for pesticides works in a rolling programme so that not all fresh produce is tested each year. But because lettuce has been such a persistent offender, and farmers have been caught using pesticides illegally on salad crops before, the Pesticides Safety Directorate (PSD) has been conducting special tests on them. It says that UK 'glasshouse lettuce is particularly prone to fungal attack during the cool, damp winter months. There is a limited range of products approved to combat disease and in the past growers have been tempted to over-use approved products (resulting in exceedances of statutory MRLs) or turn to products not approved for use on lettuce.'

The PSD's survey of UK lettuce for 2001/2002 shows that the problem is continuing. Nearly one in five lettuces exceeded maximum residue levels and 6 per cent contained pesticides not approved for use. The PSD considered that in two cases the pesticide levels presented 'possible safety risks' but no action was taken because the growers had followed the manufacturers' instructions for use on the label. An organophosphate, which is illegal in the UK, was found in several samples and at ten times the EU-permitted level in one of them. Residues of two carbamates, which work in a similar way to organophosphates, were also found at levels over the MRL. Organophosphates are under review because of concerns about the way they work on the nervous system. Direct exposure to them has been linked by some experts to Gulf War syndrome and to serious nervous disorders among farmers.

The effect of pesticide residues on our health is disputed. The government's Pesticide Residues Committee says that most residues are present at such a low level that they do not 'present a concern for consumer health'. The FSA's advice is that while about 40 per cent of fresh fruit and vegetables contain residues, they typically occur at very low levels, that is, at parts per million, and that people eating small amounts of pesticide residues in their diet are not at risk. It does however recognize concern over the so-called 'cocktail effect' of residues from different sources and asked the government's committee on toxicity to look into the risks. The committee concluded that it was extremely difficult to assess the risks because the data was not available, but highlighted groups of chemicals of specific concern. These include insecticides that work by blocking nerve receptors – the organophosphates and carbamates; certain fungicides; and the range of chemicals which are endocrine disrupters – in other words, precisely the sort of residues that have been found in salad.

The committee on toxicity agrees that endocrine-disrupting chemicals may be implicated in declining sperm counts and increasing rates of breast and testicular cancer. A Royal Society report also said that it was sensible for pregnant women to minimize their exposure to endocrine-disrupting chemicals.

Other experts are less sanguine. Dr Vyvyan Howard is a leading toxicopathologist at the University of Liverpool and a member of the government's advisory committee on pesticides, who has studied the effects of pesticides on unborn children. He points out that the average Briton has between 300 and 500 chemicals in their body which were not present fifty years ago. 'We have substantially changed the chemical environment of the womb.

Pregnant women are now exposed to completely novel molecules that their grandmothers were not. Quite a number of these are capable of hormone disruption and it takes only extremely low doses to cause effects.' He believes there is ample evidence that the pesticide cocktail effect is producing enormous change. Exposure to endocrine disrupters in the womb could be one of the reasons for the much-decreased age of puberty in girls. Early onset of puberty is linked to breast cancer later in life. In the 1960s women had a one in twenty chance of getting breast cancer, now it is one in nine. Dr Howard recommends minimizing exposure to pesticides on a precautionary basis.

The problem for the supermarkets is that despite their protestation that they are doing everything to cut down on pesticides, they are on a chemical treadmill. Friends of the Earth campaigns on pesticide use in food and says that the retailers' demand for cosmetic perfection forces farmers to use more pesticides than they would otherwise. Although retailers have acknowledged public concern, and Marks and Spencer and the Co-Op have notably said they would work with suppliers to phase out some of the most worrying chemicals from their crops, FoE analysis of data from the PSD in 2003 showed that supermarkets have not achieved any overall reduction of pesticide residues in the last five years.

Meanwhile, a briefing paper on the Spanish horticulture industry written for Defra noted: 'A heavy reliance on chemical pest and disease control is still standard practice among Spanish growers . . . It is likely that a number of chemicals will lose approval [when an EU review is complete], particularly those currently used in the production of edible crops.'

From the Costa Blanca, I moved east to see the Almerian miracle at its most intense, along the Costa del Sol.

Roquetas de Mar, like every other resort town along Spain's south coast, has been swallowed up by its *urbanizaciones*. An uninterrupted strip of time-share tower blocks in Malaga pink and Moorish beige competes with wall-to-wall package-holiday hotels to cover every inch of the seafront from here to the next town in either direction. Their balconies point towards the Mediterranean where jaunty straw parasols, painted brochure blue, shade rows and rows of yellow sun-loungers along the beach.

For a few euros you can take a toytown train inland a few hundred yards. It toots up the main street of bars with its central reserve of palms and carefully tended shrubs just as far as the roundabout where the barren desert intrudes again, and then turns straight back down to the front. Alternatively, you can tour the high rises in traditional horse and cart, complete with singing driver in sombrero.

You can buy your place in the sun here for as little as 65,000 euros. A few chunks of plaster have already fallen off some of the new tower blocks, but in the brilliant light and haze of cheap Sangria, no one's noticing. Arsenal v Liverpool is showing on Sky at the Colossimo pub where Brits enjoy an early-morning pint, and *Waffeln mit Kirschen* are being served to Germans in the café next door.

Less than a mile away, on the other side of the roundabout, the good road, and with it the world of holidays, comes to an abrupt halt. Drive over the patch of rough ground beyond, and you find yourself plunging instead into the sea of plastic greenhouses that have drowned the wide coastal plain for miles around.

I came up here on my first night in Roquetas, having been warned to take care. It's easy to get lost in this featureless landscape. The roads through the hothouses all look the same after a while – a maze of cracked tarmac corridors fading into unmade edges. But what the friendly advice had meant was this is another country. It is a segregated universe, alarming to locals, that stretches for miles across the province of Almeria and into neighbouring Murcia in which 70,000 (by official estimates) or more migrant labourers live. They squat by the side of the roads for hours, from dawn till dusk, in the hope of being picked up for work on the vegetables.

I had arranged to meet Gabriel Ataya, a Senegalese organizer for the Rural Workers' Union, and his friends here on the edge of town where the migrants have colonized old houses abandoned by the Spanish.

It was dark and there was no more hope of work that day, but there were still people by the roadside, refusing to give up. Some of them were slumped against telegraph poles, snatching sleep, others stared listlessly at the ground, raising their eyes briefly at each passing van.

Outside Ataya's house, a tall black man, hearing me call out in French, came up and begged for food. He told me his name was Drame Diongo. He had arrived from Senegal one month before, having left his family and paid a man in Dakar about £1,000 to borrow his papers. He'd queued every morning by the road for work but had never got picked by the Spanish farm owners. He hadn't eaten for two days. He was big and looked strong, but his weary voice was hard to catch. He had no idea why he didn't get picked and asked me what I thought.

Perhaps it was that his jeans, specially saved for and bought for his new life, looked too new; perhaps it was that his beard and Islamic cap made him look like a caricature of a terrorist, or perhaps it was just that he didn't speak Spanish. I suggested Ataya might be able to explain how the pecking order worked.

Inside Ataya's single-storey, rough-plastered old house, it turned out that Ataya knew Drame and had already helped him. Several other men appeared to have adopted the house too and drifted in and out of the sitting room past the large sacks of rice in the hall, while I talked to Ataya's friend Spitou.

Spitou had been a Spanish teacher in Senegal, but he had had to support two families since his brother died and found he could not survive on his official salary back home. He managed to get a visa from the French embassy in Dakar which he was able to use to come to Spain: 'It's easier for people like me to get visas because I had a good job.' He too was tall, with handsome, even features and a soft voice. He had worked for nearly three years on farms where they grow tomatoes for export to the UK and Holland. The work was never guaranteed but when he was needed he was paid 30 euros (about £20) for eight or nine hours' labour – the daylight hours – thinning the fruit so that the tomatoes left on the vines would grow uniformly, and harvesting. It's backbreaking work and unbearably hot as the temperature is usually 45–48°C under the plastic. The irrigation water, which comes in a huge new pipe, is computer-controlled, mixed with pesticides and fertilizers and constantly drip-fed to the plants to keep them healthy, but there's no drinking water for the workers. The boss knew Spitou by a false identity, and Spitou was paying tax and insurance, but against this false identity, on another man's papers. 'The boss doesn't care but he wants to stay the right side of the law.

'The police don't bother you if you stay here in the agricultural area, but if you stray into town it's another story,' he said. 'You feel persecuted on all sides. You have no papers, so you limit your movements; you fear being stopped and deported, so you hide. You can take no leisure, you cannot be yourself. You give up all idea of yourself. Many people break. We survive by supporting each other and by remembering the injustice.'

I asked him why, when conditions were so hard, he stayed. His eyes filled with tears. 'I cannot go back. I have paid to come. The borders are closed. You cannot come and go and come again. I cannot save, I have just enough to send back each month for my responsibilities.'

The tears were slipping down his cheeks now, just visible as they gleamed in the half-light of the lamp, and he paused to steady his voice. But he didn't want to stop. 'Every night when I go to sleep I dream of home, of my children, of my friends. There is never a day when I do not wake up dreaming of my home, but I expect to be here as long as the West is better off than the South.'

Ataya wanted to take me out to meet the English-speaking migrants who live nearby. Spitou cycled off into the night with a cheery wave, the homesickness my questioning had brought to the surface suppressed once more, the bicycle a sign of success, while we wandered down a narrow lane which twisted between abandoned houses along the edge of a patch of wasteland. A few old lamp-posts cast a weak, sulphurous-yellow light at irregular intervals. Electricity cables had been strung loosely across the street and between the low roofs. The moon was just beginning to wane in a clear sky, and the sounds of a warm African night came from glassless windows all around. The end of one house had been converted into a makeshift shop-cum-telephone exchange selling a few essentials – pieces of soap, oil, sugar, chickpeas, Dettol, and lightening body lotion. Along one wall was a line of wooden phone booths for those who wanted to call home.

Sammi from the Congo had come to buy cigarettes, and conducted a trilingual conversation in Spanish, French and English, swaying slightly as he sized me up with his huge bulging eyes. He was wearing an old English cloth cap, and a tweedy-patterned cotton shirt-jacket over a scruffy polo shirt. He adopted a mock county drawl – 'Eeoohh, how interesting' – when he was told why I was here, but declined to talk to me further because he'd 'had a spot of bother' in Madrid and it might be better if he didn't. 'Allow me however to introduce you to Jacqueline. She is the fine lady in charge of giving a good time to everyone.'

Jacqueline was from Nigeria and was dressed in an Adidas bomber jacket and skintight short trousers over an ample frame. Her straightened hair was dyed pinkish-red on top, and crimson toenails peeped out of impossibly high platform sandals. She mostly worked in the big tomato-packing factory up the road, putting tomatoes into boxes for export to England, Belgium and sometimes Australia. The money's good when there's work, sometimes 40 euros a day if you work twelve hours. But sometimes there's no work, then you have to make do where you can. Her two children were back home, looked after by her mother. 'Does their father help?' I asked. 'How would I know? I'm here,' she shrugged.

Breakfast at the hotel on the beach next morning was a self-service, flat-rate, 6-euro buffet, constantly replenished from 8 a.m. until 11 a.m. Here the chefs were on display behind a giant hotplate frying fifty eggs at a time, flipping 100 pieces of bacon as they turned a sugary brown. The white bread rolls were stacked like a game of sticks, so high that you couldn't remove one without disturbing the whole pile. There were twenty different kinds of pastry and a dozen processed cereals. Buckets of baked beans sat next to platters of meat. And yet this free for-all plenty had induced a kind of frenzy. We were pouncing on the counters like hunters, cutting across one another, grabbing tongs, barging for plates. There was no conversation but every third body spoke the same story – here were the diseases of affluence, the epidemic of obesity afflicting Western nations, writ large.

There was a diet counter where people trying hard to lose weight were loading their plates high with 'reduced-calorie' cheeses and slabs of liverish-pink 'low-fat' sausagemeat, filling their bowls with tinned fruit cocktail, and inspecting the labels of artificially sweetened yoghurts ('New! Added calcium for healthy bones!').

A humming electric cube delivered ersatz orange juice, with its tell-tale 'mouth-feel' of flavourings and sugar, even though fresh oranges grown nearby cost only a few cents. Eastern European waitresses moved silently up and down the tables clearing away plates as fast as eaters pushed them aside.

Out in the foyer, the big-name package tour companies offered day trips – 'to the Carrefour supermarket for retail therapy . . . here you shop to your heart's content' – and to the Sunday market where you can 'buy a little bit of real Spain' to take home.

Sunday is in fact still a day of rest in Spain. This was the only time I could meet the migrants who live right in among the greenhouses, when the farm managers were away having their traditional long family lunches. So I had to forgo the market and my piece of real Spain and head back to the sea of plastic instead.

I found I could navigate my way through the plastic maze by using the dozens of billboards advertising agrochemicals as markers. I took a left at the DuPont sign for 'Lannate r' systematic insecticide with triple action for complete crop security.

There are few trees and no fields here. All is grey and dusty brown, except where the endless line of sheeting is broken here and there by large rubbish tips on to which hundreds of brightly coloured chemical containers have been dumped.

I wandered over a fenced-off dump and gingerly kicked the containers. Some still had dregs left in them. Here were the big brand names again. Others were recognizable for the notoriety of their active ingredients. Endosulfan, a persistent organochlorine pesticide, acutely toxic and an endocrine-disrupter. Metam sodium, a soil fumigant that acts as fungicide, herbicide and worm killer, also acutely toxic; Metomilo, a carbamate – highly toxic. There were dozens I'd never heard of, and lots of emptied cartons of nitrate and phosphate fertilizers, and ground disinfectants, all displaying their hazardous chemical warning signs and instructions on careful disposal. The Spanish government has been trying to improve its record on waste, but these were still awaiting attention.

On the next road along, mountains of rubble and soil excavated from the greenhouses when the land has become exhausted had been dumped on another tip, along with old contaminated plastic sheets and more pesticide containers. A farmer had driven his white van to the middle of the tip where he was feeding his sheep plant waste, the tomato vines and pepper stalks collected from the greenhouses once the crops have been harvested. The practice is banned because the plant waste contains chemical residues which then accumulate in the animals' fatty tissue, thus building up in the food chain, but it's common all the same.

The next dump a few miles on looked like the entrance to hell. A huge crater had been carved out of one end by diggers, a heap of spoil was being turned at the other, and plastic and concrete debris was everywhere. A foul smell of rottenness was rising up from it. On one edge of the pit there was a small pile of broken wood that looked as though it was part of the heap, but as I got closer, five men emerged. This was their home. They were all Moroccan. Half a broken door and a few uneven planks had been lassoed to some dead tree branches and shorn-off water pipes. A torn boat tarpaulin, black with oil and smoke, had been tied over them. A scavenged mattress on top provided a desperate bulwark against wind and rain. Inside they were cooking their Sunday lunch. One of them checked the flat bread they had made and wrapped in a towel before tucking it up in their bed to prove, while a pot of couscous and herbs simmered on a stove of bottled gas. A pair of jeans, an anorak and track-suit bottoms hung from a line of nails hammered into the cardboard walls, over a row of photographs from a mail-order fashion catalogue. Upturned vegetable crates did for furniture. Hanging by the door was a broken child's blackboard, chalked with Arabic and Spanish – they had been giving one another lessons.

They had all arrived in boats, having paid the going rate of £1,000 to intermediaries to secure a place with the smugglers. They had lived there in the shack for two and a half years, and three of them had managed to get official papers. They were legal. Most of them were in debt after their journey, their families back home providing surety. They had jobs on the big farm down the road. When there was work they earned 30 euros a day. If there was enough work, they ate, if there wasn't, they didn't. There was no water or sanitation, only closed irrigation pipes for the crops, so they collected water from a tank for agricultural effluent. They were often ill with headaches and stomach trouble.

What if the farmer discovered them here, I asked. Would they be forced to move on? 'But he knows, he comes to pick us up in the morning in his van,' they said. They were getting nervous, so I went back down towards the road, happy to escape the stench, and passed the water tank. It was scummy, with three empty pesticide containers floating in it.

After a few hours, your eyes become acclimatized and you can begin to distinguish the piles of rubble which are inhabited from those which are not. Any expanse of concrete is likely to have been made into a shelter. Those who had been there a short time were still sleeping on upturned crates, lined with cardboard; those who had been there a bit longer had managed to carry home stained mattresses from the tips. When it rained most of them got wet. Apart from Mohammed.

Mohammed was a craftsman and an optimist. I found him on a rubbish tip near some greenhouses of particularly fine construction, owned not by a small farmer but by a big company. He shared the tip with about fifty Moroccans, who all lived in rickety shacks of plastic. But Mohammed had managed to find a rusty saw and had used it to build a hut from the pallets used to transport crates of vegetables on juggernauts. It was good new wood. He then covered the outside with a double layer of plastic sheeting and lined the inside with carefully cut cardboard, screwed into place with 'top-quality nuts and bolts'. 'It doesn't leak,' he declared in triumph.

The bedroom was perfect for three men, so he invited his uncle over from Morocco to join him. There was no water or sanitation here either but he had found a way to tap into the main irrigation pipe, a huge conduit of clean water running alongside the greenhouses. With some nifty work with a nail and a replaceable plug he had provided safe supplies for all of them. 'It comes out in a terrific gush,' he said, provoking laughter from all the other men. He offered me the fried aubergine and corn bread his friend was making for their Sunday lunch.

If they could survive here for five years and prove they had been here that long by showing they have made regular remittances home, these migrants would be granted residence. For those with relatives already in Spain, it's quicker – just three years.

Abdel Majid had done two years already. He was thirty-seven, dressed in American basketball shirt and plastic shoes. He had worked on the cucumbers and tomatoes but he had only once succeeded in sending money back to Morocco, so he might have trouble proving it. The jobs had been erratic, but he was still getting up to queue by the roadside each morning. Home for him was an abandoned Andalusian farmhouse, its roof long gone and its walls reduced to jagged teeth, that he shared with twenty-five other men. They had put plastic over the top, weighted down with stones, and made tiny tables from scavenged chair legs and old planks. Two of them were burning plastic and rubbish on a huge bonfire outside when I arrived, releasing acrid fumes. Abdel invited me to sit in his cardboard room and drink green tea. A young boy with him was making bread – his mother had taught him how to do it, wanting to give him a skill before he chanced his life in the boats. Hundreds of Moroccans drown each year trying to cross from Africa to Spain.

Abdel wanted me to know that they were respectable people. 'I do not live like this at home. It's true I have no papers. But we are quiet and law-abiding. We work hard and sleep a little. What do you think of all this, have you seen this before?' I did not know what to say. My French was inadequate to the task, leaving me silent. I had seen this before, but not since a visit to an aid project in the slums of Delhi over twenty years ago, and amidst all the African French and Arabic I was struggling to remember that I was in Spain, less than a mile from the Costa del Sol. So I borrowed Spitou's words, and said I thought it unjust, danger-ously so, but that I was impressed by their dignity. Abdel smiled encouragingly before replying: 'I think of myself as a slave. I go to sleep dreaming of work. I live amongst the rubbish like a rat. But I remember that I am a man. Wherever I live, whatever anyone thinks, I am a man.'

About 40 kilometres west, the greenhouses of Roquetas merge with those of El Ejido. El Ejido is a small, conservative Spanish town inland from the coast, stranded in the sea of plastic. Its narrow, straight main street is lined with plane trees and unremarkable shops. But its outskirts are swollen with new construction built with recent agricultural wealth. The value of its horticultural production has tripled in ten years.

In the hour before dawn, nothing much was stirring in the centre. But up by the petrol station café on the new highway that skirts the perimeter, farm managers with flat caps and old-fashioned moustaches were downing a quick brandy. A police vehicle was already cruising up and down, its headlights catching the shifting shadows on the pavements. Its passing beam showed 100 or more people queuing on the edge of the road. They had been walking up for nearly an hour, arriving from all directions, first the early birds, mostly black men wanting to improve their chances by picking the best spots, then Moroccans, then white men and a few white women, mostly in pairs. As the sun rose and the traffic picked up, they shuffled forward a bit. Then a white van pulled up and stopped near the white men. A farmer got out and pointed at the four he wanted. They climbed into the van and set off for work. An ordinary car pulled up and a man got out to talk to the women. They turned away and he drove off. Another van pulled up, the crowd surged forward, a bit more aggressively now, and another five white men were chosen. Some moved down into the light thrown out by the bakery, just opened, hoping to be seen first next time. The rest waited. And waited. The police patrol passed by again. One more van came and took another three, who looked Moroccan. But then there was nothing for over an hour and a half. By 9 a.m. it was clear that most of the rest of the crowd would not have work that day. The police patrol car was back: the cue for the majority of them to fade away. But a few squatted down for the day, just in case.

In February 2000 there were three days of rioting in El Ejido. A Moroccan man with severe mental health problems stabbed a twenty-six-year-old Spanish girl to death. The killing followed the arrest of another Moroccan two weeks earlier for stabbing two agricultural workers to death. After the young woman's funeral, Spanish men marched through El Ejido shouting racist slogans. Then they went on the rampage burning shops and cars owned by Moroccans and attacking any migrants they found. It took more than three days to quell the riots, during which more than thirty people were injured. Moroccan workers subsequently organized a strike, demanding their rights. The disturbances shocked the government into issuing permits to many migrants. They also provoked a series of studies highlighting conditions. More than 90 per cent of the agricultural workers in the region turned out to be immigrants, and well over half of them had no access to drinking water or sanitation. Since then, according to some academics, such as Emma Martin Diaz, professor of social anthropology at the University of Seville, there has been a delib-erate policy of segregation and harassment to keep migrants out of the town, but also a move to recruit more eastern Europeans who are less visibly different. 'This situation is only different from South African apartheid in that it is not sanctioned by law,' she says, a claim that I thought extravagant until I saw the conditions.

The horticultural industry has made one of the poorest regions of Spain wealthy but it cannot survive without a large number of migrants. It requires not just cheap labour, but cheap labour in excess. In order to turn labour on and off at will, you need to have people waiting at all hours, frightened enough to be docile and grateful enough to do whatever they are offered.

Just as previous revolutions in trade have led to mass move-ments of labour from the land into new cities, so globalization has been accompanied by waves of migration. The free movement of goods across borders and rapid improvements in transport have inevitably gone hand in hand with the movement of people. Today's food industry has not just drawn people into Spain, the UK and the rest of Europe, but has seen migrations within developing countries too. I have visited food factories in Thailand

and Kenya where a newly urbanized workforce serves the boom in global sourcing and food for export from spreading slums.

Global trade has created the potential for new wealth. But in Europe it is as though we have gone back to the dark days of the early nineteenth century. In the name of a 'flexible workforce', we have effectively thrown away two centuries of reforming legislation. We have bypassed the Factory Acts and employment regulations that were introduced to curb the abuses and excesses of the Industrial Revolution, so that its enormous contribution to the affluence of society as a whole would not be undermined by squalor and suffering.

We have allowed a structure to emerge that enables our shops to be resupplied at short notice by casual labourers picked up from the roadside whatever the hour in the Costa del Sol, or collected from their Dickensian housing in rural England. These workers are at the mercy of pecking orders as brutal as those in the turn-of-the-century American docks. We are told this has happened because people want cheap food.

The paradox is that our fresh food is not cheap any more. By the time it has been packaged and transported, and the retailers have added their margins, it is very expensive. Ninety-nine pence for a few leaves is a lot of money. But 99p for an unlimited supply of servants to wash and pick over it all, hidden not as in the old days below stairs, but in remote caravans or underneath plastic hothouses – that is cheap.

3. Beans

The link in the chain that connects fluctuating orders to casual labour around the world is the supermarket distribution centre. It is at the heart of a revolution which has swept away the old and varied structures that used to bring our food to us and replaced them with a new centralized system controlled by a mere handful of operators. Yet, like the call centre that crept into our collective consciousness long after it had rewritten the notion of customer service, the distribution centre has effected its revolution without us noticing.

The jargon of 'supply-chain logistics' is as tangled and ugly as Spaghetti Junction. 'Efficient customer response', 'constant replenishment', 'just-in-time deliveries', 'vendor-managed in-ventories', 'factory-gate pricing', 'global standard inner unit and outer-case barcodes' – the phrases are hardly the stuff of bedtime reading, which perhaps explains why we know so little about the stranglehold the major supermarkets have acquired over the distribution of food in the last two decades.

This new system is miraculous in its scale, speed and efficiency, but it is built on a fatal flaw. It is dependent on the unsustainable use of that most politically volatile of substances: crude oil. Not only is our intensive farming dependent on the byproducts of petroleum for its raw materials – the agrochemicals and plastics it uses in proliferation – now even our most basic foods cannot reach us without burning up food miles. We have made our supply lines extraordinarily vulnerable.

It took three visits to different distribution centres before I could take in the complexity of it all. It was after watching more than a tenth of one retailer's total fresh produce for the UK move through just one depot in a few hours that the enormity of the implications sank in.

I toured the Safeway nerve centre at Aylesford in 2003, hot on the heels of the then Transport Minister, John Spellar, who was reportedly equally awed after his private visit. Aylesford is one of just six hubs from which the Safeway supermarket chain was supplying its 480 or so stores around the country, while its fate was being decided in the boardrooms of rival retailers. From this depot, ten times the size of Wembley stadium, 170 38-tonne lorries are shunted into and out of 120 cavernous loading bays in an endless cycle, day and night, 363 days a year. The lorries transport up to 1.7 million cases of groceries a week and, with the rest of the supermarket's fleet, clock up over 120 million kilometres a year.

Tesco lorries belt up and down our motorways to an even greater extent – they covered 224 million kilometres in 1.2 million journeys in 2002. Asda juggernauts travelled 148 million kilometres in the UK that same year. Add together the millions of journeys made by the fleets of the grocery retailers and between them they accounted for nearly 1 billion kilometres on our crowded transport network. Between 1978 and 2000 the distance food was transported within the UK by lorry nearly doubled.

Between 35 and 40 per cent of lorries on UK roads today are involved in producing and distributing food. Twenty years ago many of them would simply not have been there. And the numbers are growing. The supermarkets Asda, Marks and Spencer, Tesco and Nisa-Today increased their fleets by 20 per cent in the year 2002/3.

The Safeway regional distribution centre (RDC) at Aylesford is not the biggest or newest centre but it was one of the first, in the late 1970s, to create this new centralized way of getting our food to us. Now all the major retailers have rationalized distribution into similar operations and are constantly centralizing further. Sainsbury's, for example, is currently replacing a score of depots with a handful of huge 'mother depots' or 'fulfilment factories' serving the whole country. One of its new RDCs will be at Greenham Common on the site of the old US base. In December 2001 a second generation of rather well-heeled Greenham protestors tried unsuccessfully to fight off the 700 food lorries which will flow in and out of the site every twenty-four hours.

The depots for fresh produce are not warehouses – almost nothing is held in stock. Instead, millions of boxes of goods are ordered 'just in time' from suppliers and fed in and out of the distribution centres along the motorway network within twelve hours.

But for the procession of lorries, you might not notice the Aylesford RDC. Off the slip-road at junction 6 of the M20, then up a side road, it is just another industrial shed, marked with a supermarket logo, doing something you had never much thought about. Then, when you drive up to the entrance, the scale of the place suddenly overwhelms you. The guard in his sentry box towers 10 feet above your car. The welcome sign near the barrier with its gantries of lights is not just in English but in French, Spanish and Italian, and is at juggernaut height.

When I visited at 9 p.m. the chill room, a giant refrigerated shed on the site, was working full pelt. In the darkness outside dozens of trailerless cabs scuttled across the yard, casting unearthly shadows on the sheer floodlit walls. Steam from the ammonia refrigeration plant hung over the roof. Lorries constantly came and went, a hollow rattle signalling those speeding back empty, a heavy growl accompanying those hauling out fully laden. Inside, an army of men was demolishing piles of fresh food, pulled from the maw of containers docked to the side of the building. A thousand of them work myriad shifts. The chicken tikka masala was in from Newark. Broccoli had made it from Spain. So too had iceberg lettuce but that had been rejected and lay waiting for its Continental producer to truck it back. Imported salad, washed and packed in Lincolnshire that morning, was being stacked ten crates high.

As fast as the 'tippers' – men with fork-lifts – emptied pallets from the containers, so more lorries backed up to the bays and opened their doors, constantly replenishing the heaps. Then barrow men, the 'pickers', ant-like in dark caps and black fleeces, trundled up on the snub-nosed lifting machines to deconstruct the piles. They carried off their loads in a continuous column. Holding down the tillers of their electric barrows, they moved back and forth on tiny platforms. Like the automata in Fritz Lang's *Metropolis*, they followed no discernible orders, but appeared programmed to advance from one pile to another. They skated off round corners, stopped suddenly to avoid collision, reversed, side-stepped round one another and filed on.

The label on each crate was zapped with a scanning gun as it arrived, generating a string of new numbers in the glass control room. Numbered strips in the vast hangar represented each of the Safeway stores served by this centre, and the goods, choreographed by barcode, moved from the arrivals section to departure lanes.

To 9848 Peckham, sweet and sour chicken. To 7013 Gibraltar, mushroom stroganoff with rice. Sirloin steaks for 9847 Brighton. Bangers and mash for 7818 Guernsey. Some higher intelligence had divined how many cabbages would be required on a cold day in Cambridge and how many kievs would be consumed in Colchester.

The pickers worked relentlessly, silently. An evaporator threw out icy air with a constant roar and fans the size of aircraft turbo engines pushed it around. Occasionally the cold was pierced by the blast of dozens of horns. When a barrow dropped a load, the pickers responded with a prolonged honk of tribal derision. But the diversion was brief. The piles were accumulating again and could not wait.

Last to dock, between 10 p.m. and 11 p.m. each night, were

the lorries from the consolidators. These are the companies which run separate sheds taking smaller deliveries from suppliers around the world and putting them together in categories before trucking them into the distribution centres. They arrived in constant flurries. The doors opened, the tippers zoomed up and back. There was a pause and much shaking of heads. One load had been piled too high by a consolidator keen to keep his costs down. Some of the boxes were crushed. To sort the good from the broken would require stopping, taking time, and that might hold up a lorry going to two or three stores. It would be quicker to reject the whole lot, but they'd save what they could tonight, they said. Once the final loads were unpicked the operation went into reverse. The loading of vehicles started. Now the supermarket trailers were backed up and filled with pallets. By dawn the following morning all the piles would have gone from the lanes. There would be no trace of the night's efforts. And then the cycle would begin again.

Up in the transport control room, Steve Bethel was the planning manager responsible for over 300 lorry movements a day. He was looking at a screen showing a map of the M25. Red and orange arrows were flashing all around it, warning that speeds were down to less than 5 m.p.h. here, 10 m.p.h. there. The log-sheets showed thirteen lorries out between 5 a.m. and 5.30 a.m., and another thirteen between 5.30 a.m. and 6 a.m., each with its time slot like traffic control at a busy airport. It takes half an hour to load a 38-tonne trailer and turn it round and the supply trucks have to be out on time. Bethel keyed a global satellite positioning command into his computer. Within seconds a marker had appeared on the screen pinpointing the location of one of his lorries. If necessary, his next load could be reallocated to a driver who had not been held up.

Bethel was executing the 'Aylesford falldown'. Before the 1980s big supermarkets used to stock about 8,000 products, mostly delivered direct to each shop. Then hi-tech information systems and the humble wooden pallet combined to rewrite the system. Stacking pallets which can be forked on and off lorries dispensed with the need to load and unload individual boxes, while creating a centralized RDC removed the need for storage at the back of the shop. Then the retailers worked out a way to revolutionize the 'picking' at the depots. Instead of starting with an order from each store and gathering what that store needed from stocks kept in different parts of the warehouse, they started 'picking by line'. Now each product line – bananas, let's say – comes in and is immediately distributed around the depot to lanes allocated to the different stores so that it can go straight back out. Where depots used to hold a day's stock of fresh food they now hold none.

All this is possible because instant information about stock is transmitted electronically from the computerized checkout tills back to the distribution centres and directly to the suppliers. Many of the products sold in stores are now delivered twice a day. This is the new concept of 'constant replenishment'. Without the need for room for stock, a big supermarket store can now keep 40,000 or more products on its shelves.

The 'falldown' begins when a customer buys something in one of the Safeway stores. Scanning the barcode at the till creates a new order for the product. The information is transmitted to head office, electronically collated several times a day and instantly converted into a delivery schedule for the farmer or manufacturer for the following day. The supplier will have estimated how much food to produce, but will only get a final order a few hours ahead of the time he or she is expected to deliver to the depot. It might be in the evening for delivery early the following day, or at noon for delivery that night, for example. The orders can vary dramatically. A spell of good weather can, for example, double the demand for lettuce. Failing to meet a retailer's order in full can result in a financial penalty. Suppliers can find themselves losing thousands of pounds. But then unexpected rain might halve your order. If you end up with a surplus there's hardly anywhere else for it to go, since the big retailers control so much of the country's total market. Wholesale markets are a shadow of their former selves and are used to dump surpluses, often at low prices. The need for a workforce that you can turn on and off like a tap, and if necessary keep at it for as long as it takes to fulfil your order, becomes clear.

This system has also imposed a huge strain on our transport infrastructure. It has been one of the factors driving much of the expansion of road networks across Europe, and will continue to do so as new countries join the European Union.

I had a further chance to test the dry statistics, that 35–40 per cent of freight on UK roads is now involved in the production and distribution of food, when I hitched a lift in a vegetable lorry travelling to the Asda RDC at Dartford, Kent. I had been watching the Christmas Brussels sprout harvest in Lincolnshire and wanted to see it right through the process. Asda felt unable to let me into their depot at such a busy time, but the 'con-solidator' agreed to let me go along for the ride. Martin Tate is one of three men who runs Lincolnshire Fresh Produce. He organizes a group of other growers to provide seamless supplies of fruit and vegetables to Asda so that the supermarket doesn't have to deal with them direct. 'Asda doesn't have the time or experience to deal with that number of growers. We've built the relationships here and in Spain. It's about commitment, vision, passion. The two most important things are availability and value. Our business is to deliver the promise,' he explained. 'Spalding is central. We can hit all depots from here to Scotland and Cornwall. Our fleet is forty units plus fifty trailers. Forty-four tonnes is the maximum UK weight limit. It was traditionally what you could carry on the road if travelling from a rail terminal to a port. 'Course that doesn't apply now. But you'll see, trucks aren't horrible big belching things any more.'

So it was that I found myself 12 feet up in the cab of Bob's articulated lorry. Air-suspension seats like armchairs, a nice little bed behind, acres of leg-room, spotless wrap-around windscreen, computer controls, it was an exhilarating £90,000-worth of machine attached to a 40-tonne trailer full of vegetables, sitting on an 800-litre tank of diesel.

You could live in there, and Bob practically does. He averages 180,000 kilometres a year, he reckons. He has been driving lorries for forty-three years, food trucks for twenty-five of them. 'There have been a few changes,' he said.

We negotiated our way out of small lanes near Spalding, giving way to international food lorries coming in the opposite direction, and settled in for the long, slow drive from the pack-houses of East Anglia to the Asda distribution centre on the edge of London. Down the A1, then the A14, M11 and M25. The traffic wasn't too bad because it was holiday time, but the speed limit for lorries, carefully monitored by the legally required tachograph, is 55 m.p.h., and we'd got ourselves behind a Nisa-Today lorry also doing 55 m.p.h. 'We're stuck staring at his backdoor for a few hours now, I won't be able to get past him.'

We idled away the time with a game, counting lorries going by on the other side of the carriageway. While we talked about the difference half a century has made to our supply chain, I tested how many of the lorries were to do with food.

We scored a hat-trick of points instantly. Asda, Safeway, and Iceland colours were emblazoned on the first three juggernauts to thunder by. Then came a vehicle from Bob's own company. 'That's four in a row,' I said, surprised.

Bob was nonchalant. 'Well, it would be. Before supermarkets came along and put them to sleep, I used to do the wholesale markets. Every town had its wholesale market. But there's nothing much in town centres any more. The depots get bigger and bigger. We'd be taking in everything grown locally round here. The time scale was the same. It'd be from field to the market one day and into the shop the next. But there were more corner shops then and we used not to get caulis in winter. There are no seasons any more. You don't look forward to the new season's potatoes now.'

'Look, there's a James Irlam lorry.' No refrigeration unit, so I guessed that wasn't food.

'No, you're right there. That's not food. That's the packaging for food. They're big in that. Everything's packaged now, isn't it? When I was young we used to just put a hand in a sack if we wanted potatoes. But those packhouses, they employ no end of people. Eddie Stobart's big in packaging too – plastic, glass jars, you name it.'

Co-op. Tesco. Asda again on the other side of the road. Eight out of eight. Oh no, nine, there goes Padley's Frozen Veg.

'Everything is so big these days. There are a lot of jobs in it. Matthews. That's Bernard Matthews. The cars are the worst though. They are getting faster, we're going slower. Imagine what this road'll be like in ten years' time.'

Shopping for food has made its contribution to the increase in traffic too. We are in fact all driving further to buy our food. In the ten years between the mid-1980s and mid-1990s, the average distance travelled to shop went up from 14 kilometres to 22 kilometres as small and local shops came under pressure from out-of-town retail stores and closed.

'George Kime,' I called out.

'He's a Boston veg merchant. NFT – that's Northern Foods, they do a lot of distribution. Dairy Crest. Kenyon European translink. I don't know that one.'

Thirteen out of fourteen so far.

'You get a lot of European lorries now, taking more of our work – their petrol's cheaper and their labour's cheaper. The German Willi Betz is one of the big European food hauliers.'

Turners Temperature Controlled. That must be food. BOC, that's not. Fourteen out of sixteen.

'We do a bit of backhauling now – picking up some onions from a farm on the return journey rather than going back empty – but not much. Here we are, the M25, the biggest car park in the country.'

I had thought that Christian Salvesen lorries with their blue

crosses on white were from some sort of Scandawegian pharma-
ceutical company but no, they do distribution for the retailers
and recycling of supermarket waste, Bob assured me. Fifteen out
of seventeen. Bob does a long day, twelve hours or so and then
a short one of eight or nine hours, four days a week. It's stressful
with all the traffic and he wouldn't want to be starting out now,
he said. There is a serious shortage of drivers at the moment. And
the new working-time directive restricting drivers' hours will
make it worse.

We counted Fletcher Frozen Foods from Hull, several more
supermarket lorries, then an Esso tanker before puzzling over
TransAmerica Leasing. Bob didn't know who they were.

By the time we reached the Dartford bridge we were in thick
grey fog. As we swept down into the Asda depot, the mystery
was solved. We spotted two TransAmerica Leasing lorries parked
up, waiting to unload.

Of course our food doesn't just travel up and down the
UK. During the 1990s there was a 90 per cent increase in the
movement by road of agricultural and food products between
the UK and Europe. And we don't just trade in food we cannot
produce ourselves any more. Whereas in the 1960s we drank
milk we produced locally, today we both import it and export
it. International trade in food has almost trebled in the last three
decades. Caroline Lucas, the Green member of the European
Parliament, has studied what she has called 'the great food swap'.
She gives another example: in one year Britain imported over
60,000 tonnes of poultry meat from the Netherlands while
exporting 33,000 tonnes of poultry meat to the same country.
Live animals are not spared this food swap. Some 44 million
cattle, pigs and sheep are traded across the world each year.
Millions more are transported long distances within countries
and over borders.

Our increasing dependence on processed food has also made its
contribution. A ready-made lasagne can contain around twenty
different ingredients which may have come from all over the

world, as Tara Garnett of the sustainable transport trust, Transport 2000, pointed out.

In terms of energy efficiency and damaging emissions, the dramatic rise in air freighting of fresh produce is perhaps the most troubling aspect of this global movement of food. Air fuel, unlike most petrol, is not taxed. In November 2000 a UK motorist paid 80p for a litre of petrol, while airlines paid just 18p for a litre of fuel. Thanks to this hidden subsidy, it makes economic sense to fly our food in from distant continents at short notice, to meet the demands of the retailers' distribution systems, or to fly food out to countries where labour is cheapest. The packhouses of Kenya are just one of several examples I have seen of this dynamic working outside Europe.

Many of the fresh vegetables available in the supermarkets today are sourced from Africa. They will typically have travelled between 4,000 and 6,000 miles to reach us. My favourite example of the phenomenon of food miles was a product I found at Marks and Spencer for £2.99. It was an elegantly small plastic tray of baby vegetables, each tiny bundle of asparagus shoots, miniature corn, dwarf carrots and leeks tied together with a single chive. The chives were first flown from England to Kenya. The plastic trays and packaging were flown out too. There, African women worked day and night on long and unpredictable shifts in refrigerated packing sheds, next to Nairobi airport, turning the green stems into decorative ribbons around topped and tailed Kenyan produce. Then they were cling-wrapped and air-freighted back to England again, a round trip of 8,500 miles.

The company supplying the chive bundles to Marks and Spencer was Kenya's leading exporter of cut flowers and vegetables to the UK supermarkets, Homegrown. One of its directors, Rod Evans, generously offered to show me how his company 'added value' to the hundreds of tonnes of green beans and other vegetables he grows for Tesco, Safeway, Marks and Spencer and other supermarkets.

Homegrown was the first company to turn strawberries into a commodity traded year round, thanks to an extended African season. From a beginning piggybacking on half-empty tourist flights returning to Europe, Homegrown has gradually built up its volumes of food exports to the point where it can charter its own freight flights. This is the pattern right across the world. More and more food is being air-freighted, complementing the air pollution from our roads with noise pollution of the skies above us.

Today the mainstay of Homegrown's business is the green bean. The supermarkets email over the orders about midday for what they want put on the flight from Kenya that night, depending on how much their computerized tills tell them they sold the day before. Once again, they can eliminate nearly all financial risk from their end of the chain. Like most other suppliers, Homegrown has no written contract with the supermarkets specifying quantities. The orders can go up or down dramatically. 'They might increase by five or six coffins. At Christmas it can be a three- or four-tonne increase in one day for sliced or topped and tailed beans. You've just got to get on and do it or you lose the business,' David Wakaba, manager of the packing operation, told me. 'Coffins' is the name given to the crates in which the vegetables are transported the 4,250 miles to the UK. A flexible workforce to fill the coffins is essential.

Homegrown is one of the better employers in Kenya. It has worked with the Ethical Trading Initiative to look at labour standards and is regularly audited to see how it measures up. But Evans admitted he wouldn't want to be starting out now, trying to establish terms with the retailers. The pressures imposed by modern distribution systems and the retailers' demand for constant price cuts are considerable.

To air-freight delicate vegetables and fruits, you have to pack them. Most food is packaged in plastic, and plastic is made from crude oil. Packaging in fact now makes up about a quarter of household waste; nearly 70 per cent of that is food-related. As

Britain runs out of landfill space to bury this waste, controls on the industry have been tightened and charges for disposal of waste are being increased. Food processors are now required to make their plastic trays recyclable. Although the ratcheting up of taxes has encouraged some efforts to find either more degradable plastics or other packaging materials such as starch or chalk which do not depend on fossil fuels, in practice very little packaging is recovered and very little comes from sustainable sources. The food industry still generates the second highest waste level of any UK industrial sector.

Homegrown defended the food miles its produce clocked up. Its exports make a significant contribution to Kenya's parlous economy. Moreover, the company argued, because Kenya has the benefit of a warm climate, this sort of production is no more extravagant with fossil fuels than growing green vegetables in glasshouses in northern Europe through the winter months when farmers spend as much fuel on heating. There is truth in that. The issue of food miles is not entirely straightforward. If you are considering energy use, you need to take into account not just distance travelled but also refrigeration during transport, farming methods and method of transport. But the point is that when they become routine, both the out-of-season salad grown by artificial heat in winter *and* the air-freighted green bean represent an unsustainable use of finite fossil fuels.

Of course we have always imported food that we cannot produce ourselves. But the traditional form of transport for the bulk of imports was shipping, which is much less environmentally damaging in terms of emissions than air or road freight. What is new is the supermarket-driven creation of a permanent global summer time and the volume of food being imported at times when we could supply our own.

The cost of this kind of distribution is not simply paid in human terms by those on the lowest incomes. It dramatically changes our environment. At the micro level it is part of a car culture that condemns us to living in traffic-clogged and polluted towns and villages. At the macro level it is a significant contributor to climate change.

There is a newish 'local' supermarket near where I live. It's on an awkward corner, a junction of two main roads, where one road narrows from two lanes to one on a major through route. These are old coaching roads into London, never designed for the weight of traffic, or for the size of lorries, they see today. The lorries have a habit of mounting the pavement and cutting the corner as they squeeze past cars turning right. When the supermarket juggernaut arrives to deliver, it blocks the road almost immediately so that an angry queue of honking commuters builds up behind. This sort of scene is familiar to most city dwellers in Britain. The explosion in freight in the last twenty years has had a dramatic impact on the quality of our lives. With rural lanes and suburban streets given over to 44-tonne lorries and cars, many parents feel the roads are no longer safe for young children to negotiate by themselves. Study after study shows that our children have much less freedom than previous generations, with the result that they are less active than ever. It is fear of traffic as much as fear of 'stranger danger' that restricts them.

Inside my 'local' store, at the height of the English apple season, there were no apples from this country on sale, but instead varieties shipped or air-freighted and then trucked from New Zealand, South Africa, the USA and, slightly nearer home, from France.

The fresh vegetable displays offered asparagus and mangetout from Peru, a journey of 6,312 miles; baby corn from Thailand, 6,643 miles; and green beans from southern Africa, 5,979 miles.

I have on previous occasions, without trying too hard, filled a supermarket shopping basket with a typical range of twenty fresh foods and found that they have accumulated over 100,000 miles before reaching me.

Even the organic movement, one of whose founding principles was sustainability, has been sucked into this system. Over 80 per cent of organic food now comes from abroad. Supermarkets depend on global sourcing of organic fruit and vegetables and truck it around the country just as much as conventional produce.

We have all become accustomed to the idea that we can have any fresh food at any time of year. So we purchase Israeli or Egyptian potatoes that have travelled over 2,000 miles when we want 'baby' potatoes in the winter. We buy tomatoes from Saudi Arabia, over 3,000 miles away, or broccoli from Spain that has travelled nearly 1,000 miles to reach us.

Most of us imagine we are buying the freshest of new-season produce this way. Ironically, the baby potatoes are quite likely to have been in store for six months or more and not actually just lifted from the ground – but do you know when the Egyptian potato season is? (Or the Argentinian pear season?) I always imagined the baby potatoes were new potatoes, but in fact the label does not make that claim for them, often just calling them 'salad' potatoes. Just as English carrots can be kept well in cold store from September to May, so some foreign crops can be brought in from store over an extended period. The reason for sourcing them abroad is not just related to season; it may be that costs are lower in developing countries or that foreign climates are better suited to particular varieties that retailers are promoting. The ability of retailers to source food from wherever it is cheapest at the touch of a computer key has had a perverse effect. Even when fruit and vegetables are in season in the UK, they may no longer be available. The British Potato Council estimates that the UK imports about 350,000 tonnes of potatoes a year, many of these coming in even when British potatoes are available. About two thirds of the tomatoes we eat are imported, according to the British Tomato Growers' Association, and again, many are brought in when British producers could be supplying the market. UK growers have found themselves pushed out of business, with the result that our self-sufficiency in fruit and vegetables has fallen dramatically. In the last twenty-five years, it has dropped to just 4 per cent in fruit, and 52 per cent in vegetables. Moreover, the need to transport produce long distances has skewed the market to varieties that will travel and keep well. Taste, texture and variety have been sacrificed to permanent global summer time. As has ripeness. Fruit that has to journey thousands of miles to reach us needs to be picked hard. Just one variety of strawberry, Elsanta, now dominates sales, accounting for three quarters of the strawberries on offer because it travels well and has a long shelf life.

Previous generations would have known what the British seasons were. When I published a plea in the *Guardian* to buy more local food in season, I received a deluge of mail from people saying they no longer knew the seasons and needed a guide. I realized I needed one too and rang round various food and farming experts, only to find they were pretty vague on the subject as well.

I'm not denying that this permanent global summer time has its attractions. A northern friend whose childhood was spent largely without the benefit of modern food supplies remembers clearly the shock of first discovering that broccoli came not just in yellow but also, when imported fresh, in vivid green. Nor am I suggesting that we should never eat imported or out-of-season food, only that if we understood the impact our choices made on other parts of our lives, we might make slightly different choices.

Knowing the effect long-distance transport has on the quality of our food might make a difference for a start. For just as packaging has been found to affect the nutritional content of salad, so the distance travelled by fresh food appears to be taking its toll. New research suggests that the more food miles fruit and vegetables have clocked up, the more their vitamin content is reduced.

The FSA advised recently that frozen broccoli contains more nutrients than fresh imported broccoli that has undergone a long refrigerated journey. Their comments followed research by the Austrian Consumers' Association which found that the nutrient content of a whole range of 'fresh' imported vegetables was lower than frozen versions of the same produce. The vitamin content of frozen broccoli, peas, cauliflower, sweetcorn and carrots was significantly higher than in 'fresh' versions of the vegetables imported from Italy, Spain, Turkey and Israel.

Dr Andy Jones, author of the groundbreaking report *Eating Oil*, has made the sort of calculations that bring home the absurdity of a system that regularly brings vegetables to northern Europe from the other side of the globe when we could be eating our own season's produce. He points out that it takes 88 calories in the form of fuel energy to fly 1 calorie of carrot to the UK from South Africa. And importing just 1 calorie of lettuce from California burns up 127 calories of fuel energy.

The way we transport and distribute food now has a significant impact on climate change. The food industry is the UK's third largest industrial energy user, according to a Transport 2000 study. The government's report on Climate Change estimates that the food chain's contribution to greenhouse gas emissions represents 12 per cent of the UK total. Another study puts it far higher at 22 per cent.

American oil interests may still dispute the link between global warming and greenhouse gas emissions, but almost all scientists are now agreed that global warming is already underway. The Intergovernmental Panel on Climate Change (IPCC), made up of some 2,500 of the world's leading experts on climate change, concluded in 1995 that 'the balance of evidence suggests that there is a discernible human influence on global climate'. In the last few years, the evidence has become even clearer.

Since the Industrial Revolution, we have managed to increase the atmospheric concentration of carbon dioxide and other greenhouse gases by about 50 per cent. By burning fossil fuels in our cars, lorries, homes and factories, we have taken the level of carbon dioxide in the atmosphere from 279 parts per million at the end of the seventeenth century to 372 parts per million today, a level higher than at any time in the past 420,000 years. The most rapid increases have taken place in the last twenty to thirty years and the rate of increase is still accelerating. Carbon dioxide emissions from the consumption of fossil fuel increased by over 20 per cent between 1980 and 1999.

The result has been that global temperatures are rising as extra solar radiation is trapped at the earth's surface. The ten hottest years on record have all occurred since 1991. So far there has been a temperature rise of about 1 °C since the nineteenth century. This apparently small rise in temperature has already had a dramatic effect. Glaciers are shrinking, and permafrost melting. Sea levels are rising. Extremes of climate are becoming more common. Warm air holds more vapour than cold, so evaporation increases, causing drought, which is then followed by flooding when the vapour finally condenses. As temperature rises, wind speeds increase, and storms become more violent.

The IPCC has predicted that temperatures will continue to rise, increasing between 1.4 and 5.8°C over the next 100 years. Mark Lynas, author of *Hide Tide: News from a Warming World*, has recorded the impact of global warming in his travels around the world, from the death of up to one sixth of tropical coral reefs, including some on the Australian Great Barrier Reef that were 700 years old, to dust storms which now sweep up from Mongolia carrying China's top soil with them. He points out that it was a global rise in temperature of 6°C that triggered a global warming episode 250 million years ago that wiped out 95 per cent of all species. Even at the lower end of the predicted increases, large areas of farm land will become unusable.

That we are facing a catastrophic loss became clear with the publication in *Nature* magazine in January 2004 of the results of two years of global research on the impact of warming on different species. Scientists looked at the effect of different scenarios proposed by the IPCC in which by 2050 global temperatures will have increased by a minimum of 0.5°C or by a maximum of 3°C, depending on what we do about emissions. The researchers estimated that more than 1 million species, or one in ten of all plants and animals, will be lost by 2050. Lead author Chris Thomas, professor of conservation biology at Leeds University, admitted he was shocked. 'It was far, far worse than we thought.' Much of the loss is now unavoidable because of the greenhouse gases already in the atmosphere. But some of the worst effects could be mitigated if emissions were dramatically cut.

Professor Thomas concluded that the only response to climate change that made any sense was to minimize the amount of warming by converting to cleaner technologies rapidly and widely. Twice as many species will become extinct if temperatures rise at the higher rate than if they rise at the lower rate. The scientists' estimates had looked at loss of species up to 2050. As much global warming again is expected to take place in the fifty years after that, with the result that the Earth may become hotter than it has been for 10 million years.

The government's chief scientific advisor, Sir David King, has also warned of the particular effects of global warming on the UK. Writing in the journal *Science*, he said that climate change was a more serious threat to the world than terrorism. Britain could face thirty times the current risk of flooding by 2080 so that the sort of flood levels which until now have been seen only once in every 100 years would instead recur every three years. The use of the Thames Barrier has already increased from once a year in the 1980s to an average of more than six times a year now, because of increased storm surges. France suffered 15,000 premature deaths as a result of the extreme heatwave in the summer of 2003. But millions more around the world, he argued, will be exposed to the risk of flood, hunger and drought, particularly in poor countries, if consumption of fossil fuels continues to grow at present rates. He reiterated the climate experts' call for the world's developed economies to cut emissions of greenhouse gases by 60 per cent of 1990 levels, in order to avoid far more expensive and disruptive changes later. 'Delaying action for decades, or even just years, is not a serious option,' he said.

Such dire predictions from eminent and generally restrained sources tend to induce individual paralysis. They so clearly call for concerted international action. But the Environment Agency has pointed out that if every driver took one less car journey a week averaging 9 miles, this would cut carbon dioxide emissions from traffic in the UK by 13 per cent. Transport of food within the UK alone – both in lorries and in shopping trips by car – makes a significant contribution (3.5 per cent) to total carbon dioxide emissions in the UK, as Transport 2000 points out. We not only travel further now to shop but make our car trips to supermarkets more often. In the mid-1980s, the average was one and a half times a week; by the mid-1990s that had gone up to two and a half times a week. In the last three years the value of food imported by air grew by nearly 50 per cent. Air freight is expected to increase at a rate of 7.5 per cent a year to 2010. Fruit and vegetables were the largest category of commodity being imported this way. Choices about how we shop and where we source our food do make a difference.

'Transporting food long distances is energy inefficient. One imported basket of food could release as much carbon dioxide into the atmosphere as an average four-bedroomed household does through cooking for eight months,' Andy Jones calculates.

There was particular irony in UK farmers being forced to import large quantities of lettuce from California during the normal British season in the summer of 2003 to meet supermarket orders. The record high temperatures and drought that afflicted much of Europe that year, widely seen as evidence of global warming and climate change, had a devastating effect on harvests, and so producers resorted to the air freight that makes such a damaging contribution to carbon dioxide emissions, which in turn will have contributed to more global warming.

The food industry, meanwhile, is lobbying hard to be allowed to use our roads even more. At present many cities impose night curfews and other restrictions on lorries over a certain size travelling through residential areas. For example, Steve Bethel's juggernauts from the Aylesford RDC are only allowed into London on officially designated trunk routes. During my visit to the distribution centre he and his colleagues gave me a taste of some of the lobbying officials no doubt receive. 'We're a twenty-four-hour operation and we're in residential areas, but more curfews are being imposed by local authorities. The deliveries are shoe-horned into shorter and shorter times. It creates rush-hour traffic jams. If we could reduce morning deliveries and bring more in at night, we could stop adding to the problem. Central government is in favour of it but local government isn't,' Dave Timpson, systems effectiveness controller at Safeway, explained. Steve Bethel later showed me a map of the London and M25 area. He explained that in order to deliver to his supermarket's Holloway Road branch from Aylesford, he cannot take the direct route down the A2, a journey of 134 kilometres. Instead, he must send his vehicles all the way round the M25 up to the A1, then down again, which is 214 kilometres. 'It's a busy store, we go twice a day, or four times a day at the back end of the week. That's 58,000 extra kilometres a year. If you look at all the London stores, we're doing an extra 242,422 kilometres a year, just one way. Half a million extra kilometres in all! Think of all the extra congestion!

I found myself asking the idiot's question: Why couldn't they deliver to Holloway Road from the north or operate smaller warehouses instead of trucking everything round and round the country? 'Because by going bigger we can reduce the cost of produce in the stores. And reduce congestion of course.'

After leaving them, it took me fifteen minutes to crawl up from the slip-road on to the M20. On the other carriageway, there was a 6-mile tailback, waiting to get on to the M25. There appeared to be no reason for the queues, just sheer volume of traffic. I passed endless supermarket lorries stuck in the jam on the other side. A Tesco lorry boasted 'You shop, we drop'. I passed under a bridge on which the traffic was tail-backed too. For a moment there were food lorries above, to the side, in front, and behind me all at once. The juggernaut above sported a different logo: 'Why pay more?' The answer to this rhetorical question is of course that we already pay more, maybe not at the checkout, but in so many other ways.

Shifting back to older systems of supplying local food to local shops is likely to become harder and harder. The retailers are tightening their grip on the distribution of food in other ways. The latest buzz in the logistics business is 'factory-gate pricing'. Until recently manufacturers transported their goods to the retailers, or if they were small companies without their own fleets paid logistics companies to do so, and then agreed a price with the supermarkets which included the cost of transport. But recently retailers, led by Tesco, have imposed a new system on manufacturers and suppliers in an effort to make their own transport systems more cost-efficient. They now require suppliers to quote them a factory-gate price which excludes the cost of transport and they can then decide whether to collect in their own lorries or not. Even the major manufacturers have blanched. David Ingram, the head of logistics for Unilever Frozen Foods, described the experience to the *Grocer* magazine. 'We got the infamous letter asking for very detailed information on the costs in our supply chain – which made us nervous because we didn't understand why we were being asked. Tesco was underwriting its fleet to the tune of some £400 million, almost twice as much as anyone else was spending. It has a lot of empty trucks and wanted to see a reduction in core costs.' Eventually Unilever agreed to a reduced factory-gate price to the retailer. 'We didn't have our own transport fleet, so we had a flexible approach.' Unilever now describes the scheme as hugely successful. Others are not so happy. Independent wholesalers point out that it will become less and less economical for manufacturers to run their own fleets, making it harder for them to distribute their goods to independent retailers.

*

But perhaps the most obvious danger of building a system in which supplying even the most basic of foods depends on oil is that oil is running out. Everyone agrees that this is the case. (Every year we use three to four times as much oil as we find.) How long it takes before we face a critical shortage is the subject of much debate.

The pessimists think the energy crisis is imminent, with a permanent and deepening shortage beginning in the next few years. Dr Colin Campbell is the leading exponent of this view. A geologist with nearly half a century of experience working with oil companies, he says: 'From 2005 onwards, we will see the beginning of the long-term decline in conventional oil production. I think it will probably fall roughly three per cent a year. Demand on the other hand is growing at two per cent a year. By about 2020 there will be a shortfall of something like forty per cent.' This view is supported by many in the oil industry and tallies with the model developed by Shell geologist King Hubbert in 1959 which plotted the depletion of world reserves as new discoveries fell and existing reserves passed their peak. As shortages bite, oil prices will continue to rise, and with them food prices, and economic slowdown will become inevitable.

Others argue that pessimists have predicted that oil will run out before and have been proved wrong as new reserves have been discovered or new technologies developed to exploit previously inaccessible or uneconomic reserves. This argument is less persuasive than it used to be, however. Just as the technology to extract oil has become more sophisticated, so has the technology to map world reserves. As Richard Hardman, vice-president for exploration for American oil producers Amerada Hess, has said: 'People have cried wolf in the past many times. I believe this time the wolf really is at the door. And I believe that because for the first time we have a systematic survey of all the major sedimentary basins in the world. And we've got a calculation of what reserves they can contain.'

Recently Matthew Simmons, chief executive officer of the

world's largest energy investment bank, Simmons & Company International, whose clients include American oil giants such as Halliburton, said in an interview with the US investigative website, From the Wilderness: 'We may be finding out that we went over the peak in 2000. Over the last year I have obtained and closely examined more than a hundred very technical production reports from Saudi Arabia. What I glean is that Saudi Arabia has very likely gone over its peak. If that is true, then it is a certainty that planet earth has passed its peak of production. What that means in the starkest possible terms is that we are no longer going to be able to grow.'

Whether an oil shock is nigh or already upon us, there is no disputing that oil is one of the most politically charged of substances. Almost two thirds of oil reserves are in the Middle East. As supplies diminish, the struggle for energy is likely to distort our decision-making and lead us into more conflicts than in the past. In the current climate, to be making our food system dependent on ever-greater consumption of oil seems madness.

Since the September 11 terrorist attacks on New York, security experts have studied the global supply network. In its Implications of Terrorism Report 2003, risk consultancy Aegis warns that 'modern, low-inventory, just-in-time supply chains could easily be thrown into disarray'.

Just how insecure our food system already is became clear when the UK had its own very British fuel crisis in 2000.

As violence in the Middle East drove the price of crude oil to a ten-year high of $35 a barrel, a handful of angry farmers and hauliers blockaded oil depots around the country in protest at petrol price rises. The government was caught on the hop and appeared to be in a state of alarming ignorance about how our food reaches us these days. *The Times* reported that the chief executive of Sainsbury's had written to the prime minister warning that the petrol crisis could leave stores without food in days rather than weeks. The public was accused of panic buying as staples disappeared from the shops. Their panic turned out to be a well-founded fear that food would run out more rapidly than anyone was admitting. A senior member of the government has since admitted privately that the country very nearly did run out of food.

In the end it was not a question of days, but hours, according to the Federation of Bakers. John White, the Federation's director, told me, 'We came very close to not getting bread out in the fuel strike.' Bakeries, like supermarkets, order 'just in time' these days and keep little in stock. 'If you haven't got flour, you can't make bread. The whole supply chain was suffering in the same way. But there was great confusion at the ministry [MAFF as it then was]. There seemed a complete lack of understanding about how reliant every part of the chain was on everything else. We were on the phone to them all the time, but the civil servants just didn't seem to realize how interconnected it all is. Then some fuel was released and we were put to the top of the pile so we could get the deliveries going. But we were within just a few hours of the country not having a loaf to eat.'

Who knows how much influence this searing experience had on Tony Blair and his government? But it's small wonder that understanding supermarket distribution is now an urgent part of any Transport Minister's brief.

4. Bread

The wholemeal bread from the supermarket in-store bakery felt springy, but as I cut it, the top of the loaf squeezed down to half its height like a damp sponge and stayed there. I pulled it back into shape, put a slice into the toaster and watched it pop up, light as anything again. I found myself wondering, not for the first time, how *do* they do that?

How do they take wholemeal flour, yeast and water and make the mixture into something like boiled flannel? Why isn't it more like the wholemeal bread you can buy, if you are lucky, from a local craft baker, or the stuff you make yourself at home, with its nutty taste and dense texture? The labels, when I have inspected them, have been curiously silent on the subject. They generally have just one added ingredient listed. Flour treatment agent.

'Boy, that's pouffy. There's a lot of air and water in there,' Elizabeth Weisberg, master baker at the Lighthouse Bakery explained, as she too squeezed the specimen I had brought her. 'How do they do it, well, they use chemical so-called "improvers" to put the air and water in, and fat, hardened fat, to hold them up.'

We were standing in the bakery at the back of the small shop Elizabeth runs with her partner Rachel Duffield in south London. The scent of dough and freshly baked bread draws you in from yards away. You have to queue for it, but that's part of the experience.

Rachel and Elizabeth toyed with the idea of running a delicatessen before setting up a bakery. Bread won in the end because they liked the idea of re-creating the ritual of buying your daily bread from a small local shop where everyone gets to know everyone else. It is a ritual that binds communities together, one considered so important to the fabric of society by the French that their government has taken action to protect small bakers. But it is a ritual that we have almost completely lost.

While you patiently wait your turn outside the Lighthouse, you have time to agonize over which of the thirty or so types of bread you'll choose when you get to the front of the queue: will it be Gloucester rye or old English spelt, seven-seed cob or stoneground wholemeal for the goodness of the whole grain? Or for the luxury of real white, will it be farmhouse or sandwich, cottage or bloomer? A board outside tells you that all the breads are made and baked on the premises daily without the aid of 'any artificial enhancers or chemical improvers'.

The queue moves forward slowly because Rachel knows nearly everyone, and she stops to chat with them. Likely as not, someone will be holding up the front of the line maddeningly while they gossip with another customer they know. But then you find yourself doing the same as someone familiar greets you.

Out at the back, Elizabeth works non-stop, getting up at three most mornings and baking right through the night on Friday for the weekend rush. Not many people are prepared to do that any more.

Trays of willow baskets holding balls of sourdough which were started the day before go into an old steel oven for another day's fermenting before baking the following day. Elizabeth pulls from a bucket a lump of baguette dough that has been proving for several hours. It stretches and droops from her hand and then flops on to the counter. She kneads it gently with her knuckles, folds it to pull it back, pushes away, and gives it a quick roll with the heel of her hand. It is springy and soft, and although it looks wet, is dry to the touch. Knocking back like this redistributes the gas bubbles produced by the yeast, helps the gluten to develop and sets the yeast going again. Once replaced in tins, the dough starts coming back to life. Then it will be left to prove and rest overnight so that it ferments slowly and acquires the full flavour that comes from the traditionally made loaf. This is how our bread has been made for centuries.

The only ingredients required are flour, yeast and water. Bread has sustained generations. It was called the 'staff of life' because, when well made from good-quality ingredients, it contains so many of the vital nutrients we need for good health, the essential fats, fibre, protein, vitamins and minerals (over twenty of them) and carbohydrates that our bodies need to function properly. Since staples by definition account for a large proportion of our intake, if the staple of the diet is healthy, it is much easier to ensure that the diet overall is healthy.

But bread made like this also needs time and space, and in mass manufacturing, time and space mean money. Only a tiny fraction of our bread is made this way now.

Look at the supermarket shelves displaying dozens of loaves, and you might think that you are confronted with unlimited choice, but the vast majority of the breads on offer have emerged from the same factories and been made by one industrial method. Perhaps instinctively we know this. We spend on average less than one minute in the bread aisle when we shop.

Like much of food manufacturing today, the bread sector has become highly concentrated. By 2003, eleven factory baking companies, or 'plant bakeries' as they are called, were making 81 per cent of the 9 million or so loaves we eat each day in only fifty-seven factories around the country. Two giants dominate the market, British Bakeries and Allied Bakeries, which between them produce two thirds of British bread.★

Supermarket in-store bakeries account for 17 per cent of the bread market. The lure of bread fresh from the oven is used by the supermarkets to pull customers in; it whets their appetites

★ British Bakeries is part of Rank Hovis McDougall which owns the brands Hovis, Mother's Pride, Nimble, Granary and Mr Kipling, as well as supplying burger buns to McDonald's, pizza dough to Pizza Hut, frozen partly-baked brands, and own-label breads to the supermarkets.

Allied Bakeries is part of the Associated British Foods group which owns the Kingsmill, Sunblest, Allinson and Burgen brands, supplies own-label breads to the retailers, and also encompasses Silver Spoon sugar and Twinings tea.

and encourages them to spend more. But the illusion of freshness can be deceptive. Figures are hard to come by, but the baking industry reckons that half of the big retailers' in-store bakeries are using 'prebaked' dough and 'baking it off'. In other words, their bread is made by one of the plant bakery companies, and partially baked at its factory, then simply finished off in the oven in the supermarket store. Nearly all the remaining in-store bakeries make their bread from 'premixes', with flour, yeast, fat and improvers already measured out by a factory, to reduce the level of skills needed by workers in the supermarket to a minimum.

That leaves 2 per cent of our bread to be produced by independent bakers, but even that figure is misleading because only a small number of them genuinely bake from scratch, many depending instead on the same factory 'premixes' of flour and additives. Today there are only 3,500 individual craft bakers in the UK, compared to about 35,000 in France.

At the beginning of the nineteenth century most bread was made in the home. But with increasing urbanization, long working hours and the high cost of fuel needed to keep ovens warm, the baking industry began to develop. In 1850 nearly all bakers were independent master bakers, who baked bread and sold it on the same premises. By the beginning of the twentieth century a few large factory bakeries were emerging – some, like J. Lyons, making bread for their teahouses, others supplying their own shops. The pace of change accelerated in 1932 with the arrival in England of Garfield Weston, a successful Canadian biscuit manufacturer. He started buying up independent bakeries and shops, importing Canadian wheat to supply them, and in 1935 he formed Allied Bakeries Ltd. Before that only the Co-operative Movement in Britain owned both mills and bakeries; the other big millers, Spillers and Rank, had no bakeries. But now, finding their flour markets threatened, they also started buying up bakeries and shops, and established their own factory bakeries. The rush to integrate had begun. Smaller millers were gradually squeezed out, particularly after the war when government subsidies and price controls on flour were removed. Independent bakers struggled to compete with the larger companies which were taking advantage of the launch of commercial TV to promote their brands of bread to a nation just recovering from rationing and the nutritious but heavy wartime National Loaf.

Although the sector was rationalizing rapidly, the bread its factories produced was nevertheless still made in a way recognizable to home bakers: dough would be left to ferment and prove over extended periods. Then in the early 1960s a method evolved that revolutionized the centuries-old process. Researchers at the British Baking Industries Research Association in Chorleywood developed a way of making bread that had first been used in the USA. It dispensed with all the time and expensive energy required by traditional methods. Instead of allowing two to three hours' fermentation, they found that air and water could be incorporated into dough if it was mixed with intense energy at high speeds in mechanical mixers. Double the quantity of yeast was needed to make it rise; chemical oxidants were essential to get the gas in; and hardened fat had to be added to provide structure – without the fat, the bread collapsed in early experiments – but the process removed labour, reduced costs and gave much higher yields of bread from each sack of flour because the dough absorbed so much more water. Cheaper British wheats, with lower protein content than the North American grains that had become standard, could also be used.

By 1965 the Chorleywood bread process, or CBP as it was known, had become widespread. It could not be used for wholemeal bread because regulations prevented the addition of anything to wholemeal bread other than 100 per cent wholemeal flour, yeast, salt and water. But in the late 1980s, once the use of improvers had finally been permitted in wholemeal bread too, production of that switched to the same instant industrial process.

The technology of the chemical improvers on which modern bread depends has developed rapidly since.

Improvers had first emerged in the 1920s as 'yeast foods'. By the 1930s the industry had found that soya flour whitened bread and softened the crumb. Then, when chemical oxidants were needed to make the short, intense mixing in the CBP work, it made sense to incorporate them into a premix of additives with soya flour as the carrier for the chemical ingredients; most of the improver manufacturers in fact started out as soya flour millers. The improver or 'flour treatment agent' was also the logical way to add the fats needed in CBP breads.

Ingredients manufacturers and bakers regard their improvers as commercially sensitive and are not overeager to tell you what is in them. Bakers' technical handbooks, however, are an instructive source.

They explain why industrial bakers have used hydrogenated fats for years: the CBP requires the addition of a hard fat with a high melting point to give the bread structure. The fat has to remain solid at temperatures of up to 43°C, hence the need for artificially hardened or hydrogenated fats. (Unfortunately hydrogenating fat creates trans fats that are known to increase the risk of heart disease, see Chapter 7.) The fat also needs to be present in the dough in a highly dispersed form. So manufacturers of bread improvers and other industrial baking ingredients blend hard and soft fat and either spray-dry it or disperse it through a carrier such as soya flour. Hydrogenated fat may sometimes be listed simply as vegetable fat on a label, but since it counts as a processing aid and may be part of a mixed 'flour treatment agent', it is not necessarily declared separately.

The ingredients manufacturers still advertise 'pumpable fats in returnable bulk tanks' with 'high slip point fat for use in CBP . . . to provide increased volume, texture and improved fresh keeping . . . made with hydrogenated oil, water and emulsifiers E471, E475, E476'. But they also now offer alternatives for manufacturers 'where trans fats are an issue'.

The alternative is generally 'fractionated fat', which is replacing hydrogenated fat as both the industry and public wake up to the latter's dangers. Fractionated fat is typically made from palm oil that has been cooled until fat crystals form so that the solids can be separated out. This palm stearin used to be considered waste but then it was found to have the high melting point that is so useful in food manufacture. Its hardness is double-edged, however. Like hydrogenated fat, it has been associated in some literature with heart disease, although the palm oil industry disputes the link.

The CBP also needs emulsifiers. These perform a similar function to the fat. They plug the gaps, enabling the dough to retain more air while also slowing down staling. The most commonly used group of emulsifiers in bread are the data esters, relatively novel and complex compounds, made from petrochemicals.

Double the amount of yeast is also used in the CBP to make up for the lack of fermentation time. Champions of real bread have suggested a link between this increase in yeast and its residues and the rise of infections such as thrush, which is produced by the yeast organism candida albicans. But there is little research in this area.

Salt goes into bread to add flavour, at up to 0.5g per 100g for white sliced, making it a high-salt food by government health guidelines. Although levels have been reduced in the last ten years, they have remained high. Traditionally flavour develops during the fermentation time, so when you eliminate that you need higher levels of salt.

Legislation has gradually been introduced to restrict some of the more damaging additives manufacturers used to depend on in the CBP. Potassium bromate, which was used for years as a bleaching and oxidizing agent but also destroyed valuable nutrients, has been banned, for example. The only oxidizing agent that may now be used during mixing is ascorbic acid, often labelled as vitamin C, although any vitamin C content is destroyed in the baking.

It took from 1927 when a government committee first recommended a ban until 1998 to stop the use of flour bleached with chlorine compounds. Manufacturers liked chlorinated flour, not just because of the bleaching effect but also because it allowed higher levels of water to be added. When it finally lost these props the industry accelerated research into enzymes and other novel ingredients to find alternatives. The Associated British Foods group that owns Allied Bakeries, for example, also owns Cereform which in turn owns AB Enzymes, the first company to supply enzymes, or 'tiny invisible helpers' as it calls them, to the baking industry.

As enzymes are destroyed in the baking process they do not have to be declared on the label. Their use in food is increasing rapidly, thanks to the introduction of gene modification techniques. Naturally occurring enzymes – proteins that speed up biological reactions – have been used in food preparation for centuries. The combination of pineapple and ham may seem a culinary travesty but it evolved because the enzymes in the fruit have a tenderizing effect on the meat. Since the 1980s, however, companies have been using genetic modification to mass-produce customized enzymes. Many of the enzymes used in baking today are produced by genetically modified organisms (GMOs). It is the microorganisms that produce the enzymes, however, rather than the enzymes themselves that have been modified.

A report in the technical journal *New Food* highlights some of the benefits of these enzymes. It describes how certain hemicellulase enzymes 'enhance bread volumes' and control the softness of doughs so that manufacturers can incorporate more water, 'giving high percentage volume increases with relatively low-grade flour'.

Getting water into the dough is one of the keys to profitability. The CBP white loaf is made with about 3 per cent more water than one made by traditional methods. When the government's Food Standards Committee looked at water in bread in 1978, the average percentage of water in a loaf ranged from 36 to 40 per cent. A subsequent study in 1986 found the average percentage had risen to 45 per cent.

The comparisons looked even worse when a traditional wholemeal loaf was put alongside a CBP wholemeal one. The CBP wholemeal had 6.5 per cent more water than the traditional loaf. Bread is sold by weight, and water is pretty heavy stuff.

Most of our bread is now made by the CBP. Over 80 per cent of it is wrapped and sliced and of that three quarters is white sliced. At the time of writing a white sliced loaf can be bought in a supermarket for just 24p. Until the droughts of 2003 sent the European harvest plummeting and the value of wheat soaring, the price of a loaf had been stuck for months at 19p.

Chemical wizardry and economic efficiency have undoubtedly produced cheap daily bread. Yet for all their power and despite all the new hi-tech methods to help them make money, the bakers are under pressure, as I discovered when I went to a large white-sliced bread factory.

The great silos and chimneys of the Erith bread factory look imposing as you walk up the leafy hill towards them from the suburban station of Barnehurst in outer London's Bexley Heath. But close up, the factory entrance, set amidst nondescript housing, is modest enough, as is the assessment of our culinary aspirations displayed on its welcome sign. 'Consistent products, contented customers,' it announces above a rollcall of brand names – Hovis Great White, Mother's Pride, Nimble – that manage to sound both weighty and light.

The loaves that come out of here are certainly consistent. Ten thousand of them an hour, a quarter of a million a day, travel in an endless line through giant mixers and moulders into the gas oven, following a schedule which allows for no interruption from each Saturday afternoon until the early hours of the following Saturday morning, when the plant closes down briefly for cleaning and maintenance before winding straight back up again.

This is where 10 per cent of all British Bakeries bread is made. Here 13 tonnes of fats and 12 tonnes of chemical improvers are used each week to turn 820 tonnes of flour into the sort of bread that can fill 1.5 million factory bread bags, marked either with the company's own brands or with own-label logos for Tesco, Sainsbury's, Safeway or Marks and Spencer. Because the volumes are so enormous, bread is one of the few foods that retains its own distribution system. Eighteen articulated lorries take the bread from Erith to the British Bakeries' distribution centre at Dagenham for it to be trucked on to hundreds of supermarkets across the south of England, hitting a precise delivery window between 3 a.m. and 5 a.m. to miss the night curfews but still be in time for the stores' opening hours.

Nigel Dalmon, the site manager at Erith, showed me around together with John White from the Federation of Bakers, the industry lobbying group. Dalmon started in the baking business thirty-three years ago, as an apprentice aged fifteen. We began in the store room. It was surprisingly small – the flour comes in throughout the day in a 'just-in-time' delivery system. Most of it is British these days. UK wheat used to be considered too soft for breadmaking, and harder American wheats with a higher protein content were favoured, but the CBP, and the ability to separate out and then add back in gluten from other sources, has made it possible to use a majority of homegrown grain. It's much cheaper because the EU subsidizes British grain farmers, and imposes tariffs on imported wheat.

A solitary worker put on his mask and weighed and sieved ingredients from one yellowy plastic tub to another, stirring up a ghostly cloud of dust. The range of technical possibilities was engraved on a row of bins marked 'BB Longer Life', 'BB Improver', 'Gluten', 'Bred [sic] soy'.

We went into the main plant room beyond, muffling our ears against the din. Here conveyor belts rose and fell, turned and advanced through every conceivable angle and plane, shunting the bread through its different stages. At any one time there were 35,000 loaves moving through the factory in various states of being, and the machine must not stop. 'Hold up any one part of it for more than five minutes and you lose the whole plant,'

Nigel explained. Pipes and tubes wormed around the ceiling carrying yeast from pumps and flour from hoppers to the mixers. Most of the mechanical shunting was mere marking of time, keeping the stuff moving while it warmed up or cooled down. To stop would require labour. There were 100 people on each shift, but for the most part they were invisible presences.

The actual bread mixing was over in a blink. This is the wonder of the CBP. It replaces hours of waiting while the dough ferments. Two industrial steel mixers were being fed 225 kilos each of flour, plus water, vinegar, salt, yeast and the contents of one of the yellowy bins – layers of powders of different textures and a large glob of greyish fat. Then the vast bowls vibrated furiously for just three minutes before swinging up high, turning and disgorging an enormous lump of instant dough like a giant ball of chewing gum.

John White explained that 'hydrogenated fat is not an issue for us, we don't use it. There might be tiny amounts of partially hydrogenated fat in some flour improvers, but in such small quantities . . . the ingredients manufacturers are looking at getting rid of it.' They now use fractionated fat.

The ball of dough emerged from the mixers to be rolled up into a hopper from where it fell down through a divider. It was allowed to recover on the belt for ninety seconds before passing into the moulder where it was squashed to a pancake, and passed through a set of knives to divide it into four triangular pieces, each on its own lane, for white sliced bread. Wholemeal is made in one piece but white sliced is made up from four pieces of dough because 'it gives a more open texture with less shadow which makes it look whiter'. Further along, the four lanes converged and were joined by another tier bearing empty tins on a belt which glided up from underneath to meet them. Once brought together, the loaf moved for fifty-four minutes through the prover, then on through the lidding machine – for the laying on of lids – flat-top or dome depending on the supermarket client, or top left open for the independent sector. From there the bread passed on into the oven where tracks carried it back and forth past rows of gas burners for a precise twenty-one minutes.

The greatest expenditure of energy goes into cooling. The loaves have to be cold before they can be sliced or they collapse, and it takes 110 minutes to bring them down to the right temperature to pass through the high-speed blades of the slicer and be received into their plastic bags.

It was not good baking weather when I visited. The incinerating heat of a record summer and the blast of the furnaces had made it too hot. Nigel held a slice of bread up to the light. It had a few gas bubbles in it, yet looked uniform enough to me, but his practised eye was not happy. 'Our product has got to be the best on the shelf.' You can add more cold water but there's not much else you can do in a plant this size to keep the temperature down.

We walked past the coat-hanger-like racks of wrappers wearing the colours of the major retailers who have the white sliced loaves made here. I asked Nigel about the secret of the longer-life loaf. It is sprayed on the outside with either sorbate or calcium propionate – both antifungal agents which inhibit the growth of moulds. The latter has been associated with allergic reactions in workers. This factory uses the former, but not on its own brands of loaf.

I liked Nigel. He was running an efficient factory providing good jobs. He was passionate about his staff and concerned about his neighbours' best interests. A keen cyclist himself, he was committed to doing something about the traffic nuisance caused by his lorries and shift workers driving to the factory at the crack of dawn – if only the council could get some public buses running at that time of day.

When we had finished our tour, we went upstairs to talk more about the pressures on the market.

Nigel offered me a plate of ham sandwiches in white bread.

'Your own bread?' I asked as I took a bite.

'Yes indeed.'

The bread was doing that curious thing sliced factory bread does, moulding itself to my teeth and the roof of my mouth and setting as though it were dentist's putty. I decided not to ask about the ham but worked furtively with my tongue, hoping to dislodge it without looking too rude, while Nigel and John sighed and tutted about the Atkins Diet.

The diet, a weight-loss programme originally devised ten years ago by an American doctor, Robert Atkins, had hit the bestseller lists again following an article in the *New York Times* magazine headlined 'What if it's all a big fat lie?' The *NYT* piece compiled evidence challenging the orthodoxy in the USA that excess consumption of fats in the diet was at the root of that country's current crisis of obesity, diabetes and heart disease. It posited instead the theory that the problem was an excess of carbohydrates, especially sugar and over-refined white flour, white rice and pasta, just as Atkins had maintained. Bread was in the firing line and the summer of 2003 had become the season of culling the carbos.

The theory behind the Atkins Diet is that to lose weight you have to avoid foods which come high on the glycaemic index (GI). This is a system for measuring how fast a food triggers a rise in blood sugar and has been used for years by dieticians around the world working with diabetics. Put simply, we get energy from glucose in the blood, or blood sugar. When we eat carbohydrates they are quickly absorbed by the body and converted to glucose in the blood. Refined carbohydrates and sugars are converted fastest. But fats and proteins do not induce a significant rise in blood glucose.

Insulin is the hormone which transports glucose from the blood to cells, either for immediate use as energy or to be converted by the liver into glycogen (for short-term use in the muscles and liver), or to fat (for long-term storage around the body). The main chemical constituents of this stored fat are triglycerides and high triglyceride levels are a risk factor for heart disease and strokes. As the glucose level in the blood rises, the pancreas releases insulin, which reduces the blood-sugar levels. Simple sugars and starches from white bread, white rice, cooked potatoes and refined cereals are converted to glucose very fast. Fibre from unrefined carbohydrates meanwhile slows down the entry of glucose into the blood. Excessive consumption of refined carbohydrates overstimulates insulin production, leading to highs and lows of blood-sugar levels, which leave you feeling hungry and eventually cause the glucose-regulating mechanism to break down. The liver then converts more glucose to stored fat and you end up both overweight and with diabetes.

The GI takes glucose as the benchmark with a value of 100 and foods are rated high, medium or low depending on how they compare with that. White bread is a no-no with a score in the 70s, but wholemeal bread scores only 50 and stoneground wholemeal is lower still at only 30. How a food is grown and processed makes a huge difference, according to the exhaustive GI published by the *American Journal of Clinical Nutrition*, in which carrots from Romania eaten raw score a very low 16 but rate 92 when peeled and boiled by Americans.

Whatever the anomalies, Nigel and John could see that the propaganda war was running away from them. In fact there is surprising unanimity among nutrition experts, government advisory committees and diet gurus. Official health policy is that complex, as opposed to refined, carbohydrates should form a significant part of our diets if we wish to avoid the diseases of affluence that afflict industrialized nations, and that we should cut down on fats. Even Atkins, whose diet has been attacked by health experts for being high in fat, recommends wholemeal bread and whole grains once you have regained a decent weight.

The food industry, however, has been hoist on its own petard. Since most of the bread we buy is white sliced, it is hard for the big corporate bakers to argue back about GI ratings or the merits of wholemeal. So the industry maintains a line that there is no such thing as a bad food; a balanced diet is the key to health.

But the nutritional gulf between a well-made wholemeal loaf

and a white sliced factory one is enormous. It's not just what goes into the white loaf, it's also a matter of what's been taken out.

The whole grain consists of an outer fibrous layer of bran; the germ (the embryo from which a new plant would grow); and the inner white endosperm. The bran contains the fibre, some protein, fat and minerals. The germ contains most of the oils, some protein and the highest concentration of vitamins and minerals. The endosperm is mostly carbohydrate and some protein. The oil of the whole grain has traditionally been one of the most important sources in the diet of essential fats, which are vital for healthy brain and nervous tissue function, but when whole wheat is milled to white flour, the most nutritious part of the grain is taken away.

There is method in this madness, however. The oil-rich germ can go rancid and requires more careful keeping. You can also make much more from grain by separating it into its constituent parts and selling it several times over. The holding groups of the baking and milling companies have included subsidiaries that are agricultural feed companies. It is no coincidence that baking companies have also made pet food. In fact, the pigs have the best of it. The wheat germ, in which the nutrients are concentrated, and the bran are sold as animal feed for the likes of them.

During the milling of white flour, over twenty vitamins and minerals present in the original wheat grain are reduced by half or more, according to the official bible on the composition of foods. Concern that this refining might be leaving humans malnourished compared to their livestock was first expressed in 1919. It was not until 1940 that the government decided to do something about it. The tussle between private profit and public interest in the food industry was evident even then. When Lord (then plain Mr) Boothby rose to his feet in the House of Commons to announce that vitamin B1 would be added to bread for the sake of the nation's health, he reassured the Honourable Members that he had resigned as chairman of the company that made the vitamins when he was first appointed a junior minister.

The government now requires millers to put back two of the B vitamins, B1 and B3, and iron and calcium. But they are not restored to the levels found in wholemeal flour. Calcium is whacked back in generous proportions – chalk is cheap – and goes in at nearly four times the level in the original wholemeal. The more expensive B vitamins, however, along with iron, are only restored to a percentage of the levels present in wholemeal.

John Lister is the miller serious chefs and bakers turn to for their flour. He runs Shipton Mills, a company which works from a restored watermill in the Cotswolds, producing some of the country's finest flours. Ancient stones still grind his wholemeal and his white flour is matured by careful storage, not by additives and enzymes. He believes a country's bread is a barometer of its culture. By this measure the state of ours is none too healthy.

Lister explained the significance of good milling to me. 'When you stone-grind flour the grain goes in at the top and comes out the side twenty seconds later. You know you've got the whole lot.' For thousands of years flour was ground in this way. It's a relatively gentle process that leaves most of the nutrients intact. But a pair of stones can only grind 250 kilos of flour an hour. In 1834 a new method was invented which made mass production possible – the steel roller mill. Now the vast majority of bread flour is ground in roller mills. A steel roller can make 20 tonnes of flour an hour passing wheat up and down through a sequence of rollers that gradually get bigger and bigger. As the grain passes through, the bran, wheat germ, white and finer white parts are separated and collected in different bins. 'You can use roller mills more softly and have fewer rollers, but for CBP flour you do an enormous amount of grinding under huge pressure, to break open all the starch molecules. The flour ends up very fractured and grey. Then it absorbs water like a sponge. It's critical to modern baking to get lots of water in.'

When you make wholemeal on a roller mill, you go through the same process, taking the wheat right through to white flour and then mixing all the different grades back in, but you don't necessarily end up with exactly the whole grain and you get much more damaged starch than you do from a stone-grinding. That's why stone-ground wholemeal tastes different and one of the reasons why a CBP wholemeal loaf can vary so much from a traditionally made one.

Like so much of our industrialized food system, CBP amounts to a great experiment. 'It didn't take 2,000 years to develop the process of making bread for us just to bin it without consequences. The question is, have we made our staple indigestible?' Lister says.

He has done some work with local doctors on gluten allergy, the prevalence of which seems to be growing alarmingly. 'It's the fermentation time that makes wheat digestible. When we made bread that had been given thirty-six to forty-eight hours to ferment, it did not cause a reaction in people who suffer from gluten allergies. We know we also have many more yeast-related illnesses today than in the past.

'We have factories turning wheat into its constituent parts – pure starch, pure powdered gluten. Pure gluten is like chewing gum, they add it to give the flour enough strength to survive the factory process. We have bred wheat varieties for the dominant CBP processes in which the proteins are not as malleable as they used to be. Year on year since the introduction of the Chorleywood process, bread consumption has declined. At the end of it, the bread just isn't nice any more.'

The industry view is that people wouldn't buy white sliced bread if that were not what they wanted. But of course it's not that simple. The economics of the bread market are so distorted that for many people there is no real choice.

The baking industry, despite being so concentrated in the hands of the two main players, is now at the mercy of the forces that really control our shopping today: the big retailers.

At the root of the problem is 'loss leading'. On the back of this piece of supermarket speak has come a transformation in shopping habits that has squeezed the life out of high streets and markets. The unintended effect has been that many of the most vulnerable in society no longer have access to fresh food. Supermarkets are not solely responsible for the change, but they have been one of the main driving forces behind it.

Loss leading is what supermarkets do when they sell products below the price it costs them to purchase them from manufacturers. It is illegal in most European countries. France, Belgium, Greece, Italy, Luxembourg, Portugal and Spain have banned it completely. Other European countries including Germany, Austria and Ireland have placed tight restrictions on it. An inquiry by the UK's Competition Commission into the British supermarkets found the practice operated against the public interest. But it did not make any recommendations to stop it.

It works like this. Everyday groceries, such as bread, butter, milk, sugar, are classified as known-value items (KVIs). These are the key purchases whose price shoppers know and by which they judge which shop offers the best value. Most prices are no longer marked on packets but only appear on the shelves, where we notice them briefly. As a result, most of us have no clue what other items cost.

Supermarkets cut their prices on KVIs to bring people into their stores rather than anyone else's. Loss leading builds up their image as retailers offering the best value and has the same effect as predatory pricing: it knocks other shops, particularly small specialist shops, such as bakers, butchers and greengrocers, and convenience stores, out of business. Professor Paul Dobson of Loughborough University has made a study of the practice. Leading UK supermarkets operate with about 100–200 items being sold below the price they paid for them at any one time. A further 370 lines are typically sold at a gross margin of less than 5 per cent – in other words, below a price which would generate a decent profit for the store. Sainsbury's told the Competition Commission inquiry into supermarkets in 2000 that 25 per cent of its own-label products were sold below cost. On a sample day, Asda had 215 items for sale below cost. Tesco had 160.

White sliced bread is one of the supermarkets' key competitive weapons and has been sold below cost for the last few years. In July 2003 the cheapest white sliced bread on sale in the major multiples was being sold at 19p when the cost to the retailer was between 22p and 26p. If the supermarkets had been selling it with a typical retail margin, it should have cost 28–33p. The price had dropped as low as 7p in 1999. Bread in England is half the price of similar bread in France and a third of the price of the German equivalent. The cheapest bread is nearly always an own-label loaf, which gives the supermarkets more bargaining power over the suppliers since it undermines the manufacturers' own brands by making them look bad value and increases competition between suppliers.

All of which sounds fine at first hearing – good healthy competition which apparently gives us cheaper food. Except that retailers are in the business of making profits, and their losses on KVIs are made good in higher prices elsewhere – on those items we can't remember the cost of. Ironically, the practice reduces competition as people are encouraged to compare the price only of loss leaders between supermarket stores rather than look across a whole range of things they buy.

Bread is not the only food affected. Milk has been used as a loss leader, as have baked beans. Before the baked beans war broke out between retailers and manufacturers, the cheapest own-label cans of beans sold at 16–19p and accounted for 13 per cent of the market. Prices fell to 9p, increasing the own-label share to 37 per cent of the market, undermining the more expensive brands. At one point they went as low as 3p per can. Nestlé told the Competition Commission that at this level they literally could not can fresh air for the price supermarkets wanted. The end result was that Nestlé closed its Crosse and Blackwell canning operation and withdrew from that area of its business. Just one example of how loss leading tends to produce more concentrated markets that favour large retailers, not more competitive ones.

People on low incomes spend a much higher proportion of

their money on cheap staples such as bread, milk and baked beans than more affluent households. If loss leading effectively subsidized the food items poor families bought most at the expense of a few manufacturers' and richer people's tastes we might see it as a useful if unintended piece of wealth redistribution. The idea that the poor benefit from the supermarkets' cheap prices is one of the arguments always thrown at those arguing about their effect on the quality of food. In fact it is those on low incomes who suffer most.

Loss leaders are frequently the least healthy purchases – overrefined cereals, highly processed products full of salt, fat and sugar. Healthy foods, such as fruit and vegetables, and wholemeal bread tend to have the highest retail margins. As Professor Dobson points out, the introduction of persistent selling of white bread below cost has been accompanied by a decline in the consumption of wholemeal bread. Loss leading also drives a race to the bottom. It undercuts quality foods so much that it distorts the market in favour of the cheapest and unhealthiest.

It is perhaps the loss of other places apart from supermarkets to buy food that hits the poorest hardest, however. The supermarkets' practice of loss leading has taken custom away from other shops and alternative distribution systems such as doorstep milk deliveries, so that they have been unable to survive.

Sometimes the effect has been rapid and obvious. When the institution of the universal milkman died out as shoppers increasingly switched to the cut-price pinta available in the supermarkets, there was a wave of nostalgic regret. But it seemed a little half-hearted. People mourned the loss of the social function – the milkman who knew everyone, checked up on the old ladies each day, noticed the burglars. But they didn't stop patronizing those who ruthlessly undercut him.

A senior director of one of the leading supermarket chains admitted to me privately that the late opening hours adopted by his company were not profitable – that wasn't the point. You opened late to stop people shopping elsewhere. Late opening is a way of making sure you are the biggest beast in the jungle, of mopping up the opposition, however small. Supermarkets' loss leaders don't just take away a bit of business, they have a habit of taking away the whole lot. The milkman was just the beginning. Where every high street once had a butcher, a baker and a greengrocer, now only a fraction of the post-war numbers of these specialist shops remain. Pharmacies, newsagents and off-licences look like the next target. Supermarkets have lobbied hard and won the battle to scrap retail price maintenance on certain proprietary medicines and now want to dispense prescriptions as well.

Since the 1940s around 100,000 small shops have closed and every year their number drops by a further 10 per cent. Between 1995 and 2000 independent fresh food specialists, including bakers, butchers, fishmongers and greengrocers, saw their sales drop by 40 per cent as supermarkets consolidated their grip on food sales. Nearly 60 per cent of high street butchers disappeared between 1985 and 2000. There were some 47,000 independent grocery retailers in Britain fifteen years ago. Today there are only 28,000.

Independent retailing in the UK is reaching a crisis point. Seven out of ten English villages are without a shop. The decline seen in the 1980s has accelerated through the 1990s, but the independent think-tank the New Economics Foundation has warned that it could reach a 'tipping point' in the next few years. Once the number of local shops falls below a critical mass, the amount of money circulating within the local economy plummets to the point where people can no longer do a proper shop locally and are forced to travel elsewhere.

The dynamics can work in a way few of us ever imagined. If a new supermarket opens on the edge of town and half the residents do one third of their shopping there, retail revenue can drop by about 17 per cent in the town centre shops. The people who go to the supermarket may still do two thirds of their shopping in the town, and the other half of the population may do all its shopping in the town centre, but a fall in revenue of

17 per cent is enough to start killing off the town-centre shops, according to the NEF analysis. Once that happens, more people feel forced to switch to the supermarket, because they cannot get everything they need in the centre, and the town begins to shut down. As individuals we feel helpless to buck the trend.

This is the law of unintended consequences. It doesn't take many people changing their habits to force a change on a whole community that no one really wanted. The loss is not confined to the process of buying our food. Local shops perform dozens of social functions. They are places where neighbours who might not otherwise meet bump into each other and talk; they are somewhere for the elderly or those stuck at home with young children to go to; by using them we find familiar faces that make us feel safe in our areas. When these shops go out of business, we are left with boarded-up shopping parades or high streets full of charity shops, fast-food outlets, graffiti and litter. Whole areas can become food deserts where there are almost no shops selling decent fresh food. This is not what we foresaw when we leaped into our cars to do our weekly shop where KVIs were cheapest.

Other European countries have been much quicker to spot the damage done to the social fabric by allowing big supermarkets to acquire a stranglehold on retailing. It was the end of the 1990s before the UK tightened up its planning laws to stop new out-of-town developments. In France, by contrast, local authorities were given the right to veto the construction of supermarkets over 1,000 square metres in 1973. In 1996 the French government introduced a law that required a public inquiry for any outlet of 6,000 square metres, to protect 'the social and economic cohesion and the fabric of society'. Supermarkets were also banned from advertising on TV in France until the EU forced the country to lift its restriction at the beginning of 2004.

Supermarkets argue that it is the customers who have chosen what kind of shopping suits them best. For many working women, life without the convenience of a weekly one-stop shop with parking, would be virtually impossible. Supermarkets have also been able to offer much wider choice. Many of the small grocers they have replaced had become pretty depressing places, with tired and unimaginative offerings.

Those sufficiently well-off to own a car may feel that the loss of the high-street shops is sad or mildly inconvenient, but that the benefits outweigh the disadvantages. For people on low incomes, however, many of whom have no cars, the loss of other outlets can represent a devastating loss of a basic service as their areas turn into food deserts. They often end up spending a significant proportion of their weekly food budgets on taxis to carry their food home.

Food deserts are things the supermarkets would like us to believe are nothing to do with them. The lobby group for the big retailers, the British Retail Consortium (BRC), recently announced the results of research – part funded by J. Sainsbury – by the University of Southampton into a deprived area of Leeds where large numbers of residents had no access to shops until a new Tesco opened recently. The study found that a complex range of factors affected people's shopping habits and that while the new supermarket improved their diets, it did so only marginally, suggesting access was not the only factor in poor diets. 'Food deserts a mirage,' the BRC press release accompanying the study publication trumpeted to a seminar it had organized of dozens of MPs, health professionals and government policy advisers. The authors of the study weren't quite so sure that was what their research had shown. They acknowledged that food deserts exist.

My interest in the politics of food was first sparked over twenty years ago by a pioneering public health nutritionist, Caroline Walker. In between working for government advisory committees she was involved in a project in the East End of London to tackle the disproportionate rates of cardiovascular disease suffered among its poorer communities. They were living in one of these 'mythical' food deserts and could not afford decent food, so were filling up on junk instead. Caroline's warning that a debased, industrialized diet was taking a terrible toll on the nation's health, and that the government needed to act to change what we ate, was dismissed by the industry as food Leninism. Two decades later, as epidemics of obesity and diabetes take hold and the relation between diet and other diseases such as heart disease and cancer becomes clearer, her warnings and those of other experts are harder to dismiss. Caroline died young, so it was something of a pilgrimage for me to go back to the East End and the areas that had been her stamping ground. The present government has now designated these areas as food and health action zones.

Outside West Ham station the Dolphin fish bar's windows are obscured behind the small mesh of security grilles that characterize so many areas in decline. The convenience shop next door selling Wall's ice cream and lottery tickets has a few tired vegetables on its half-empty shelves. Further along, a video shop selling wine and fizzy drinks offers photocopying. A new small convenience store, built in the station under the footbridge over the main road to catch returning commuters, is better stocked but expensive. These are the only shops within easy walking distance of a whole network of housing estates in the London borough of Newham.

Lilian Rowley has lived nearby in West Ham for thirty-eight-and-a-half years. She's a widow on two pensions – her husband's occupational one and the state pension, so she counts herself better off than many of her fellow septuagenarians. She spends £10 a week on food, eating lunch at a pensioners' club. She remembers shopping round the corner just after the war, at Mr Jones's grocery where the assistant was called Doris or at Mr and Mrs Shannon's the greengrocers where they would always pick out a nice Laxton for her and sell her 'scrumpy ones for cheap'. 'Of course, as a child, everybody knew everybody and we'd go out to shop on our own. The manager of the shop would be on the step making sure everyone behaved. There was a baker – I can remember the smell. They used to sell off stale loaves so you could have a bread and butter pudding very cheaply. But that's gone, it's all gone. We've still got a few shops in the Plaistow Road but they're expensive convenience places. The butcher's closed.'

Lilian is active and enjoys nothing better than a weekly dance, but like the majority of her friends she has no car. 'I have to get the bus to Stratford to the nearest supermarket four or five times a week because I can't carry heavy loads. That's twenty-five minutes, but at least the bus is free. It gets me out but it's not sociable at all now. I smile at people in the supermarket but I think they think you're a bit funny, you know. The trouble is I'm five feet tall and I just cannot reach the top shelves. There are staff somewhere around but not where you want them. I've thought of taking one of those clipper things on a handle you get to help you put your socks on, but I'd feel foolish. The fruit is so expensive – I always bought apples but not any luxury items. The peaches were forty-nine pence each last week! I don't buy cheap bread. I like good seed bread, the other stuff's like glue. I do drink a lot of milk. On a budget it's a good way of getting cheap food, but my doctor's told me to cut down on the fat.'

Lilian's lifeline has been a new food co-op set up on a nearby estate. It has enabled her to increase dramatically the amount of fresh food she can buy locally. It's also a place to go and help and get to know new people.

The co-op scheme was started here by Eric Samuel, a Caribbean-born Pentecostal minister who has made this food desert his unofficial parish. He took me on a tour, providing a commentary on what we saw delivered with preacher's zeal but at rapper's speed. 'Come here, come, come with me, look at this. It's a total food desert. There's a tiny parade. It cannot compete with the supermarkets. The prices the supermarkets charge for fresh healthy food are wicked. We have terrible rates of diet-related disease here but it has become impossible for ordinary people to live well.' The co-op started when he decided to go to Spitalfields at the crack of dawn each morning to buy good cheap fresh fruit and vegetables and bring them back for those people who had no cars or could not afford to shop elsewhere. His temporal reward has been an honour and the attention of a whole posse of government advisers and their schemes.

With the help of money from the Labour government's new deals for regeneration and action on health, the co-op project has expanded. Ironically, it is the taxpayer who is now picking up the bill for successive governments' failure to tackle the power of the supermarket retailers and to protect the public from the consequence of the demise of high streets and town centres.

Lita Webb, another East End dynamo, helps run the food co-ops now and supplies fresh fruit and vegetables to the school breakfast clubs so that children can start the day with something good in their stomachs. She also drops bags off to the elderly who can't get out. Local doctors prescribe fresh fruit and vegetable vouchers from the co-op for those diagnosed with diabetes, heart disease and cancers, to help them change their eating habits.

The hub of the West Ham scheme is an old community shed, with those ubiquitous mesh grilles and a spiked metal fence, that turns into the local greengrocer once a week. It's the sort of place where neighbours come and gossip, where Lita will say hello to everyone, and if you find yourself £2 short you can owe it till next week. When I got there the people using it were in danger of being overwhelmed by co-ordinators and evaluators with clipboards, and press minders wanting to know what they thought. But eventually they melted away, and Lita and I chatted over a cup of coffee while people filled their baskets. Some of the people who came to use the co-op were people on benefits; many were working in low-paid jobs in social services or were students.

Love Anderson arrived with two of her four children. She's a care worker with the elderly, bringing home £200 a week while her children are at school. She stocks up on staples at the co-op – plantains, sweet potatoes and fruit. When I asked her what difference it had made to her and where she used to shop before, she dissolved into emotion. 'I'm speechless. It's made such a difference. It would cost much more before. We had to walk to Canning Town, but there isn't much there. Food takes all my money. I used to go hungry and we used to live on white bread and rice. The children don't like them any more, they can have all this.'

Isaac Hewett is a twenty-one-year-old dental student, with an income of £12,000 a year, £7,000 of it made up of debt in the form of student loans. When he came in at the end of the day, he was dressed all in black from his shirt and tie to his trousers and big shoes, and with his shoulder-length ginger hair he looked the archetypal student, except for the buggy from which his sixteen-month-old son Hudson stared out with huge eyes and a pale, sleep-bleary face.

'My wife and I spend £18 a week on food for the three of us,' Isaac said. 'I live in Stratford so I'm near shops, but I walk down here to get the weekly supplies of fresh fruit and vegetables. We can eat them now. We used not to. We can't afford the fresh stuff in the supermarkets. And I like the idea of it. Stratford was one of the homes of the early co-operative movement. There have been times when you go without because you want the best for your child. It's not that we're completely desperate, but it may be that we've chosen to have a bit of a social life and have gone out together for once in a while. Then we can't afford fresh fruit and vegetables, and we have to fill up on white sliced bread and the cheapest things.'

I walked to Canning Town afterwards to see the loss of shops and the degeneration they had all talked about. It's a desolate high street, with the pillars of the A13 flyover marching right through the community. The old Kwiksave building is being gutted, and shuttered shops along the high road are interspersed with takeaways advertising themselves with the smell of cheap fat and fried chicken and trails of debris. 'Two pieces of chicken and chips, only £2.29. Kid's meal of nuggets and chips and fizzy drink only £1.50.' The Rathbone market was just a car park when I passed, but sells mostly clothes, not much food, when it does splutter to life, according to an office cleaner emptying bins. Nail bars and pawnbrokers have filled the gaps between run-down shops selling yams and plantains. The Titanic Café is left to speak of the neighbourhood's ambitions, in between the Light of This World Church and hairdressers flogging cornrows and braid. The only beams of light are the golden arches of the McDonald's beyond the traffic lights, illuminating a road sign to Becton, and its new superstore, three miles away.

5. Apples and Bananas

The apple trail through Kent, Garden of England, was perhaps the most famous of the old guided orchard tours, although Hereford and Worcester were also known for the beauty of their fruit trees in flower. Late spring would bring the show – clouds of white and carmine petals set against emerald buds, or twigs flushed their length with pink, depending on the apple type: James Grieve, Crispin, Chivers Delight, St Edmund's Pippin, Cox and D'Arcy Spice – the names of the traditional varieties as poetic as the blossom along the bough.

Nick Swatland's apple farm near Sittingbourne used to be as fine a sight as any. But no more. A couple of years ago the Kent Tourist Board said the blossom trail would not run again, since so many of the orchards had been grubbed up. And in 2002 Nick too packed up his apple business. His last year, 2001, was ironically one of the best ever, with a huge and good-quality crop, but he saw little from it. He was supplying the supermarkets through a marketing organization, but the prices just kept getting lower and lower. 'We were being given twenty to twenty-one pence a kilo, they were selling them in the stores at twice that, and we needed thirty-two pence to break even. The prices would change by the day, and then they'd take sixty to ninety days to pay you, when you'd already paid your labour. If you were a very good boy you'd get some money eventually. It was not good for the heart. It was a combination of things, I suppose, that finished us: the global economy, dominant supermarkets and the strength of the pound.' It was a wrench selling most of the farm – his father had started out in 1941, but in the end he, like Nick, was just relieved to be out of it.

John Dickson is a fifty-six-year-old farmer in Cambridgeshire.

He is hanging on with his apples, pears and plums, but only just. He averages a seventy-hour week for an income of about £18,000. His farm now has orchards with 10,000 trees, that are home to owls, hawks and much other wildlife, but he hasn't earned enough to pay income tax in three of the last five years. He used to supply the big supermarkets direct but got delisted, for complaining, he says. Most people are too afraid to speak out. He now supplies smaller supermarkets through a packhouse.

'You'd agree a price at the beginning of the season, then the week after it would be cut, then it would be cut again, till you say, very sorry but I can't take that kind of money, and you get dropped. Most of the time you feel you have no choice about going along with them, because once you've been dropped you can't get back in at a decent price. And you've got all their bloody packaging and have had to pay for it.

'Last year, I had to do a "promotion" on apples, three pounds for the price of two pounds, and I had to take the loss. I also had to pay two-and-a-half pence extra for each sticker that went on the pack boasting about the offer. The supermarket said they knew I was making a loss on the apples but no one would pay more and they could always get them somewhere else abroad if I didn't want to do it.'

But perhaps the most maddening thing was the beauty parade. A supermarket apple must look good in front of the camera or risk rejection.

A Dutch company provides packhouses with the machines, which cost hundreds of thousands of pounds, to measure cosmetic perfection. The 'Greefa Intelligent Quality Sorter' has cameras that take up to seventy colour pictures of every apple as it passes along a conveyor belt to determine the 'blush of non-equally coloured fruit', and to grade it by size. It can detect deviations of as little as one square millimetre. So if the supermarket specification says that an apple of a particular variety must be 15–17 per cent blush red on green, for instance, it can 'grade out' or reject any apples that are 18 per cent red on green or a miserable 14 per cent red on green. Its promotional literature cheerfully explains the reason for the beauty parade: 'Nature has many surprises . . . Buyers, however, require uniform fruit and vegetables of standard size.'

The beauty parade often means the difference between profit and loss for the farmer. Anything 'graded out' for failing the test ends up, if the farmer is lucky, as fruit for juice at giveaway prices of 3–5p a pound, but as often as not it will just go to waste.

Then there's the penetrometer. It's a spring-loaded little tool that measures the resistance of the fruit. John Dickson is eloquent on the subject of the penetrometer. 'I had the buyer round and he said my pressures were out. He admitted my Coxes were the best he'd tasted, but they weren't hard enough for his shelf life, and he told me I'd have to pick the fruit earlier,' he said. 'All the ripe ones have to come off when we go through the grader. No wonder people complain fruit doesn't taste of anything. They also get tested for starch and sugars and all that. I test mine the traditional way, with my front teeth. I can't get very excited about all this.'

The triumph of appearance over flavour has gone so far that the World Apple and Pear Association recently announced that it was considering drawing up 'an international organoleptic standards' label. Fruit that tasted of something would quality for the new logo.

It's the same with the plums. John grows thirty-two varieties, can start picking on his wedding anniversary, 13 July, and still have plums at the end of October. But the supermarket English season only lasts a few weeks, and they'll only take three varieties. 'The market for Victorias used to work really well. The largest went to the fruit market, the middles to canning and the smalls for jam. Now the smalls get thrown away, and most of the middles do too. They've got to be thirty-eight millimetres, unmarked, with stalk, to pass muster. The specification covers two sides of A4. The shape must be "typical", they must be more than fifty per cent coloured but they've also got to have a four-day shelf life. Well, that means they've got to be picked rock-hard. Plums need to be picked and eaten within a day or two to taste good. I can see an enormous supermarket from my fields. I asked if I could supply it direct with plums that were actually ripe, in peak condition. It can't be done.'

Size matters too. Assuming the fruit can survive the penetro-meter, it must conform to the supermarkets' vital statistics. For John this presents its own problems. 'When I was a boy, sixty millimetres was considered the ideal size for an apple – that would be five or six apples to a pound; you'd sell larger sixty-five-millimetre ones for a premium. But sixty-five millimetres gave you four apples to a pound. Now the supermarkets want a minimum of seventy-millimetre apples from me, so you only get three to a pound. Which of course means most customers end up buying more: to get four apples now you need to buy one-and-a-quarter pounds rather than the traditional pound.

'But to achieve those bigger apples I have to prune my trees much harder, and overfeed them. The apple is less well balanced because of the excess fertilizer; it loses its flavour. Then you get bitter pit – that's brown spots – and I have to spray all the time with calcium to prevent the markings.' A Cox may have been sprayed up to sixteen times by the time it reaches the shops.

The supermarket 'grade out' has become a source of great dread to farmers around the world. Enormous quantities of food go to waste because they do not meet the very narrow specifications now demanded by most big supermarkets. I have watched smallholders in Kenya's Machakos hills grading green beans for export to the UK supermarkets. They stood in a simple traditional building on the edge of a triangle of rough ground, shaded by mango, jacaranda and pepper trees, measuring the vegetables against wooden slats to check that they conformed to the requirement that a green bean should be 95mm in length and between 5 and 7.5mm in diameter. And they had to be straight; curved green beans would not do. The packer and exporter, Homegrown, explained that 35 per cent of beans failed to make the supermarket grade, and while a few of the rejects went to cattle feed, or into the local market, most went to waste, even in a country where people go hungry.

A leading Lincolnshire supplier of Brussels sprouts to the supermarkets is allowed two sizes for his crop, 25–30mm or 30–35mm. A neighbouring supplier who grows carrots for the supermarkets told me that his typical waste figures were even higher. For every 30 tonnes of carrots harvested, just 10 tonnes are used. As well as the vegetables rejected because they are marked or damaged in some way, anything that is bent, or has a slightly green top, gets graded out.

Organic farmers have been hit particularly hard by this demand for cosmetic perfection, since they cannot resort to heavy chemical use to achieve it. No one is immune, as I discovered on a trip to Highgrove, to see the Prince of Wales's organic farm.

'You are entering a GMO-free zone,' reads the sign on the track as you swing into His Royal Highness's estate near Tetbury in the rolling Cotswold hills. Prince Charles bought the land here in the 1980s and gradually converted it to organic farming a decade ago. Home Farm is run, as has long been the tradition on rich landowners' estates, as a model farm where new ideas and enlightened agriculture may be tried out. The Prince is opposed to genetic modification. He is also patron of the British organic farmers' organization, the Soil Association, showing guests around Home Farm to persuade them of the cause. 'All the things I have tried to do in this small corner of Gloucestershire have been the physical expression of a personal philosophy,' he has said. The traditional crop rotations are used to maintain soil fertility and health. Hedgerows and trees have been planted with an artist's eye. The farm manager, David Wilson, who had farmed conventionally before he worked with the Prince of Wales to convert to organic farming, says that now he has tried both methods, organic farming 'just makes complete sense'. He looks back with amazement at his agricultural college textbooks with their adverts for the agrochemical companies. It would be hard not to be converted by the well-tended beauty of the place that HRH has 'put heart and soul into'.

Like guests at a Jane Austen tea party, we gathered in the sunshine for our tour of farm and gardens followed by picnic lunch, in the absence of the patron himself. The charabancs pulled up one by one on the gravel outside a large barn, as beautifully preserved as a National Trust tea room. Few had been able to resist the excitement of the outing. There was the adviser from Number Ten, the top civil servant from the Department of Health, the man in charge of 'better regulation', various leading lights from the organic movement, a big cheese from a French food multinational. They emerged from their vehicles, all as instructed by the invitation wearing sensible boots, some of which looked suspiciously clean. Then came the school-dinner lady who had transformed meals at St Peter's primary school in Nottinghamshire; the corporate but socially responsible face of a large supermarket, and my friend from the bakers' federation, together with an OAP who was saving allotments in Hastings.

First we had tea and talk with Duchy biscuits, then David Wilson led the party off through the grounds. We admired the Highgrove Ayrshire dairy cows, chosen he said partly because HRH didn't want to see any more black and white Friesians blotting the landscape, and partly because he is troubled by the overbreeding for high yields that has narrowed the gene pool, made animals prone to sickness, and diluted traditional breeds. Home Farm has had considerable success with its experiments in bovine homeopathy. These low-yielding cows glowed with good health. They were brown and white and becoming against the gentle rise of the pasture. But commercial reality intruded here as everywhere. The Highgrove farm has been hit like all other dairy farmers by the collapse of the milk price. But for the power of his own brand, Prince Charles would be selling his organic milk at less than the cost of production.

We ambled back down the fields to the vegetable areas where the onion beds had just been hand-hoed, though it's hard to get the staff these days. 'We had to get a gang in on Monday, Iraqis and Indians in a minibus from Birmingham. Of course we can't get messed up with anything illegal,' Wilson said, sparking a discussion among the farmers in the party about the price of casual manual labour and the difficulty of competing against others who might be tempted to cut corners. Anyone working on the Duchy farms is very carefully vetted.

Foursomes and couples were forming now, breaking up, coming together again, rearranging themselves in the ritualized dance of a day's networking, and I found myself catching a curious jumble of half-absorbed snippets: government health policy priorities being addressed . . . nitrogen imbalance . . . public sector procurement rules framed within EU parameters . . . slug egg predators . . . unravelling regulatory red tape . . . worm resistance . . . the role of the American soy bean association in setting subsidy levels . . . clean sheep bottoms . . .

We paused to inspect a field of winter wheat, where poppies are allowed to flourish and long grass margins give shelter to small mammals and teeming insect life acting as natural predators to pests. And my, what a lot of insects there were this summer, we agreed, as we flicked them away.

And now, just as the party was flagging a little in the midsummer heat, a 4×4 carriage appeared, drawing a trailer behind it, with bales of straw arranged in two rows as rustic seats, to pull us up a small incline from where we could admire the royal carrots and potatoes. The party safely installed, we proceeded at a sedate pace up the hill, waving cheerily to the Iraqis resting next to the carrot field they had been weeding that day, while an Indian ganger drew on his fag next to his B reg minivan. The gangmaster, I learned later, was Zad Padda (see Chapter 2). When we were level with the potato fields, the talk turned to the dreaded 'grade out'.

Prince Charles has had his vegetables rejected by the supermarkets too. In fact the Highgrove grade outs are currently running at about 40 per cent. Sometimes the rejection is justified but sometimes it seems not, it might be just that the skin on a potato is a little ugly . . . whereas the odd scab was acceptable a few years ago, now it isn't, the quest for perfection has gone too far. As an organic farmer you can only get rid of scab by doing things that damage the soil or use too much water. Prince Charles had been asking for his rejected vegetables back – he'd like to feed them to his cattle. He also makes Duchy crisps (£1.59 a pack at Sainsbury's or Waitrose), but once they have gone into the system it can be rather hard to find them again.

Later, in the formal kitchen garden, where fragrant roses grow in among decorative herbs and summer vegetables, I chewed over the state of the rural nation with the Soil Association's director, Patrick Holden. The imbalance of power between producers and retailers is having a devastating effect on organic farmers. It was a conversation we had had before. 'It's not a food chain so much as a fear chain. The supermarket directors live in fear of losing market share and not being able to deliver endless growth to their shareholders, the supermarket buyer lives in fear of not meeting his or her targets and always wants to buy cheap and sell expensive, the packer lives in mortal fear of being delisted by the supermarkets, the grower lives in mortal fear of having his goods rejected or the price falling below the cost of production. How do you rebuild trust in a chain which is dominated by aggressive players and practices? This is what happens with the twin pressures of globalization and concentration of power. It's a crisis affecting every farmer in the land.'

The impact is indeed widespread. Britain is suffering from an agricultural slump. Figures from the Department of Environment, Food and Rural Affairs and the National Farmers' Union show that in England over 17,000 farmers and workers – or nearly 5 per cent of the workforce – left the land in the twelve months to June 2003. Total job losses for the farming industry since 1996 have exceeded 80,000.

Not only have rural incomes collapsed, traditional landscapes, wildlife and biodiversity are under threat. The demise of the

English orchard is just one typical case. You could see similar patterns in many other sectors – from dairy farming to poultry production. We have lost nearly two thirds of our apple orchards in less than thirty years. There are 6,000 varieties of dessert and cooking apples and hundreds more cider apples, but many of them have been lost to commercial production and survive only in the national fruit collection at Brogdale in Kent. By the end of the twentieth century just ten varieties accounted for nearly all the eating apples in UK orchards, with 70 per cent of production being Coxes and Bramleys.

Supermarkets increasingly buy their apples abroad, even at the height of the English apple season. A survey of supermarkets by Friends of the Earth in 2001 found that in late October and early November most were importing the majority of their apples and pears, despite a bumper English harvest. Less than one third of Tesco's and a quarter of Safeway's apples and pears came from British orchards. British farmers have meanwhile been receiving EU grants to grub up their trees, as retailers switch to global sourcing.

The crisis affecting farmers in Europe is in part the shake-down from the post-war productionist era. Before the Second World War, there were about 500,000 farms in Britain, the vast majority of which were small and mixed, raising both crops and livestock and using rotation to maintain soil fertility and contain pests and disease. Spending on feeds or fertilizers from agrochemical companies was minimal. Manure from animals was used instead to feed the crops which in turn provided fodder for the animals in a sustainable pattern of land management that was centuries old. By planting different crops each year the life cycle of pests was disrupted and diseases were by and large prevented from building up in the soil. Where that failed, labour-intensive husbandry was needed to nip problems in the bud.

But then the war brought shortages and rationing as Britain was cut off by Hitler's U-boats. The Ministry of Agriculture, working with the National Farmers' Union, took control of producing the nation's food, including its price and distribution. An all-out drive to boost farmers' incomes and maximize production began. Emergency measures were introduced to increase yields. After the war, these were formalized in the 1947 Agriculture Act, which gave farmers both guaranteed prices and guaranteed markets. The government was determined that Britain should never face food shortages again. Farmers were paid subsidies, first by the British government and then by the Common Market, for the quantities of food they produced. To obtain maximum yields, farmers started to specialize. Livestock were moved indoors where their conditions and feeding could be controlled. Mixed farming was gradually replaced by monoculture. With prices fixed, farmers were freed from the need to grow different crops as an insurance policy against glut or disaster. They were set on the path to industrialization.

The war had also seen the rapid development of chemical works to process nitrates for the manufacture of explosives. In peacetime, these companies were looking for a new use, and so the mass marketing of nitrate fertilizers for agriculture began. Organophosphates, developed as poisonous nerve agents against the enemy, could be marketed as new pesticides.

The Green revolution made it possible to produce much more food. But the combination of subsidies and the intensification it encouraged soon led to oversupply, as farmers became disconnected from their markets. Prices could only be maintained by expensive interventions. European farmers showed they could be highly efficient, using new technologies and agrochemicals to replace labour and boost yields phenomenally, but the legacy has turned out to be one of environmental degradation and decline in rural economies.

Each cow may produce twice as many litres of milk a year, each chicken may grow twice as fast, and each hectare of wheat may yield nearly three times as many tonnes as fifty years ago, but in that time, 60 per cent of ancient woodlands, 97 per cent of meadows with their rich flora and fauna, and 50 per cent of birds that depend on agricultural fields have gone, as have nearly 200,000 miles of hedges. Not only has intensive farming polluted water courses (see Chapter 2), it has also created problems of soil erosion and flood. Its industrialization of livestock has left animals prone to devastating epidemics of disease.

Meanwhile, other countries with more propitious climates, cheaper labour and sometimes differing standards have been able to undercut the prices offered by British farmers. But the distorting effects of subsidies are only half of the picture.

Bill Vorley, senior research associate at the International Institute for Environment and Development, has studied the underlying causes of the slump in farm incomes. The cause is partly oversupply, but he thinks one of the most important factors, concentration of power in processing and retailing, has slipped under the radar.

Attention has been focused on the way protectionist trade policies, such as farm subsidies and tariffs in the USA and the Common Agricultural Policy in Europe, have distorted markets and penalized poorer farmers. But in his report on agribusiness, *Food Inc.*, Vorley points out that 'even if unjust trade rules were to be reformed, disparities in bargaining power, scale, market access or information [would remain]'. Farmers are playing to the rules of the new global market and 'perfect competition' in which profits are supposed to go to the most efficient, but their customers, the food processors and retailers, are now part of oligopolies or complex monopolies which enable them to set the rules of the game and suck all the profit out of it.

The crisis is not unique to Britain. It is hitting rural economies across industrialized countries. France lost half its farmers between 1982 and 1999. In Germany the number of farmers has declined by a quarter in the last ten years alone. The USA has lost over 4 million farmers since the 1930s. And of course the slump is not confined to the developed world but has affected developing countries even more severely.

In less than half a century, the food chain has been turned

upside down. The money made from it has shifted dramatically from the millions of producers at the bottom of the chain to a few corporations at the top. With 2½ billion people out of a global population of about 6 billion dependent on agriculture around the world, the distribution of profits in the chain is not just an academic matter but of vital importance to global stability and development. Food processing and retailing are vastly profitable today, but across Europe farmers are going bankrupt despite their vast subsidies, while in developing countries farmers can barely keep alive.

In the UK the top six supermarket chains, Tesco, Asda, Sainsbury's, Safeway, Morrisons and Somerfield, controlled three quarters of the grocery market by the beginning of 2003. Half the country's food is sold through just 1,000 huge stores. With Morrisons cleared to take over one of those other five retailers, Safeway, the UK market is set to become even more concentrated. By the end of 2004, just four chains will control three quarters of the market – Tesco, the clear leader with over a quarter of the market, and the other three, Sainsbury's, Asda, and Morrisons/Safeway, battling it out with 16–17 per cent of the market each. Few city analysts expect it to stop there. To end up the loser in fourth place in the supermarket stakes after a takeover battle is to risk extinction. The year 2004 was being seen as make or break time for Sainsbury's. The reason for the drama was simple: buyer power. Unless a supermarket group can keep up with the buyer power of the dominant players, it cannot hope to survive in the big league.

The battle of the bananas is a classic example of the dynamics of retail concentration at work.

In 2002, Wal-Mart, the world's largest retailer which owns Asda in the UK, renegotiated its banana buying. It invited the biggest distributors of bananas to bid for a global contract to supply its stores in several countries. Control of banana trading had been taken over by the end of the 1990s by an oligopoly, with more than three quarters of global trade in the hands of just five companies, Chiquita (26 per cent of the market), Dole (25 per cent) and Del Monte Fresh Produce, Fyffes, and Noboa (8 per cent each).

Bidding for the international Wal-Mart contract was ferocious. The size of the contract meant that it alone would dramatically alter market shares in favour of the winners. Del Monte Fresh Produce, sourcing bananas from Latin America, won a large chunk of it and, because of the scale of the business on offer, promised Wal-Mart a deal that would enable the retailer to slash its prices to customers, including its Asda shoppers.

Bananas are British retailers' largest-selling and most lucrative item. According to the fairtrade non-profit organization, Banana Link, for every £1 of bananas sold at retail, the supermarkets keep 40p while growers receive just 10p. Bananas are, like bread, 'known-value items', one of the few items whose price shoppers remember and use to make comparisons between different shops and whether they offer good value or not. So if you cut prices on bananas you put intense pressure on your competition. As the price of bananas in Asda shops fell from £1.08 per kilo in the summer of 2002 to 81p per kilo in March 2003, other retailers were forced to scramble to keep up.

Sainsbury's said it was losing £22 million a year on bananas as it tried to match Asda prices. Its orders could not touch the scale of Wal-Mart operating globally, and it could not extract the same deal from suppliers. Moreover, it had been sourcing many of its bananas from the Windward Islands, where the fruit is produced on family farms with fewer chemicals but correspondingly greater labour costs. The Windwards could not match the prices offered by Latin American countries, where bananas for export are produced on large-scale plantations which depend on routine aerial spraying of pesticides and where infringements of labour rights and environmental abuses are both notorious and well documented. Nowhere have abuses been greater than in Ecuador, from where some of the bananas for the supermarket price war were to come. Banana Link calculated how much money would be left for other links in the food chain if bananas were being sold in shops in the UK at 81p per kilo. At this price it is impossible for a grower in Costa Rica to be paid the set legal minimum for a box of bananas, and impossible in turn for that grower to pay his labourers a legal minimum wage. 'International buyers are in effect obliging all banana-exporting countries to reproduce Ecuador's poor labour and environmental conditions,' it says.

The stranglehold that supermarket buyers now have over the food chain is graphically illustrated in a diagram drawn by food industry consultant Jan-Willem Grievink. It is an hourglass shape, with a wide line at the top to represent the 160 million consumers who make purchasing decisions in Europe, and another wide line at the bottom representing the 3.2 million farmers and producers who grow food for them.* But the lines connecting the two ends of the food chain, the consumers and the producers, are not direct. They narrow into a tiny pinch-point in the middle of the hourglass where just 110 retail buying desks decide what manufacturers may sell to us and what will be available in the shops for us to buy. This pinch-point is highlighted in Grievink's diagram with a large arrow marked 'Power'.

The concentration of retail power has not just taken place in the UK. It is a global phenomenon. The top thirty grocers in the world now control a third of all food sales. Supermarket chains have rushed to expand into other countries and strengthen their position, generally by merger and acquisition. Wal-Mart is not just the world's largest retailer; it is the world's largest company by sales. In 2002 its sales were $245 billion, bigger than all but thirty of the world's largest national economies. As global director of Deloitte Research Ira Kalish says, 'There is nothing

---

* 160 million is the number of consumers in the EU in 2003, plus Poland and the Czech Republic, who make decisions about what groceries to buy. The total number of eaters whose access to products is funnelled through just 110 buying-desks is 430 million.

like Wal-Mart. They are so much bigger than any retailer has ever been that it's not possible to compare.' The company is nearly four times the size of the next biggest global retailer, the French group Carrefour, which is itself awesomely large, with net sales in 2002 of $65 billion. Not far behind in the pecking order is the troubled Dutch group Ahold, with net sales of $60 billion. Four other US firms, Kroger, Target, Costco and Albertson's, together with German groups Metro and Rewe and UK-based Tesco, make up the rest of the top ten global retailers.

Tesco, which has been expanding rapidly in central and eastern Europe, south-east Asia and China, is the only British supermarket group to make the top ten with net sales in 2002 of $40 billion. Sainsbury's, with only a small international presence through a group of grocery stores in the USA, comes in at number twenty with an estimated $26 billion sales. The global buying power of Asda, through Wal-Mart, and of Tesco, with its chains in several countries, has undoubtedly helped these companies consolidate their positions as Britain's leading retailers. At the time of writing, Tesco had increased its market share of the UK grocery market to over 25 per cent, thanks in part at least to the acquisition of a chain of convenience grocery shops, which was unopposed by the regulatory authorities.

This emergence of retail power as the dominant force in food has taken place in the last two to three decades. It parallels the extraordinary concentration that took place earlier in food manufacturing (see Chapter 4). But it is retailers who rule the roost now.

If this power enables supermarkets to buy goods more cheaply and pass the savings on to customers, does it matter that only a few companies control so much of the global food system? UK shoppers certainly did very well out of the banana wars, after all. Food prices generally have fallen as the supermarkets here battle for market share, so, the argument goes, this must be good for ordinary people.

The competition authorities in this country have certainly

focused on prices and adopted this narrow definition of public interest when judging whether the concentration of power is anti-competitive. The late 1990s saw a flurry of activity but the retailers survived pretty much untouched.

During this time, supermarkets were being accused in the press of being responsible, together with banks and car manufacturers, for a 'rip-off Britain'. Complaints that prices were higher in the UK than in neighbouring European countries or the USA grew louder and louder. When New Labour came to power in 1997, both Tony Blair and Stephen Byers, who was Trade Secretary from 1998, took up the cause. The Office of Fair Trading (OFT) was asked to look into the grocery market. By spring of 1999, it had asked the Competition Commission to conduct a full-scale inquiry. That same spring, the chief executive of Wal-Mart visited England, and explored how a takeover bid for Asda would be received politically. He and his team were invited to tea at Downing Street. When criticized for entertaining them, the Prime Minister said he made no apology. 'We are overpriced compared to the USA and the reason, in part, is that there is too little competition.' Welcoming in a price-cutting US giant was seen to be championing the cause of the people. Within a month or two, Wal-Mart had announced its takeover of Asda and triggered a shake-up of the whole supermarket sector.

The main complaint over supermarkets had been the disparity between prices they paid to farmers and prices they charged consumers in the shops. When the Competition Commission published the results of its inquiry in late 2000, they ran to some 1,200 pages of detailed analysis. Needless to say, few people managed to wade through all of them, and it was the summary of findings that was widely reported. The headlines showed that the retailers were off the hook. 'Supermarkets given the all clear,' said the BBC. 'Shoppers getting a fair deal,' announced another press report. The large supermarket chains had spent about £20 million in legal and other costs defending themselves. The Commission found that there had been a decline in the real price of food of

9.4 per cent from 1989 to 1998. It concluded that the retailers were broadly competitive and did not make excessive profits.

Prices in the UK supermarkets were higher than some European counterparts, as much as 12–16% higher than in France, Germany or the Netherlands, but land and building costs were higher and together with exchange rates helped account for the difference.

Byers defended the two-year investigation, saying that since it started there had been significant changes in the industry, notably the entry into the UK market of Wal-Mart which had led to price cuts worth about £1 billion to customers.

A senior member of the government has since admitted to me privately that there was disappointment that the Competition Commission had not come down harder on the supermarkets. This lingering sense that they had got off lightly may have been behind the outburst by Tony Blair six months later. It came at the height of the foot and mouth crisis that had engulfed much of the country and was crippling English farming. Meeting farmers on a tour of the West Country, he blamed the supermarkets for much of the pressure on British agriculture. 'We all want cheaper food in our shops, but on the other hand the supermarkets have pretty much got an arm-lock on you people at the moment.'

The letters to Downing Street from supermarket bosses came thick and fast, as did the government backtracking. The retailers had pretty much got an arm-lock on the government. They could point out that the exhaustive Competition Commission report had cleared them. The government's Curry Commission into sustainable food and farming, set up in the wake of the foot and mouth disaster, looked extensively at agricultural subsidies, but barely touched on retailer power.

However, a closer look at the full 1,200-page Competition Commission report shows that the Commission already had some serious concerns about power, despite its overall findings. It had not only said that some pricing practices pursued by the supermarkets were 'against the public interest', in particular the practices of selling certain products below the cost of production and of charging different prices in different stores depending on the strength of local competition. It also reported that there were a 'substantial number of serious concerns' about the relationship between supermarkets and their suppliers, that is, about how they used their enormous buying power. Astonishingly, it recommended no action on the first two problem areas. It did recommend a code of practice to regulate the way supermarkets dealt with suppliers, and went so far as to say it would have to have legal force in order to work. However, once the inquiry had started, the supermarkets, who could see which way the wind was blowing, rapidly developed their own codes of practice to pre-empt its findings. In the end, only a voluntary code was introduced. A year later, the consensus among suppliers was that the code was so weak as to be useless.

Buried in the dense economic analysis of the report are some extraordinary insights into how the business works these days.

The Commission had heard many allegations about the way the big supermarkets treated their suppliers. It found 'a climate of apprehension among many suppliers founded on their view that there is an imbalance of power between them and the multiples'. It has also proved a struggle for the Commission to extract information despite its statutory powers. Suppliers, even large multinational manufacturers, were extremely reluctant to come forward for fear of being delisted, and needed absolute guarantees of confidentiality. Even with those guarantees, many suppliers still refused to give evidence for fear of the consequences. This climate of fear is one that journalists are familiar with. It is hard to get anyone to go on the record about how they are treated by the big multiples.

According to the report, 'many suppliers commented on the purchasing power of the [main supermarkets] and their ability to drive down prices to uneconomic levels and what they saw as their general high-handedness.'

A small supplier commented: 'The power of the multiples, especially of young buyers [aged twenty-five to twenty-eight] without experience, is frightening. [They have] the power to dictate prices and margins, display or not, allocate space and threaten covertly.'

One supplier organization said the supermarkets 'talk about partnerships but these do not exist, and they ruthlessly erode suppliers' margins with no consideration of the damage they are doing to that company or its employees. Multiples switch their buyers around every six to twelve months in order that loyalty to suppliers can be avoided. The new buyer is given carte blanche to delist suppliers who are frequently treated with complete contempt.'

Another supplier said that it had been asked by one multiple to make three separate cash contributions to the supermarket's profits. The third, requested by telephone, was for a sum over £100,000 and was claimed as 'a contribution towards profits'. The same supplier said the multiple had introduced other charges, none of which had been negotiated and all of which had been deducted from their next payments without agreement. They felt that if they complained they would 'upset the relationship'.

The Commission investigated fifty-two alleged 'coercive and abusive business practices' used by the supermarkets. It found that twenty-five of them operated against the public interest. Not all the main supermarkets were guilty of operating all the anti-competitive practices, but the practices were widespread and all the supermarkets practised several of them. The practices gave rise to 'a second complex monopoly situation', the report concluded.

To outsiders some of the practices and lack of action to stop them are mind-boggling. Suppliers are asked to pay listing fees just to get their products on the shelves. They are also asked to pay extra for better positions on the shelves.

Promotions and price cuts are funded by suppliers and produce for special offers is often predominantly paid for by suppliers. In

1999, for example, Safeway wrote to suppliers of 1,000 of its most popular lines soliciting an immediate payment of £20,000 per line to help fund its new marketing campaign. Some suppliers had more than one line of products in the supermarket's stores and so were expected to make enormous contributions. Safeway defended itself by saying the scheme had been intended as 'voluntary'.

Suppliers face threats of delisting if they do not agree to price reductions. They have restrictions put on trade with rival supermarkets. Elsewhere suppliers were also found to have been asked to 'contribute to the costs of store refurbishments or openings'.

Among the most controversial of practices is the supermarkets' demand for 'overriding discounts'. These are discounts on the agreed price if sales reach certain volumes. Discounts are also often sought retrospectively, yet there appears to be no corresponding sharing of risk, for supermarkets also demand compensation from suppliers if sales are less than expected. Suppliers complained of having amounts deducted from their invoices without agreement, and of having the cost of complaints from shoppers passed automatically back to them without investigating who was at fault.

Asda, Morrisons and Somerfield were found to sell produce with labels which might be taken to indicate that the produce came from the UK when it in fact came from overseas, putting genuine UK produce at a disadvantage.

When you find yourself in the company of any supplier, it never takes long for the conversation to turn to these practices and the devastating impact they have. Since the voluntary code of practice to improve relations, the situation has actually worsened for many. I have been told recently of a major supermarket requesting £1 million up front from a large dairy co-operative in order for negotiations about listing its milk to begin. One South African wine supplier has said that it was required to pay £100,000 to have its bottles moved up just one shelf. A food manufacturer with a turnover of several hundred million pounds a year told the supermarket it supplied that since its costs – wages and raw materials – had gone up, it needed to increase its prices by 1 per cent. The reply was that not only was a price rise unacceptable, a cut of 3 per cent was in fact needed and if it wasn't forthcoming, the manufacturer could clear its products off the supermarket's shelves immediately. Pea farmers in the north of England, who had contracted to supply a supermarket at an agreed price at the beginning of the season and planted accordingly, were told on the eve of harvest that their price would be halved.

Some of the requests are surreally funny. A Tesco letter several years ago has become legendary. It told its suppliers that its Dudley Moore TV advertising campaign promoting chicken had been so successful that it would like a contribution for it. Nick Howell, a fish supplier in Cornwall, received a letter saying his contribution would be £2,000. 'I wrote back saying I don't supply chickens and we've never discussed this, get lost. Then a letter came saying "Thank you, we will be deducting it from your monthly payments." And they did.' Tesco said the issue was raised at the time of the Competition Commission report, when it had refuted it. 'We do not require suppliers to contribute to advertising retrospectively. Positive long-term supplier relationships are key to our business and we work hard to maintain them,' a spokesman said. The Competition Commission said it had not always been able to resolve the differences between suppliers' and supermarkets' accounts of how business was conducted. But for most suppliers, the way power is exercised over them is anything but funny.

They are bearing the brunt of the current price war between the big supermarkets as the retailers battle for dominance of the UK market. Even some of the largest suppliers are beginning to say publicly that it cannot go on. The chairman and chief executive of Nestlé UK, Alistair Sykes, has complained of 'the real danger that the competition between the major retailers has become too focused on short-term unsustainable price cutting', which could destroy the profitability of brands.

Writing in the trade magazine the *Grocer*, the sales director of Unilever Bestfoods UK talked of 'the spectre' of 'deflationary pressure'. 'There can be no doubt that in part it has resulted from retailers and manufacturers making marginal reductions in prices for short-term competitive advantage . . . but we must not allow it to go too far. If too much profitability is sucked out of the chain, it will fundamentally damage the quality of the offering to the consumer by adding to the pressure felt by farmers and primary producers.' The Association of Frozen Food Producers warned the Competition Commission inquiry into the Safeway takeover that any further strengthening of the top three retailers would 'severely damage the viability of food manufacturing in the UK'.

The *Grocer* also conducted a survey of top manufacturers about so called 'trade investment'. This is a euphemism for the direct payments required by supermarkets. Almost half the manufacturers said that 'trade investment' accounted for between 15 and 25 per cent of their turnover. A £200 million supplier would expect to have a 'trade fund' of between £30 million and £50 million a year to cover such things as price cuts demanded by the retailers after a price has already been agreed, the cost of special offers, and other promotions in the stores not built into their original negotiations. The manufacturers felt much of it was going on 'wasteful promotions' and price-cutting which simply served the retailer's interest. 'Most is going towards the current in-fighting between the retailers,' one top own-label executive said.

Such is the power of the big retailers that despite the fact that they thought it was money poorly spent, most manufacturers expected to have to find more for this 'trade investment' in the next twelve months. They cannot afford not to, since there is now almost nowhere else to go if they want to reach the mass of consumers. The suppliers are in effect being forced to subsidize the supermarkets' fight for control of our spending.

Even with all the price-cutting, the leading supermarket profits are incredibly healthy. Tesco recorded profits of over £1.3 billion in 2003, driven by non-food and overseas expansion. Sainsbury's was thought to be flagging when it posted profits of £667 million in the same year, and its shares fell. Wal-Mart profits were over $8 billion that year. Asda does not announce its profits separately, but figures filed with Companies House indicate its operating profits in 2002 were £588 million. Safeway profits in 2003 were £335 million.

Increasingly, supermarket profits are coming not from margins on food sold but from direct contributions. Studies in Australia suggest that over half the gross profit of the big retailers is coming from direct payments made by suppliers to supermarket head offices. These payments are not calculated as part of the retailers' margins on produce, enabling them to argue that they are highly competitive and work on very tight margins.

The supermarkets have become the gatekeepers who control access to us, the customers. Manufacturers and farmers are being required to pay for that access.

The big supermarkets argue that they offer people convenience, value for money and unprecedented choice. It is indisputable that hundreds of products that were not widely available before are now commonplace. But it is questionable whether it is really consumers who want many of them. In Europe 10,000 new food products are launched every year, but 90 per cent of them fail to make it into their second year.

There may be any number of unusual fruits and vegetables in supermarkets today that were rarities just a few years ago – the flat peach and the purple carrot to name just two. But on a trip to the municipal market in the small Spanish town of Cartagena recently I was reminded of how much our choice has also been narrowed. On sale on a dozen stalls was an enormous range of fruit and vegetables of different qualities and therefore of different prices. You could buy local tomatoes in six different grades. They came as top-quality ones at top prices for salads, and right down through the grades and prices, from slightly misshapen ones, or slightly marked ones, to those that were fantastically cheap and a fraction of the price of the best offer in the local Carrefour – the slightly unripe ones for pickles or the slightly overripe ones which are perfect for cooking the same day.

The concentration of power is narrowing our choice in other ways too. Wal-Mart already has 32 per cent of the US nappy market, 30 per cent of the market in hair-care products, and 26 per cent of toothpaste sales. Despite the fact that large numbers of its US stores sell guns, it has decided to act as moral and cultural gatekeeper by not stocking any CDs or DVDs with parental warning stickers. It removed 'lad' magazines from sale one month last year and started obscuring the covers of *Cosmopolitan* and *Marie Claire*. The big music companies have responded by supplying sanitized versions of CDs to the stores, because you can't reach your audience if the biggest player won't stock your products.

Tesco has shown no inclination to take on the role of cultural censor but the choice of its buyers has an enormous effect on what gets sold. It sells more chart CDs than Woolworth's or Virgin and more toiletries than Boots and Superdrug combined. Over the Christmas period of 2003, the supermarkets fought a price war over beer, using cheap alcohol to draw custom into their shops. As they slashed prices on a couple of the leading brands, others were cleared from the shelves to make space. What we are allowed to purchase, from the type of music to the variety of tomato or brand of beer, is being determined by buyers operating in the supermarkets' interests rather than the consumers'.

The inexorable logic of such concentrated power in retailing is that suppliers must consolidate too, which erodes our choice still further. The competition authorities are caught in a bind here. Unless suppliers merge and combine they may not be able to survive the pressure from retailers. The recent takeover of

Express Dairies by the Danish giant Arla means that there are now only three major milk suppliers to the supermarkets in the UK: Robert Wiseman, Dairy Crest and the new Arla Food UK. Yet the takeover was given a smooth ride. As one analyst said to the *Grocer*, 'It doesn't surprise me the Commission was as timid as it was. The general consensus is the retailers don't need protecting, they're more than capable of bashing these businesses around on their own.' But none of that is good news for small suppliers or anyone new who imagined they might be able to enter the grocery market.

It would be naïve too to assume that the sort of low prices that go with a price war will continue in the longer term. The 2000 Competition Commission report showed that supermarkets already charged higher prices in areas where there was less competition. There is plenty of evidence, not just from manufacturers with vested interests, that current food prices are not sustainable but are a reflection of a market in which players are digging deep into their pockets to win supremacy.

Sainsbury's told the Competition Commission inquiry into the takeover of Safeway that by its calculations Tesco derived 73 per cent and Asda 100 per cent of their profits from their non-food business, and that by 2005 they would be making 'an economic loss' on food if current trends continue. Asda dismissed this as untrue. Tesco also denies that it has been cross-subsidizing its food business with profits from its household goods and clothes sector, but the company's commercial director for non-food, Richard Brasher, told a food retailing conference that 'the competition that is Wal-Mart has introduced a tension that makes margins thin and oxygen low'.

Moreover, the current price levels are being sustained by cut-price labour, much of it working below the legal minimum wage (see Chapter 2).

Tim Lang, professor of food policy at City University, London, predicted much of what has happened over twenty years ago, when he first realized that supermarkets were changing the economic landscape. He invented the term 'food miles' in 1992 in an effort to draw attention to the way retailers were taking over control of the distribution of food, using the motorways as warehouses and transporting it ever-greater distances. He warned of the consequences of allowing a handful of retailers to win control of the food system. He foresaw the hollowing out of town centres and suburban high streets, and the emergence of food deserts that has accompanied the supermarkets' growth. For much of the last two decades the big retailers and the manufacturing lobby, the Food and Drink Federation, have disputed his analysis.

It began when he and his colleagues conducted a two year study in 1982–4 on the diets of people on low incomes in the north of England. The team followed 1,000 people for an extended period. 'I realized that something devastating was going on in terms of the prices in supermarkets and what people could afford and had access to. People on low incomes were saying that they didn't have access to decent diets any more, and that unless they travelled further and further to supermarkets there was little on offer. Once they got there the things they could afford were the fattier, sugary ingredients.' The report created a bit of a stir. By now Lang was director of the London Food Commission (LFC). One of his priorities was to look at supermarket power and its impact on what Londoners eat.

It wasn't long before he too had been branded a food Leninist. Funding for the LFC was coming from Ken Livingstone's Greater London Council. It was the height of the Thatcher era, with its attacks on the 'nanny state' and 'loony lefties'. The Commission was in fact packed with PhDs and highly qualified experts in nutrition and agrochemicals but it was dismissed by many as a cabal of Red Ken's food terrorists.

'At the time it was considered totally deviant to say supermarkets were getting too powerful. They were seen as a force for public good because they had taken on and tackled the excessive power of manufacturers that had emerged post-war as well as the vested interests of the farmers. The supermarkets were the middle classes' friend. People would talk with excitement about a branch of Sainsbury's opening near them. They couldn't wait for all the cosmopolitan foods. But twenty years have shown we were right. They now have unprecedented power over the distribution of food and determine the shape of the entire supply chain. They have so crushed any alternatives that now consumers dance to their tune, and consumers are uneasy – they are aware they have to get in cars to shop and the experience is one of drudgery, queuing, carrying vast amounts, struggling in car parks. The mood is changing but there's almost nowhere else to go now,' Lang says.

He has watched with interest as his arguments have been taken up by the sort of mainstream economists who dismissed them earlier.

In February 2003 the Organization for Economic Co-operation and Development (OECD), the heartland of the economic establishment, held a conference in The Hague on 'Changing Dimensions of the Food Economy' and invited Lang to lecture. Top government officials, senior food industry executives, leading experts from universities and competition authorities from all round the world gathered to contemplate the future under what the Dutch Minister of Agriculture Cees Veerman described as a 'new economic order . . . that has an enormous impact on not only the community but on our lives as individuals'. The impact of this new food economy was greater, he said, than the traditional instruments designed to control it. The food economy was now dominated by global parties when competition authorities have no jurisdiction at that level.

In his speech to open the conference Veerman explained that 'the balance of power in the chain [has] been completely turned upside down. Retailers and processors now rule the chain, not the farmer.' The result is that consumers can have their choice of foods from an array that is more varied than ever before and prices are lower, 'but there is a downside to all this', he told the gathering. The issue was politically sensitive but they had to ask, were the profits being fairly divided over the chain, or could the new market structure result in the misuse of power? If they were not, the effects would be felt in policy areas across the board – in environment, labour, health, agriculture, trade and competition.

Even the assembled experts emerged reeling slightly from the implications of what they had heard over the course of the two-day meeting. Dr Grievink, the author of the hourglass diagram showing concentration of power, presented a paper on the findings from in-depths interviews with sixty-five top executives in food retailing and manufacturing and with other experts including government officials in nineteen countries. 'The majority expect the retailers to rule the food chain in the coming five years.' Moreover, he said, it would be a mere handful of global retailers who will dominate worldwide food sales.

The interviews were analysed for a report Grievink has co-authored for leading management consultants Cap Gemini Ernst & Young. Called *State of the Art in Food*, it concludes that in the near future just four or five large grocery retailers will have won global domination, with a handful of others dominating regionally. Written before the list of players had been reduced still further by takeover bids for Safeway UK and financial irregularities at Ahold, the report says the supermarkets to watch are Wal-Mart, Tesco, Carrefour, Safeway (US + UK), Delhaize, Ahold, Aldi, Lidl and Kroger.

It goes on to say that within ten years just ten manufacturers will operate globally with twenty to twenty-five global 'A-brands', along with a number of consumer goods companies that will be dominant in particular countries. Retailers will become even more dominant and will increasingly operate as gatekeepers to consumers, controlling the total food process from ingredients through production.

The battle for power will take place between dominant A-brands and the big international food retailers. Three quarters of all manufacturers surveyed said they feared the consequences of the increasing strength of retailers and even leading brand manufacturers said that they are forced to provide retailers with extra discounts or face the threat of losing shelf space. Some said this amounted to 'blackmail'.

As though to underline the nature of the relationship, retailers meanwhile said that manufacturers did not yet understand how important stores were and spent too much money marketing their own brands when they should pay more to promote their products in the retailers' stores.

The smaller conventional supermarket and even the middle-sized chain will become a relic of the past, the report continues. In order to compete with the growing power of retailers, manufacturers will have to concentrate on marketing and development of new products. The actual business of making food will become so peripheral to profit that it will probably be 'outsourced'.

Professor John Connor, an expert in industrial economics and cartels, from Purdue University in Indiana, warned the assembled OECD worthies that global concentration in food retailing, food manufacturing and raw materials for food was already at levels 'high enough to generate significant departures from effective competition'. He predicted that price-fixing scandals would become more common: 'We've entered an era when transportation and communication appear to facilitate global price fixing.'

Tim Lang described the reaction he received after speaking at the conference: 'Some economists were thinking, my God, how did this happen, how did supermarkets concentrate so fast and so internationally? Others were thinking dark thoughts about economic theory. This isn't what competition policy says will happen in free markets. Much of the discussion was about the fact that there are no structures for dealing with it.'

Another week, another high-level conference. This time at the UN's Food and Agriculture Organization (FAO) in October 2003, where experts had been asked to prepare reports from thirty-five developing and middle-income countries on the impact on health of shifts in diets and urbanization. Most of the reports were coming back saying that the same pattern – rapid concentration of power in the hands of a few supermarket groups, small and medium enterprises and family farms squeezed out of business, collapse of agricultural incomes – was being seen everywhere from Latin America to China and south-east Asia. The FAO meeting of experts was being warned that the consequences were devastating. More than half the population in the developing world is rural and dependent on subsistence agriculture or farm work. They are losing their livelihoods as processors consolidate and favour larger producers and as supermarkets take over control of the supply chain. If prices are so low that the 2.5 billion people around the world who depend on agriculture for their livelihoods cannot survive on the land, they are forced into migration, as so many British packhouses bear witness.

The political influence of the supermarkets in the UK is often blamed for government's failure to check their growing power. There is no doubt that they have access to the heart of government. The revolving door between Downing Street and the retailers has seen a supermarket owner, Lord Sainsbury, become a minister; a supermarket chief executive, Sir Peter Davis, also of Sainsbury's, chair government taskforces and sit on the policy commission on food; and senior executives move from Downing Street and the Cabinet Office to Tesco and back for taskforce and steering-group duty.

But a senior former member of government pointed out to me another reason why there is no political will in the UK to address the power of the supermarkets any more. The price war between the big retailers has prevented inflation in food, which has kept down inflation figures overall. It may now actually deliver deflation in food, giving the government another year's easy ride in that part of the economy. Retailers are expanding and providing new jobs, more jobs, for the moment at least, than are being lost in companies that have felt the supermarket squeeze

(Boots, for example, who recently cut 900 jobs at their Nottingham headquarters). For a Labour party taunted with a history of economic incompetence, nothing could be more important than that. The same could be said of the USA, where economists refer to the 'Wal-Mart effect'. Wal-Mart's relentless pressure on suppliers and wages has driven productivity across the whole economy and suppressed inflation.

Governments in middle-income countries that are currently the target for supermarket acquisitions seem to have barely woken up to the significance of the trend. International giants such as Tesco, Carrefour, Ahold, Metro and Delhaize now control 75 per cent of the Czech grocery market. There are already complaints of pressure on manufacturers and of high listing fees and late payments. Large retail chains are expected to have gained control of nearly 50 per cent of Poland's total food sales within the next two years, and the top ten retailers in that country are now all owned by big foreign groups, including Tesco and Carrefour. Supermarkets already control 50–60 per cent of food sales in Latin America. The way they operate has forced thousands of small and medium farmers, traders and truckers out of business, yet their acquisitions have been largely unopposed.

As Professor Lang says, 'The horse has bolted.'

6. Coffee and Prawns

Martin Luther used to wonder what people actually do in heaven. For most participants in the intensely competitive food manufacturing industry, contemplation of Nestlé's soluble coffee business must seem like the commercial equivalent of Luther's spiritual meditation. This is a market where Nestlé has a global share of 57 per cent, sales three times the level of its nearest competitor, and margins which we estimate at 26 per cent. Nothing else in food and beverages is remotely as good.

This Deutsche Bank analysts' view of the rich pickings in the coffee market might come as a surprise to coffee growers. In 2002, the price of coffee beans fell to a thirty-year low. Many of the 25 million coffee farmers around the world ended up selling their crops at a loss. There was, however, almost no corresponding fall in the price consumers paid for their coffee, as you might expect in a free market. Not surprisingly, the profits of the companies who control the processing of the world's coffee beans remained very healthy. For while the income from coffee to the countries that grow it had halved, the retail value of the same coffee in industrialized countries had more than doubled.

Nestlé's Nescafé is one of those global A-brands, powerful enough to stand up to the increasing dominance of the transnational retailers. The coffee market today is highly concentrated, as a report by Oxfam *Mugged*, documents. This is where you can see the other half of the picture in the battle for control of our food that the Cap Gemini report, *State of the Art in Food*, described. Just five manufacturing companies buy almost half the world's total supply of green coffee beans.

In 2000, Nestlé, the world's largest food manufacturer, bought 13 per cent of the year's global supply of coffee to roast and pack for its brands which include Nescafé and Gold Blend. The tobacco and food giant Philip Morris-Kraft (now known as Altria), also bought 13 per cent of world beans for its brands Maxwell House, Café Hag, Carte Noire, Gervalia and Kenco. Altria is the world's second largest food group, taking one dollar in every ten spent on food in supermarkets in the USA.

Sara Lee, the nineteenth largest global food manufacturer, acquired a further 10 per cent of world green coffee beans for its brands Douwe Egberts, Cafitesse, Café Pilao, Van Nelle, Chat Noir and Maison du Café. Two other giant corporations accounted for another 8 per cent – 4 per cent each – of the total world market: Procter & Gamble, owner of the Pampers and Ariel brands, which also sells coffee in the USA under the Folger and Millstone labels, and Tchibo, another top-100 food company and the fifth biggest coffee roaster, which sells mainly in Germany.

The exact profits these companies make from coffee roasting are hard to pin down since they are reported as part of the larger groups' earnings, but Nestlé's trading profit on its beverages section for the year ending 2001 was $5.5 billion, while Kraft's beverages, desserts and cereals division earned $4.9 billion.

Nothing else may be quite as good as Nestlé's instant coffee business, but the same pattern of concentration can be seen in several food-manufacturing and processing sectors. By the 1990s, three companies – Cadbury Schweppes, Nestlé Rowntree and Mars – were producing nearly 70 per cent of all the confectionery consumed in Britain. Some 45 per cent of the global grain trade has been acquired by the US-based Cargill, which is the world's seventh largest food group and also owns meat-processing, sugar, petroleum-trading, food-processing and feed and fertilizer companies. Archer Daniels Midland (ADM) meanwhile controls a further 30 per cent of global grain trade and is the world's fifth largest food company. Overall the market share of the top twenty US-based food manufacturers has doubled since 1967. Consolidation continues.

As the retailers become more and more powerful, manufacturers need to be bigger and bigger to survive. The key to success is acquisition and marketing as much as the quality of products. Concentration in food manufacturing has come about as the result of flurries of mergers and takeovers in the last twenty years as the big companies have swallowed up their rivals. They have to spend heavily on marketing and advertising, for it is only by making their brands consumer 'must-haves', those 'A-listers', that they maintain their leverage with the big retailers in the price war. By doing so, the top fifty grocery giants managed not only to raise their turnovers in 2002, but also to increase their margins very slightly

Just as with other raw materials, the money made from coffee has shifted dramatically from those at the bottom of the chain to those at the top – the big transnational food processors and manufacturers based in the industrialized world. Today, less than 10 per cent of the retail value of coffee stays with the countries that grow it. Ten years ago, they kept 30 per cent of the value.

It is a transfer of power and wealth that mirrors what has happened to farmers in Western countries, as we saw in Chapter 5. Fifty years ago, 50–60p of every £1 spent on food and drink in the UK went to the farmers. Today, just 9p in every £1 goes back to them. While the shift has taken a heavy toll on rural communities across Europe, for some poor countries it has meant the devastation of their whole economies.

The significance to developing countries of fluctuations in agricultural commodity prices would be hard to exaggerate, as a few coffee examples show. In Ethiopia, coffee accounts for over 50 per cent of total export revenues, while in Burundi, the figure is almost 80 per cent. In Uganda, nearly one third of the population is dependent on coffee sales. In Nicaragua, coffee accounts for 7 per cent of total national income. Brazil, although the leading producer, is less dependent on coffee. Nevertheless, about 3 million people in that country are directly employed in the coffee industry. The national economies of Honduras,

Colombia, Guatemala, Costa Rica, El Salvador, Ethiopia, Uganda, Burundi and Rwanda are under severe threat as a result of falling coffee prices.

Until 1989, the market for coffee was, like many other commodities, managed with quotas for each producing country set by the International Coffee Agreement, rather in the way OPEC works for oil. The idea was to keep the price of coffee relatively high and stable within a band of prices. The Agreement broke down in 1989. There was a certain amount of corruption in administering the scheme and backdoor exporting to get round quotas. But the US desire to win a bigger share of the market and in theory greater economic and political stability for Central American producers in its own backyard was also a major factor. Once the Agreement had collapsed, the market became flooded and prices dropped dramatically, except for brief spikes when frosts in Brazil led to a shortage.

The flooding of the market was largely due to Vietnam. Ten years ago, Vietnam barely counted as a coffee producer. Then, in the 1990s, came liberalization. Encouraged by the World Bank and International Monetary Fund to restructure its economy, open up its markets and invest its energies in generating foreign exchange, the Vietnamese government began an aggressive programme to encourage its farmers to move out of domestic production of rice (the price of which was volatile in part thanks to dumping of subsidized harvests from the USA) and into growing cash crops for export, particularly coffee.

Vietnam is not ideally suited to coffee production and nearly all its crop is of the lower-quality robusta type used either for instant coffee or in blends with the more expensive arabica type of beans. But by 2000, with the heavy use of fertilizers and pesticides, Vietnam had turned itself into the second largest coffee-producing country in the world after Brazil. Kraft, which buys heavily from Vietnam, has expressed concern at 'severe quality and environmental problems at all stages of the coffee production process' in that country. Rapid expansion of coffee growing has been accompanied by 'severe deforestations' and 'negative ecological effects caused by over-fertilization and wide-spread irrigation', the company says. And all this to produce an oversupply, just as the Brazilians were also bumping up their yields by mechanizing and intensifying production with a greater use of agrochemicals.

For despite its impact on quality and the environment, intensi-fication has been encouraged by international aid donors, in Latin America as well as Vietnam. In addition to the greater use of agrochemicals, strip-picking the coffee cherries in clusters, as opposed to traditional hand-harvesting of individual cherries, has become common practice. That tends to mean that a high percentage of immature green cherries, which give bad black beans, are picked along with ripe ones, reducing the quality of the coffee and increasing the risk of a particular cancer-causing fungus forming.

With dreadful irony, the net result of the efforts of the inter-national institutions and their free market ideology to help poor countries develop, has been environmental damage and a collapse in their incomes from coffee. Oxfam, which produced a detailed report on the coffee crisis, has described it as 'a development disaster whose impact will be felt for a long time. Families dependent on money generated by coffee are pulling their chil-dren out of school, can no longer afford basic medicines and are cutting back on food.' The crisis is so deep that banks in developing countries are in trouble, and governments which depend on export earnings from coffee are unable to repay debts or cover their budgets for education and health.

I went to Uganda in 2003 to see the impact of the crisis at first hand. I was particularly interested in that country because it had become the Western aid donors' darling. Its authoritarian leader, Yoweri Museveni, is credited with turning from Marxist guerrilla to prudent economic manager to put the country's bloody past behind it. Just a few years ago, despite corruption and an alarming rise in military spending, Uganda was being hailed as 'a beacon in a dark continent'. It was one of the few African countries which, thanks to an enlightened programme of public health education, seemed to be getting to grips with its AIDS crisis. It had largely done what the World Bank and International Monetary Fund told it to do. It had restructured its economy, opened its capital markets, and privatized. It had produced a strategy to reduce poverty. It was rewarded by being made the first country to qualify for debt relief under the Highly Indebted Poor Countries debt relief initiative. But then came the collapse of coffee prices.

In 1994/5 when the price of coffee was high, Uganda earned $433 million from the crop. In 2000/2001 its revenues from coffee slumped to $110 million even though it sold more beans. The value of the debt relief, paid by Western taxpayers and intended as a helping hand out of poverty, was wiped out by the collapse of coffee revenues.

In Kampala I first visited the Uganda Coffee Development Authority, housed in a down-at-heel 1960s-style block near the centre of town. Once past the armed guard on the narrow concrete stairwell, I climbed up several floors to the office of William Naggaga, the board secretary of the organization. A sophisticated former diplomat who lived in London for many years, he agreed that in one way the root of the crisis was quite simple.

'Global excess production, that's the problem. More coffee is being produced than is being drunk. It's very comfortable for the roasters. There is a carry-over from each year and they have accumulated stocks, which have now become the punishing stocks. Vietnam was encouraged to go from one million bags of coffee a year to fourteen million bags a year by the World Bank and the US government. It was encouraged to produce for a market which was already balanced. Nobody seems to have thought about it. Would you like a cup of coffee?'

He brought a tray to the table and I had my first taste of African coffee on East African soil. It was milky and very weak. 'Our earnings have fallen by more than fifty per cent,' Naggaga continued. 'It's a vicious circle: when the price goes down, the level of care farmers put into it depreciates. They don't tend their crops; the quality is low. By some coincidence the excess in production is the same as the volume of low-quality coffee being produced. But there are roasting techniques now that allow them to make use of low-quality beans. Before the liberalization of the coffee market here there was no export of black beans. We destroyed them. They don't taste good. But now they blend them to get rid of the taste, and they use new steaming methods to reduce the bitterness. We had to go to the minister to allow us to include them as an export, because they were not exportable grade in Uganda. We actually had to seek permission and a change of regulations to export black beans.'

But of course, the problem is about more than just supply and demand out of kilter. 'The roasters are taking too much out. They are so powerful they can determine the price. This is a monopolistic situation, not a free market. What makes us mad is that the retail price of coffee has never really gone down. If it had, it might have stimulated demand and brought the market back into balance. Just think of it, five men from the big companies – they are all men, I wish they were women, things might be different – sitting in a room and deciding the fate of twenty-five million coffee farmers around the world.'

One way developing countries could increase their share of the final value of the coffee sold would be to process more of it themselves. But breaking into that so-called added-value market is almost impossible. Once processed or manufactured, agricultural goods generally face punitive tariffs when imported into the West. Processed coffee from Vietnam, for example, would face these tariffs. Parts of Africa have preferential terms, so this is not the obstacle with Ugandan coffee, but there are other barriers. 'The brands are so powerful, they control the distribution chains. They've worked out their deals and discounts with the retailers. It is very difficult for anyone else to penetrate that part of the market where the value is added,' said Mr Naggaga.

I asked him if he was against globalization. 'No, globalization is good, but taken in this way it is madness. A few men should not decide what millions of people eat and drink. I'm telling you, it is us today. But it may be you tomorrow. Make some noise.'

In the streets outside, a pleasant, cooling breeze had got up from the capital's seven hills. The central hill is famous for its parks and extraordinary birds. Here the flat tops of the acacia trees have been colonized by giant Maribou storks. Like vultures with their scavenging appetites and flesh-coloured wattles, their oversized bodies seem impossibly large for the slender branches of the trees on which they have made their comfortable nests.

I took a taxi next to Ugacof, the Ugandan coffee exporters' association. Like many of the taxis in Kampala, the suspension in this one was on its last legs, and as we headed for the outskirts of the capital, it felt as though the bottom had dropped out of the car and we were bumping along the ground. Meanwhile, most of the road ahead had been taken up by a huge convoy of new Toyota pick-up trucks, each fitted with giant hoardings and pumping out music advertising Pepsi. We were forced to stutter along in its wake.

When we reached the headquarters of Ugacof, beyond the containers being loaded and unloaded with coffee beans, they looked like a colonial relic, a long verandahed building shaded by palm trees and surrounded by immaculate grass and flowering shrubs. The exporters here send coffee to the big roasters, but their margins are tiny these days, squeezed like everyone else's down the chain.

One of the managers, Claude Auberson, had agreed to see me, and while I waited, I flicked through the technical manuals on coffee production in the reception area, wondering what to make of them. 'High roasts are preferred in the US because they mask poor blending, dirty machines and stale coffee . . . bitterness is reduced by the addition of sucrose, sodium chloride or citric acid . . . Hydrocolloids in general decrease the perception of bitterness . . . The bitterness is weakened when polyphenols are introduced . . .'

Eventually I was ushered into the airy office of M. Auberson, a tall, moustachioed Frenchman, who was studying the market prices on his screen. 'The [coffee commodity trading] markets, in New York for arabica and London for robusta, were meant to help stabilize prices for producers by setting the price, but now they are the playground for speculators who have nothing to do with the industry. It's added to volatility but you can't stop people trading,' he said, shrugging and motioning me to a seat.

Auberson had worked in Africa for thirty years and was frank about the extent of corruption and its effect on any efforts to introduce stabilization mechanisms. But, as he saw it, the real problem now is that nearly all the money is going somewhere between the point at which the beans are imported to Europe and the point at which the product reaches the shelf. 'If you ask the roasters what their excuse is, they will say that thirty per cent of the retail price goes on advertising and packaging. But where is the rest going? We are too small. We have no power. These large roasters have immense power and they are pushing most of the risk down the chain. Have you heard of "vendor-managed inventories"? This is how it works now. Suppliers have to keep huge stocks available near the roasters' factories ready for just when they want them, without commitment on their side, so the manufacturers can order "just in time". The suppliers carry all the risk and cost. It's outrageous, well, I suppose it's smart business if you can get it. And they can, because they are big transnationals, so no one can stop them.'

'What about fair trade, doesn't that help?' I asked.

'It's a drop on a hot stone.'

Nestlé says that it is not in favour of low coffee prices. It argues that when the price drops, roast ground coffee becomes cheaper in relation to its instant brands and makes them less competitive. Furthermore, its costs are only partly made up of raw materials. It has much more invested in capital-intensive processing machinery and spends heavily on advertising and marketing. It has supported international efforts to stabilize the price. But the main problem, it argues, is that supply exceeds demand. 'Any solution to the low coffee price must address this basic issue, in order to reverse the disturbing increase in poverty and suffering among many coffee farmers,' a spokeswoman told me.

The following day I drove down to the coffee-growing areas near Lake Victoria, with my guide from Oxfam, Monica Asek-enye. This is where the cheaper robusta coffee is grown, to be used in blends with the better-quality arabicas or in instant coffee. We followed the thin strip of road between the oxide-red dust edges on either side. It stretched ahead, straight and empty all the way to the Congo. First came the papyrus swamps with their feathery foliage and pythons, then scenes of breathtaking tropical beauty as we passed through wooded hills and mile upon mile of smallholdings. Small shacks by the road offered handfuls of fruit. Everywhere women were tilling their patches, planting sweet potatoes, hoeing their yams, or tending the cassava growing beside their sugar cane.

After a few hours we reached Mgipi Epicenter, a tiny cluster of shacks on the road, and turned off the tarmac on to a red dirt track. Dozens of birds rose up in front of us – lilac-breasted rollers, doves, red bishops, little brown jobs too quick to identify, fleeing the rare motorized disturbance. Long-horned cattle glanced up briefly from their grazing. We rattled for half an hour along tiny, endlessly forking tracks in our own cloud of dust until eventually we reached a clearing that was Kituntu village and found the adobe hut of coffee farmer John Kafuluzi.

His coffee is organic by default, manured with cow dung and hand-weeded and hand-harvested, since he cannot afford agrochemicals. The bushes are interplanted with bananas, sweet potatoes and other subsistence crops on which he and his family live.

John's mother, children and his sister's family came out to greet us and we sat on wooden boxes to talk. On John's knee, a listless child, his youngest at just eighteen months old, drifted in and out of fevered sleep. She had malaria, as did three of her siblings. Her brother standing nearby had the tight, swollen belly of the malnourished. At the other end of the track a strange caterpillar appeared. Four small pairs of scurrying legs sticking out from under an upturned 1960s sofa were making their way towards us. Some of John's other children had been to a neighbour's to borrow seating for the foreigner.

Our translator was trying to explain to John how much a cup of coffee sells for in a London café. 'One cup, five thousand Ugandan shillings?' A confused smile flickered across his face, registering disbelief, but then his eyes filled with tears. 'No, you mean one kilo, no, no, this is painful to hear. I only got two hundred shillings a kilo for my coffee this year.' John's eldest sons Bruno and Michael had to drop out of school when prices fell because the family could no longer afford the fees. They had hoped to train to be doctors or accountants. In the good years the cash from their small coffee crop was enough to send everyone to school. Now the children take turns to go to school instead. Their clothes were torn and stained. Some of the coffee bushes were neglected; no longer worth the effort of tending.

Inside the hut, just visible through the half-open door, an old man was lying on the floor on a thin mattress, the fragile bones of his wasted back rising prominently each time he took a shallow breath. Peter Kafuluzi, John's father, who has farmed coffee here for forty-five years, was dying, but the family could not afford medicine for him. They had spent their savings the previous year on his treatment. Medicine for the children's malaria would have cost them up to 5,000 shillings.

The soil here is fertile and alluvial, capable of producing surplus. It has ample rainfall and needs no irrigation or fertilizer. The vegetation is so lush, the birdsong so rich, it is hard to understand how people can be going hungry. In good times, the coffee made enough money for families to pay for the essentials: education, medicine, clothes and roofing materials and extra food to supplement their limited subsistence diets with a bit of meat or milk. But without coffee they have nothing to sell for cash.

John didn't know why he got so little for his crop but thought the local middlemen must be cheating. In fact, Oxfam studied the chain and discovered that at the beginning of 2002, a Ugandan farmer received 14 cents (US) for 1 kilo of beans. The local middleman who transported it to the mill took 5 cents profit, as did the miller, and the cost of transport to Kampala added a further 2 cents, making the cost of the coffee when it arrived at the exporter's warehouse 26 cents. The exporter, operating on a tiny margin and minimal return on his capital-intensive machinery to dry, grade and pack the beans, added 19 cents to the kilo, taking it up to 45 cents. Freight, the importer's costs and margins took the price to $1.64 when it reached the factory of one of the giant roasting companies. By the time that same kilo was sold in the shops in the form of instant coffee it was worth $26.40, or 7,000 per cent more than the farmer got for it.

On our way back to Kampala, we dropped in at a nursery which raises coffee seedlings. A young man approached me to say he wanted to go to school. He'd had to drop out because there was no money. 'I am very disappointed. This was my future.' Soon there was a small crowd of children around us saying the same thing.

Arabica coffee, grown at high altitudes and with a finer taste, fetches higher prices than robusta, but that has done little to insulate its farmers from the crisis. The drive up to one of the main arabica areas of Uganda took us in the opposite direction, along the road to Kenya and the foothills of Mount Elgon, the volcanic mountain that straddles the border. The road this side of the country runs past the Coca-Cola factory, built recently, with government approval, in what was a 'preserved wetland' area, despite a hunger strike protest by a local MP, then through the old colonial estates of tea and sugar plantations, where monoculture has created a sea of emerald green.

Eventually you come to Mbale, the small outpost at the base

of Mount Elgon. As we approached the town, the usual road-side procession of bare-footed women in African dress carrying fire-wood on their heads gave way to one of heavily veiled women in Muslim burqas. This is the home of the Islamic university, supported by Saudi money. Uganda has been predominantly Christian since nineteenth-century Western Church missionaries came proselytizing and offering not only religion but also free medicine and education. But Mbale also has a Muslim com-munity which is attracting converts. 'A different god has more money than yours now and offers free education,' our driver explained.

On the edge of Mbale, near the shaded streets of the faded old colonial town, we found the mill and warehouse of the now privatized Bugisu co-operative union to which many of the coffee growers of the area deliver their beans.

We arrived towards the end of the day, the hour when children file along the roads carrying their yellow jerrycans to fetch water from the wells. The notices on the door of the office next to the milling factory were not encouraging. 'Anyone opting to do industrial research here should try elsewhere because we have already had enough of them,' said one. Beneath it was another: 'Hitherto every Tom, Dick and Harry have been making personal calls using office telephones. Such calls are henceforth prohibited and non-compliance or complicity shall lead to stern punishments of the culprits, by order of the admin manager.' Peering through the window, I could see battered filing cabinets, overflowing with yellowing cardboard files, and papers and invoices stacked in dusty piles on top, but the chair behind the tin desk was unoccupied. The manager, Wamutu Samuel, had attended a funeral that week, and had been in court over a land dispute. We were told to come back tomorrow.

When we met the following day, Wamutu looked exhausted, the whites of his brown eyes covered with a yellowy film. He mumbled through his figures on prices before and after liberalization and I had to strain to hear him above the sound of constantly falling coffee beans from the mill behind. But the message was the same. The quality has declined, the multinationals have arrived at the farm gate, fairtrade and organic coffees give them a premium and offer hope to some farmers, but so far the quantities involved are negligible.

Finally Wamutu said he would find someone to introduce us to the arabica farmers and we set off, following the road that winds steeply up into a gorge on the edge of Mount Elgon. Under a bright blue sky, streaked with thin cloud, we climbed up to the wooded hills. The slopes of the mountain are planted with bananas and 'Irish potatoes', the staple crops, and everywhere is verdant. George Sakwa, his wife Topista and their family live near the top of the mountain in the tiny remote village of Buginyanya.

They had been up since before dawn, seven of them labouring in the steep terraces of their coffee garden for five hours, before returning to their hut for breakfast of half a cup of tea with a little sugar. They used to employ casual labour to help with the coffee, but can't afford it now and anyway, since there is no money to send them to school any more, the children are free to work. In a good year, George has been able to get 1 million Ugandan shillings for his high-quality arabica, but last year he got less than half that. All the spare money was then spent on his elder son Boniface's school fees. The other children were sent home because he couldn't pay.

The Sakwas sold a bit of land in 2001 to keep the children at school but that reduced their ability to earn money even further. 'We have no other source of income, which is why my house is in such bad shape,' George told me. He took me inside. One room was given over to the goats, another to his stores of coffee. He was hanging on before selling the year's harvest, hoping the price would pick up. It was dark apart from the light glinting through holes in the tin roof.

The house leaked, the timbers were beginning to rot, and the mud plaster had come off the walls in large chunks. They had patched the roof where they could with papyrus, but the children still got wet when it rained and were suffering from respiratory problems. Their clothes and blankets were so worn they had nothing left to cover themselves with at night to keep the mosquitoes off. Several of the children had malaria. They did not have enough to eat. They had also had to give up buying soap, George explained, though without a trace of anger or self-pity. He has a fine young wife, Topista – his third – and sixteen children. They would help him survive.

To the side of the house in a circular mud hut that was the family kitchen, an eight-year-old girl was feeding the tiny twigs she had gathered from the woods into a fire over which she was making a maize-meal porridge, their meal for the day. Behind the hut under the dappled shade of a stand of trees, I noticed the mounds of four tiny graves. Topista was mother to nine of George's children, but four had died already. Malaria claimed two, another died in an accident with hot water in the hut, and another of an unexplained fever. Their nearest hospital is in Mbale. They have no money for transport, none for medicine either.

Driving back to the airport the following day, I passed a government billboard, a sign erected in recent but more optimistic times, proudly declaring, 'Coffee eradicates poverty.'

When I got back to England, I bought a jar of instant and punctured its tight paper seal. A rich smell of fresh coffee wafted up. When coffee is made into instant, it is brewed, concentrated and then dried. In the process, much of the aroma is lost, but manufacturers are allowed to add volatile oils that carry the smell back into the jar. Contemplating this ingenious and perfectly legal deception, I wondered whether what I had seen could really be as simple as it seemed. These were markets that were failing. The money is being sucked out by a tiny number of dominant players. But there was the whole complex issue of subsidies and tariffs and other trade distortions to consider too.

Since the Second World War, a series of trade talks have sought to aid the operation of a free market by removing barriers to trade and by lowering tariffs. From 1947 to 1994 the General Agreement on Tariffs and Trade (GATT) was the forum for global negotiations. The World Trade Organization (WTO) came into being at the beginning of 1995, at the end of the Uruguay round of GATT talks, which were held between 1986 and 1994. It is now the forum for negotiating international trade rules. Agriculture was included in the original GATT talks but the Uruguay round's new agreement on agriculture specifically committed countries to lift trade restrictions and abolish distorting subsidies within food production.

Poor countries have been forced to open up their markets while rich Western countries have kept their quotas and continued to subsidize their agriculture. Rich countries spend nearly $1 billion a day, well over $300 billion a year, subsidizing their farmers. The EU's common agricultural policy cost the UK a total of £5 billion in 2001, the equivalent of 2p on the rate of income tax – £16 a week in higher taxes and food prices for each British family, according to research by the Consumers' Association.

Despite the commitment to reduce farm subsidies, President Bush's controversial Farm Bill in 2002 actually promised to raise them and allocated over $190 billion over the next ten years to protect US agriculture. When poor countries export to the West they face tariffs four times higher than Western countries impose on one another.

The latest round of WTO negotiations was meant to be the developing round in which tariffs were lowered and subsidies cut on agricultural produce. But vital talks are deadlocked, as the industrialized countries argue for extending WTO influence to new issues such as freer foreign investment, while the developing nations say they would like the changes they had been promised on agricultural subsidies and tariffs first.

These subsidies have a devastating effect on developing economies. They encourage excess production in industrialized countries, which leads to low prices and dumping. The dumping of subsidized goods at less than the cost of production on markets in poorer countries has undermined local agriculture. Import tariffs, meanwhile, have made it harder for poorer countries to switch their production to more lucrative processed food.

The obvious answer for a Ugandan or Vietnamese coffee farmer faced with collapsing coffee prices is to grow something else. But the reality is that their choices are limited. They might grow sugar or wheat or rice but then they find themselves undercut by Western imports. And, as William Naggaga said, breaking into the more valuable instant coffee market is almost impossible.

Even when countries do move into processing, the results can be mixed. When I was investigating chicken nuggets in 2002, I visited some of the Thai poultry factories that had started exporting to Britain. Thailand deregulated and liberalized its economy in the early 1990s. It removed import tariffs and went all out to produce surplus for export. Until the Asian crash, the Thai economy experienced phenomenal growth, with a new and booming poultry industry being a major contributor. Chickens used to be a key source of cash for smallholders. Happy to forage on leftover grain, they were cheap to raise and easy to sell when money was needed. But in the last decade poultry production has become industrialized, and is now controlled by the handful of large Thai and foreign companies that have introduced Western-style intensive systems to supply Western markets with chopped and deboned chicken and ready meals. Smallholders have been squeezed out. The factories to process these intensively reared chickens are clustered around the capital, Bangkok. They have drawn workers from rural areas and slums have grown up around them, but the internal migration and concentration of industrial plants have created enormous pollution and public health problems. The avian flu crisis of early 2004 was but one of them. It followed a scandal over the illegal use of antibiotics in meat being exported to the EU. And although, in theory, the wealth from these new export-led industries should trickle down to the newly urbanized, industrialized workforce, the figures are pointing in the opposite direction. As Thailand has become richer, malnutrition rates have got worse, as have many other poverty indicators. When Thailand introduced minimum standards for labour, the largest companies simply switched production to China where labour was cheaper.

The effect of moving to food for export can also be to compromise a developing country's own food security – that is, its ability to feed itself. After my trip to Uganda, I flew to Kenya, where growing fruit, vegetables and flowers for export to UK supermarkets has become a major industry. Horticulture is now the second largest export business after tea, earning US$300 million a year of much-needed foreign currency. It is also a major employer. But local economists are not convinced that this sort of growth is desirable.

If you take the road from Nairobi north along the huge geological fault-line of the Great Rift Valley, and climb up through the rolling hills, a spectacular view opens out in front of you as you come over the top. Naivasha, one of only two freshwater lakes in Kenya, gleams like a sheet of silver in the hazy distance below. Originally Masai grazing land, this was one of the first areas settled by white farmers and was immortalized by the Happy Valley set as one of the most beautiful places in the world. Today, huge patches of white plastic rise like blisters around Naivasha's waters. These are the greenhouses and tunnels of the intensive farms. The lake itself is shrinking and its southern shores are blighted by algal bloom. Local environmentalists blame the water problems here as in other parts of Kenya on the country's horticultural activities – on excessive abstraction to water the crops, on pollution from pesticide run-off, and on deforestation caused by migrant workers cutting wood for cooking fuel. The industry disputes this and points to studies that have suggested other causes of the ecological damage. Oduor Ong'wen, director of Econews Africa, a sustainable development organization, predicts that without radical changes in agricultural practices, the area around Naivasha will have become unfarmable in fifteen years. The net effect of Kenya's drive to food for export had been to undermine its ability to feed itself. 'Most of the productive land where people were growing food for local consumption has been turned over to land growing food for export. In the 1970s we were largely self-sufficient in food, now we are a net food importing country. That has compromised our food security,' he told me.

Compromised food security, the poor getting poorer – these are also familiar themes in discussions among Vietnamese academics about the effect of liberalization and the push for food for export in their country. For Vietnam has not just moved into coffee. It has played its part in the extraordinary evolution of the UK supermarket prawn.

Something happened to prawns in the 1990s. Like the girths of Western gourmands discovering fusion food, they started to grow and grow. Once a mere shrimp of a thing, a fiddly heap of shell for every tiny mouthful, the prawn miraculously turned into a great tiger, an effortless bite as good as lobster but at half the price. Healthy and fashionably south-east Asian, but not too exotic or rare any more, prawns flew into our lives from apparently teeming tropical seas where everything grows bigger and better.

Annual sales of prawns – or shrimp as the Americans prefer to call them – now amount to US$50–60 billion worldwide and are growing at an average of 9 per cent a year. The major retailers in the UK import them not just from Vietnam, but also from other south-east Asian countries – Thailand, Indonesia, Pakistan and Bangladesh – and from Latin America, from Ecuador, Honduras, Guatemala and Mexico.

This sudden glut in tiger, or warm-water prawns, is the result not of a natural harvest but of an explosion of intensive fish farming in southern countries. International financial institutions have promoted the trade as a way of generating income from exports, providing food for the hungry and decreasing poverty in the developing world. Selling at £18 a kilo for headless specimens, and a breathtaking £35 per kilo for the largest whole ones, there is big money for those who strike lucky.

But environmental degradation, disease, pollution, debt and dispossession, illegal land seizures, abuse of child labour and violence have afflicted the dozen or so countries entering the market. In at least eleven countries people have been killed in violence linked to prawn farming. Western diners, meanwhile, have been eating a food dependent on the heavy use of antibiotics and growth hormones.

Aid agencies, including Save the Children Fund and Oxfam, have warned of the abuses that have accompanied the introduction of prawn farming to emerging economies for some time. But the rapid growth of the industry and the scale of mangrove destruction it is now causing led an environmental charity, the Environmental Justice Foundation (EJF), to raise the full alarm in 2003.

The pattern of events accompanying the arrival of large-scale prawn farming has been the same around the world. The experience of Vietnam is typical. When I visited in the summer of 2003, there had been reports in the newspapers in the Mekong Delta of small armies of poor and dispossessed people attacking prawn farmers and emptying the ponds.

As dusk falls south of Ho Chi Minh City, the frogs start singing, and the searchlights along the dykes of the prawn ponds flicker on. Men sweat the night away on plastic chairs in new tin sheds built next to the fish farms. While they play cards and drink, guard dogs lie panting at their feet or rummage through the litter. A pale shadow climbs into a watchtower over the water here, a wiry silhouette sets up decoy mosquito nets along the mud banks there. The thieves, when they come, creep up in the night, sometimes in gangs.

Le Van Hong is an intensive farmer in Can Gio province near

Ho Chi Minh City. His dykes have plastic netting, lights and a watchtower to deter attackers. The ponds he has dug where mangrove used to be are lined with blue plastic.

He was using a boom to try to scoop out algae – a sign of pollution and disease – when we arrived. His prawns were ill. He pulled a few out to show us – they were curled up and deformed and telltale black marks were visible along the shell. He said he would apply more antibiotics with the feed next day and hope for the best. He had cleared the pond with chemicals, he wasn't sure which, before he had filled it for his crop, but they hadn't been strong enough, he thought. He explained that when his crop does well, he makes a lot of money, but it is tricky and things often go wrong.

The official picture is rather different. The Vietnamese government's television adverts promote cheap loans for converting land to aquaculture and promise that those going into prawn farming will become instant millionaires. Anaesthetized by a generation of Communist propaganda, the population generally believes what it is told. Hundreds of small farmers have mortgaged their land to join the action, under the new policy of 'renovation', which allows property to be sold once more.

The result has been a scramble akin to the Gold Rush, according to the few academics who will talk openly to foreigners. (Despite the myth that it is a relaxed tropical tourist destination with a liberalized economy, this is a country where the Party's control remains absolute and where each copy of the *Bangkok Post* mentioning government officials on trial for corruption is censored by hand with a black marker pen.)

'Only the rich make money, the big outside investors, who come because they have already polluted their own land and they need virgin territory. Then when it goes wrong here, they move on,' Dr Tran Triet, a leading ecologist at Vietnam National University in Ho Chi Minh City, told me. Smaller farmers have no technical expertise and rarely survive. The environmental damage and social dislocations, which come with prawn farming, make it completely unsustainable in its current form, Triet believed.

Most prawn farms are built in coastal areas where mangrove forests thrive. Mangroves are among the most productive eco-systems on the planet, and support a great variety of marine life. The world's coral reefs and seagrass beds – upon which two thirds of all fish caught depend – need the mangroves. But mangroves across the globe are being cleared to make way for intensive prawn farms. Nearly 40 per cent of world mangrove loss has been attributed to prawn farming, according to EJF.

When the mangroves are destroyed, local fishermen find that their catches of other fish collapse. They are also often denied access to the sea once the farms have enclosed what used to be common land. Examples of this are not confined to Vietnam. Thousands of Bangladeshi subsistence farmers have suffered from the invasion of their rice paddies by prawn farm owners, and reports of violence and intimidation of small farmers have been widespread.

In Vietnam, more than 80 per cent of original mangrove cover has been deforested in the last fifty years. Although the Americans scorched the earth with their use of the toxic defoliant agent orange in Viet Cong areas during the Vietnam war, the most important cause of destruction since 1975 has been prawn farming.

But the environmental damage goes wider than that. Prawns are carnivorous, and farming them intensively requires protein feeds of more than double the weight of the prawn produced. Inevitably, the fishmeal and fish oil required to raise the prawns further deplete wild stocks of fish. (This is the problem with all fish farming. It takes 3–4 tonnes of fish made into fishmeal to produce one tonne of farmed salmon.)

Salination and chemical pollution of drinking water and agri-cultural land also frequently result from prawn farming. The farms pump out their waste water into the canals, rivers and nearby sea water, contaminating them with pesticides, antibiotics and disinfectants. In Sri Lanka, 74 per cent of fishermen in prawn-farming areas no longer have ready access to drinking water.

Evidence from several countries suggests that the farming is unsustainable not just in the long term but after a few years. Disease sets in quickly and productivity declines rapidly.

Dr Duong Van Ni, a Vietnamese hydrologist at Cantho University, who has studied the social impact of prawn farming, was gloomy about the immediate future when I met him. 'Prawn farming will be Vietnam's final choice, because it is so damaging to the environment and so polluting to the soil, trees and water that it will be the last form of agriculture. After it, you can do nothing.'

Ponds which use more traditional methods, including exploiting the natural tides to refresh the water rather than pumping so that feeding is not required, tend to be freer of disease. But the pressure is to intensify to produce higher yields.

In a study Dr Ni conducted in the west of the Mekong, nearly half of prawn farmers had lost all their money in the past four years. Of those who did make money, 80 per cent were outsiders.

In 2001, the EJF has established, 70 per cent of World Bank-financed prawn ponds in seven Indonesian provinces were abandoned. In Thailand, more than 20 per cent of prawn farms in former mangroves are abandoned after two to four years. About 50 per cent of prawn ponds in Thailand as a whole are thought to be disused. Once the land has been salinated, farmers cannot revert to rice growing. In Thailand, 50 per cent of the land used for farming prawns may have formerly been used as rice fields. The result has been a drop in the availability of local food.

Dien, another prawn farmer I visited, had been a rice grower in the Camau province of the Mekong delta when he heard about the money to be made in shellfish. He had sold his own land and leased an area on the coast in Kien Giang, near the Cambodian border, along with several of his brothers. They had cleared the palms and mangrove and turned it into prawn ponds. Like other prawn farmers, he had applied lime to the soil and

Not on the Label

heavy doses of pesticides and other chemicals to clean it before stocking the ponds with larvae bought from traders. Tiger prawns are not native to most of the countries farming them and wild larvae have to be brought in. It takes about 100 days of feeding to raise the prawns to the size that makes them valuable on the world markets. To fetch top prices they need to weigh enough to calculate twenty to thirty prawns to a kilo. But Dien's prawns kept dying at about sixty days. He said he had been dosing them regularly with antibiotics and growth hormones but nothing seemed to work. He explained that the crop we were looking at would be his last. If it failed he would be ruined. 'It is like gambling. I have nothing to go back to except my wife and children. I cannot grow rice any more. I will have to sell my labour. My brother released 30,000 larvae into his pond earlier this month, but they all died yesterday. We don't dream of being millionaires any more,' he said.

Further along the same dyke, reachable only by flat boat, Nam and her family had been winners. She had gradually been able to buy up ponds from those who had failed. She could afford technical advisers and was applying a cocktail of chemicals which had kept the disease which had plagued her predecessor on the site at bay, although she didn't want to tell us what they were in case we passed on her secret. Another outsider from Camau province, she was cagey about the reaction she had had from local people. Less than 5 per cent of the successful prawn farmers in the area were local.

The social tension caused by migration from other areas to cash in on the boom is palpable, but there is even more resentment at the international companies moving in to set up along Vietnam's coastal regions. In the delta area just south of Ho Chi Minh City, my guide pointed out where the giant Thai chicken and fish-processing company CP, which joint-owns a chain of supermarkets with Tesco in Thailand, was developing land to clear for prawn cultivation. Its intensive farms are on a scale which dwarfs most local production. Large areas of forest had been cleared and the land bulldozed and lined with plastic sheeting in preparation for new ponds. Fencing and security lighting had sprouted up from the dykes.

Dr Sansanee Choowaew, an environmental expert from Mahidol University near Bangkok who was visiting at the same time as me, was alarmed that Vietnam appeared to be making the same mistakes as the Thai industry. 'We have suffered from severe problems with pollution and conflict between prawn and rice farmers. The government has restricted any further expansion inland as a result and so companies have looked to invest abroad for new territory.'

At the beginning of 2002, the European Commission banned all prawns from China because of fears over the use of cancer-causing chloramphenicol and nitrofuran antibiotics. When the UK Food Standards Agency (FSA) began testing other warm-water prawns, it found problems with samples from Thailand, Vietnam, Pakistan and Indonesia. Nine UK retailers, including Sainsbury's, Tesco, Safeway, Iceland and the Co-op, were asked by the FSA to withdraw some prawns from Asia because they contained illegal nitrofurans. A requirement for prawns from these Asian countries to be tested before they can be imported to the EU has now been repealed. Prawns from China are still banned, however.

But the trouble for developing countries doesn't end there. As more land has been converted to prawn farming, the price the prawns fetch on the international markets has become more volatile. The sort of bumper prices which attracted countries into the business now depend on a disaster, such as a typhoon, in another, to restrict supply. And although the World Bank has encouraged the trade, once Vietnamese yields reached lucrative levels, the EU announced that the tariff on frozen-prawn imports from Vietnam would be increased from 4.5 per cent to 10.9 per cent.

Oxfam's influential study of trade and globalization, *Rigged Rules and Double Standards*, has summarized the arguments for reform of the current rules on trade that have driven globalization. It acknowledges that historically trade has reduced poverty, and that globalization has generated unprecedented wealth, but argues that the poor are being excluded from its benefits because the rules of trade are rigged in favour of the rich. While in theory rich countries open their markets, they use subsidies and tariffs to protect their industries, yet poor countries have been pressurized by the IMF and the World Bank to open their markets at breakneck speed, and cannot afford to subsidize their agriculture. Meanwhile, transnational companies have been left free to sweep in with investment and employment practices which exacerbate poverty. Foreign investment has the potential to do good but often results in profits being repatriated to industrialized countries rather than benefiting developing ones.

Powerful voices have joined the call for reform. In *Globalization and Its Discontents*, Joseph Stiglitz, who speaks with the authority of an insider as former chief economist of the World Bank, also argues that the IMF and WTO have driven the process of privatization and liberalization in a way that has damaged the interests of the poor around the world. Stiglitz won the Nobel Prize for economics for his work showing that markets are not perfect even when supposedly free because knowledge and information are not equally shared among participants. He favours gradual opening up of markets over shock therapy. He points out that today's industrialized countries did not practise free trade when they were first developing. If you force developing countries to liberalize their trade before they are ready, you wipe out their domestic industries and risk creating the conditions for social unrest.

But there are still plenty of economists who adopt the pain-for-gain view. They argue forcefully that historic precedents show that protectionism has held back economies and that it was free trade that built the West's wealth. They also attribute the pain more to corruption and poor governance than to trade rules.

About half-way round Uganda, I had realized that I was following in the footsteps of Stephen Byers, the former Secretary of State for Trade who had not only taken on the rip-off Britain campaign but also negotiated the British position at the world trade talks in Seattle in 1999. He had just completed a private visit to aid projects in East Africa, and had been introduced to some of the Ugandan coffee farmers I had met.

When anti-capitalists rioted during the Seattle WTO talks against globalization, Byers had been one of the Western representatives arguing that globalization and trade liberalization as currently negotiated by the WTO were the only way forward for poor countries. Protectionism could not work and never had. Globalization would bring benefits, he had said. I thought I should hear the other side of the story, and I decided to ring him.

But we never did have the debate about the merits of unfettered trade, because when I got through to him, he said he had changed his mind. The journey that had taken him to Uganda and Kenya had been a personal road to Damascus. It was an entirely private visit and he sought no publicity, but I said I thought that if he really had changed his mind, people probably ought to know. He agreed to write two pieces for the *Guardian* in which bravely, and unusually for a politician, he admitted he had got it wrong. He wrote:

In November 1999 . . . I watched from my hotel room as thousands demonstrated against the evils of globalization. Anarchists clad in black marched alongside grandmothers dressed as turtles . . . As leader of the delegation from the United Kingdom, I was convinced that the expansion of world trade . . . would be one of the key means by which world poverty would be tackled . . . I believed that developing countries would need to embrace trade liberalization . . . opening up their own domestic markets to international competition.

Like many economists, he believed that only the efficiency of the market could solve the problems of corrupt or inept governments, and that as their economies grew, the benefits of the free market would trickle down to the poor.

This is still the basis on which major international institutions like the IMF and the World Bank give loans to developing countries. But Byers went on: 'My mind has changed. I now believe that this approach is wrong and misguided.

'An unfettered global market can fail the poor . . . if markets are left alone . . . liberalization is used by the rich and powerful international players.' He proposed instead a regime of managed trade in which markets are opened up, but slowly, and with poorer countries being allowed to use subsidies and tariffs to protect their agriculture and industry as they do so. Such a challenge to the current orthodoxy on development would be 'opposed by multinational companies who see rich and easy pickings in the markets of the developing world', he predicted.

I asked him what had led him to this new view. 'I was aware of the arguments, but it's not until you see first hand the consequences of policies that you see they need to be changed.' He said that when he travelled as a minister he rarely saw beyond other ministers' air-conditioned offices. It was only 'getting away from Whitehall and the persuasive arguments of trade policy experts' that had made it possible for him to meet and understand 'the plight of ordinary people in developing countries'. Once he had seen at first hand, he realized that the rapidity of the changes and the way richer nations have written the rules in their favour had made trade liberalization simply too brutal.

One of the encounters that made him rethink was with a Kenyan farmer, Peter Makokha. His one source of income was sugar cane which he was growing as a cash crop. But he was finding himself pushed out of his local market and undercut by cheap, heavily subsidized imports of sugar from Europe and the USA.

Unlike coffee, sugar is grown in both Europe and developing

countries, so that the gulf between the environment in which farmers from different continents operate can easily be seen.

The EU sugar regime that controls production in the UK and the rest of Europe is one of those labyrinthine areas of economic intervention that can probably be fully mapped only by Brussels bureaucrats suffering from insomnia, but to simplify the key points: the price of sugar within the EU has often been three times higher than that prevailing on world markets. The costs of sugar production in the EU are also up to 80 per cent higher than in developing countries. In other words poorer developing countries should have a competitive edge. However, anyone wanting to import their cheaper sugar into the EU faces very high tariffs. Meanwhile, to prevent surpluses in the EU depressing the price of sugar for its farmers, the EU encourages their export by giving exporters refunds on the difference between the higher EU price and the world price, so enabling farmers of one of Britain's most profitable crops to dump their excess at below the cost of production in developing countries. Dumping is not permitted under WTO rules, but agricultural products are exempt. The effect has been to make it impossible for those poorer countries' sugar farmers to compete, even though they produce their sugar for a fraction of the cost incurred by the beet barons of East Anglia. As with other subsidies, the European farmers who benefit are not small ones, but the large landowners. Around 70 per cent of EU subsidies go to less than 30 per cent of farmers. The sugar regime is currently under review, with the EC pushing the idea that subsidies be brought down gradually until the intervention price is in line with the world market price, and farmers being compensated for the pain with direct payments instead.

Aid agencies welcomed Stephen Byers's conversion to the cause of protecting poorer farmers from such distortions of free trade, but neo-liberal economists were quick to condemn it. The inevitable response from the incumbent negotiators in trade talks was swift too. Baroness Amos, as Britain's Secretary of State

for International Development, and Patricia Hewitt, as current
Secretary of State for Trade and Industry, wrote a letter to the
Guardian saying they were 'disappointed to read Stephen Byers's
article calling for an increased use of tariffs and subsidies by
developing countries. The bulk of the evidence shows that this
will limit their opportunities to trade . . . excluding them further
from the world economy.' They went on to say that we could
not hope to reform the EU common agricultural policy if we
were also advocating protectionism for poorer countries.

Some of the world's poorest coffee growers have not waited
to hear the end of the debate. They have grubbed up their
unprofitable coffee bushes and replaced them with a more lucrative cash crop. In Peru, as the world price of coffee beans has
plummeted, they have switched to growing coca for cocaine. In
Ethiopia, the birthplace of coffee, farmers have turned to the
stimulant khat, and in Angola marijuana is becoming a valuable
cash crop.

7. The Ready Meal

It is twenty-two years since Marks & Spencer first brought the ready meal into our lives and set in train a revolution in our eating habits. About a third of us now use these supermarket meals more than once a week. Britain is in fact the largest consumer in Europe of ready meals, a reflection no doubt not only of its position at the top of the league for long working hours, but also of changing patterns of family life. The trade has a phrase for it: 'in-home meal solutions for single-person eating occasions'.

Instant, effortless meals provided by factory kitchens have been a theme of literary utopias since the early twentieth century but in those brave new worlds the convenience meal was celebrated for its efficiency or its capacity to liberate from drudgery rather than for any sensory experience. There have been frozen versions of instant dinners before, but for today's eaters, the genius of the new ready meal is that it promises freshness and pleasure too.

I cruised down the ready-meal aisle of a supermarket the other day. A vast array of dishes, placed next to the fruit and vegetable section, offered liberal sprinklings of 'fresh' this or 'hand-selected' that. The outer packs were all gorgeous colour photography. Key words, picked out in fashionable typography, hinted at the care and quality that had gone into their preparation. Top chefs from around the world appeared to have been labouring person- ally to provide me with a choice of exotic meals. I came back with a lamb dish, a 'favourite recipe', with what sounded like a delicious gravy and stuffing.

While it reheated, I just had time to read the label. The ingredients of my lamb dish, described in such mouth-watering prose on the front of the pack, were listed in long and minute detail in the small print on the back. By law, ingredients must be listed in order of weight. This is what it contained:

Lamb (23%), water, fried potato (21%), carrot (6%), peas (6%), red wine, onion

So far so good, although rather heavier on the potato and lighter on the lamb than I had realized at first sight, then as the bold letters slipped into fainter and harder-to-read type, it became more and more intriguing:

Pork sausage meat (pork, water, rusk, wheat flour, salt, herbs, ground spices, preservative: sodium acetate, sodium sulphite; dextrose, stabilizer: polyphosphate, antioxidants: ascorbic acid, sodium citrate; spice extract, glucose syrup)

Breadcrumb (wheat flour, water, yeast, soya flour, salt, rapeseed and palm oil, vinegar, sugar, wheat gluten, emulsifiers: mono and diglycerides of fatty acids, sodium stearoyl lactylate; preservative: calcium propionate; flour improver L-ascorbic acid; dextrose, flavouring)

Redcurrant jelly (3%) (sugar, water, redcurrant concentrate, lemon juice, citric acid, gelling agent: pectin; acidity regulator: acetic acid, preservative: potassium sorbate)

Lamb stock (concentrated lamb broth, vegetable concentrate, tomato concentrate, glucose syrup, salt, flavourings, yeast extract, dextrin, lamb fat, sunflower oil)

Modified maize starch, tomato purée

Lamb bouillon (salt, dextrose, yeast extract, lamb, skimmed milk powder, onion powder, potato starch, flavourings, hydrogenated rapeseed oil, white pepper, malt extract, citric acid, paprika)

Rapeseed oil, salt, margarine, wheat flour, garlic purée, mint, rosemary, dextrose, white pepper.

Now, in case I lost you half-way through, that's at least eight mentions of different kinds of sugars and sweetening agents, seven of fats in various forms including some that have been hydrogenated, four of preservatives, and three of chemical flavourings, not to mention thickeners such as starch in different guises. Salt came in at an impressive 5.9g for the pack. The maximum recommended salt intake for an adult for a whole day is 6g, according to the Food Standards Agency (FSA).

I could have gone instead for the Mediterranean flavours of a vegetarian lasagne ready meal. As well as water (the main ingredient by weight), that contained cooked pasta, various vegetables, cheese, cream, fats which included margarine, rapeseed oil and butter, modified starch, salt and sugar, and herbs together with a vegetable bouillon of:

Salt, dextrose [a form of sugar], potato starch [a thickener], sugar [what, more?], lactose [more sweetening], yeast extract, flavouring, hydrogenated rapeseed oil, onion powder, citric acid, herbs, dehydrated celery, malt extract [more sweetening] and turmeric extract [for that Mediterranean feel or possibly handy colouring].

That ready meal managed to be made up of 15 per cent sugars.

These are not quite the ingredients I would reach for when making a lamb casserole or a vegetarian lasagne. But otherwise there is nothing exceptional about the contents of the ready meals described above. I could find others like them in any supermarket.

Frozen-food manufacturers point out that a weekly basket of prepared fresh chilled meals like this costs 40 per cent more than a basket of frozen meals made with similar ingredients. Yet many of the constituent ingredients of fresh chilled meals have been previously frozen, and fresh chilled meals often contain more additives and preservatives than frozen. Such is the power of packaging and marketing, however, that we have all bought into the illusion sold by these industrialized products of the factory line.

Ready meals, like other processed foods, are typically high in processed fats – generally derived from soya, palm or rapeseed oil – and processed sugars – derived not just from sugar but also from corn. Large numbers of them contain processed starch – also generally derived from corn. In fact, a quarter of all processed foods are made with corn in some form and two thirds of all processed foods contain soya or its derivatives.

In the last three decades, considerable research effort in the food industry has been devoted to finding ways to break soya and corn down into their constituent parts and discovering new uses for them. As the US Corn Refiners' Association explains on its website, 'Corn refining is today's leading example of value-added agriculture. Refiners separate corn into its components, starch, oil, protein, and fibre, and convert them to higher-value products.'

Added value is food-industry speak for increasing profits by doing something to simple food. You might add value by using cheap labour to grade or wash and chop your raw materials so you can charge a premium for them (see Chapter 2); or you might take cheap ingredients, process them and sell them for much more than the sum of their parts. The attraction for the manufacturers and retailers of the ready meal is that it is the incarnation of 'added value'.

The protein from corn goes to feeding intensively reared animals, to create 'added-value' meat, leaving the oil and starch. Starches are thickening and bulking agents, and are often used to replace more expensive ingredients. Starch in its natural form has technical limitations, so food technologists have devised ways to treat or modify it with various acids, enzymes or oxidizing agents to improve its resistance to heat, make it more soluble in cold water and better able to produce gels, pastes and other textures required by the food industry. (Because modified starch has been altered at the molecular level, it is banned in organic production.)

Modified starches are low in nutritional value and most are also high in calories. But this component of corn is used most widely in ready meals and processed meats.

In an article in *Innovative Food Ingredients* magazine, entitled 'Innovative uses of corn starch in food', the American Corn Refiners' Association explains the many different ways food manufacturers can make use of modified starch. 'Starches are a vital element in today's diet, used in practically every category of processed food.' When modified by enzymes to produce cyclodextrin for instance, starch can 'mask off-flavours and unpleasant odours'. When chemically modified to make 'resistant starch', it has 'excellent expansion qualities' and can be used 'as a bulking agent in reduced-sugar or reduced-fat food formulations'.

The list of merits appears endless.

Several innovative applications of corn starch involve the replacement of other ingredients that may be expensive . . . pre-gelatinized starch can be used to replace tomato solids or fruit solids. Granular or flaked starch can provide texture and bulk to simulate the pulpy characteristics of the solids they replace at a reduced cost to the manufacturer. These types of textural starches are used effectively in tomato sauces, fruit fillings, fruit drinks, instant hot cereals, potato products and baby foods. In addition, the starch can add to the product's shelf life by efficiently binding water during storage . . . Imitation cheese manufacturers can cut costs by replacing [milk ingredients] with specially modified thin boiling starches . . .

The piece goes on to conclude that 'The diversity and sophistication of food products that are available is attributable in part to the imagination of the carbohydrate chemist.'

Evidence of the carbohydrate chemist's imagination is everywhere. In October 2003, Shropshire trading standards officers decided to test the office workers' staple: the sandwich. They bought chicken sandwiches from all the major high-street retailers. 'These sandwiches are described as chicken. Some boast they contain 100 per cent chicken breast . . . In many, the very small print . . . tells another story,' their report concluded. Many of the sandwiches contained chicken which had been adulterated with starch, water and flavourings. Here's a typical example: a 'roast chicken and salad sandwich with tender roast chicken breasts' whose label declares its chicken contains water, salt, dextrose, stabilizer, E450, E451, E452, modified maize starch and whey protein. David Walker, chief trading standards officer of Shropshire County Council, explains: 'Starch has no technological function other than as a meat adulterant. It soaks up water. The adulterated chicken industry has grown up in the last two years. Very few people know. The Food Standards Agency didn't know about it. My colleagues didn't know about it. But the problem is, the technology is moving so fast, we'll never keep up with it.'

The low-fat yoghurt is another classic example of the use of modified starch to add value. Often marketed as a healthy food, a typical strawberry yoghurt version contains not just yoghurt and strawberries, but also modified starch to thicken it and replace the texture of fruit; gelatine, gums, or pectin to glue it together and make it gel; colouring and flavourings; and some form of fructose (i.e. corn sugar). (It helps to know your labelling law here: a strawberry yoghurt must contain some real strawberry. A strawberry-flavoured yoghurt has had a briefer encounter with the fruit. A strawberry-flavour yoghurt, on the other hand, has not been within sight of a strawberry.)

Perhaps the most lucrative product of the carbohydrate chemist's imagination, however, has been the corn sweetener, and in particular high-fructose corn syrup (HFCS). It was food scientists in Japan who first found a way to produce this syrup, a sweetener that can be up to eight times sweeter than sucrose from cane sugar. By the late 1970s the industry was able to mass-produce it. Greg Critser describes the effect of these technological advances in his book *Fat Land*. In the early 1980s, Pepsi and

Coca-Cola in the USA switched completely to HFCS, saving them 20 per cent in sweetener costs and enabling them to increase portion sizes dramatically as they looked to give their products a market edge. HFCS is now the commonest form of sweetener in soft drinks around the world. Soft drinks are another classic example of added value.

A manufacturer of an alternative brand of cola was kind enough to share his production costs with me. As a rule of thumb, only one third of the cost of production of processed foods is the cost of ingredients – one third is the cost of packaging and one third the cost of processing. The higher the quality of the product, the higher the percentage of the costs devoted to ingredients. But sometimes the costs of ingredients are negligible.

For example, in a can of cola retailing at between 40p and 50p, the metal can itself costs 7–8p, and the ingredients less than 2p. Sugar or sweetener makes up 10 per cent of the recipe; colouring and flavouring and other additives account for a tiny percentage more; the rest is water. The most expensive ingredient is the sugar or sweetener. A can of cola contains 30g of sugar or the equivalent in corn syrup, which at current prices would cost just 1.3p.

So much for the sugars and starches. One of the other characteristics of processed foods is that they are high in fats. These tend to be soya, rapeseed and palm oil. Soya oil is the commonest in processed foods. The USA is the world's largest producer and exporter of soya, and accounts for about 40 per cent of global oilseed exports. Once the high-protein soya meal has been extracted from the soya beans for intensive livestock feeding, the oil is left for human consumption. But manufacturing processes need fats with slightly different properties to soya oil, and so much of it is hydrogenated. Hydrogenation was developed in the 1920s as a way of artificially hardening liquid oils so that they would function more like animal fats. The oil is heated to 200°C and held at that temperature for several hours with a metal catalyst, usually nickel, while hydrogen gas is pumped through it. The hydrogen atoms penetrate the oil molecules, forming trans fats. Hydrogenated fat is exceptionally hard and plastic-like when cooled which makes it particularly useful in food processing. Rapeseed oil may be treated in the same way. But the very property that makes the hydrogenated fats so useful to manufacturers also makes them a health risk for consumers. It is now generally accepted that it is safest to avoid hydrogenated fats, because they have the same effect on your arteries as other hard fats. They are banned in organic production. The FSA advises that 'trans fats have no nutritional benefits and because of the effect they have on blood cholesterol they increase the risk of coronary heart disease . . . evidence suggests that the adverse effects of trans fats are worse than saturated fats'.

Avoiding them is hard work. Hydrogenated fats are very widely used in processed foods such as ready meals, margarines, crisps, confectionery, bakery products, biscuits and cakes.

So why all this effort to make use of corn, sugar, and soya and other oils, and why are manufacturers so keen to replace fresh fruits and vegetables or meat with these ingredients?

Corn, sugar, soya, palm and rapeseed happen to be among the most heavily subsidized crops in the world. Fresh fruit and vegetables, on the other hand, are not subsidized. The former, when processed, are blessed with a long shelf life but are high in calories and low in nutrients; the latter are high in vitamins and minerals but have a tiresome habit of going off. Straightforward economics dictate what goes into the processed food we eat today.

When we think of agricultural subsidies, we tend to think of cosseted Continental and American farmers, but these post-war interventions have done little to prevent the collapse of average farm incomes. What they have done is deliver cheap ingredients to the food-manufacturing sector while also giving money to the handful of global giants that dominate trading in and processing of subsidized commodities. Not only have subsidies undermined farmers in developing countries, they have distorted diets in the West.

The USA dominates soya as well as corn production. A new system of direct payments to American farmers in the early 1970s led to an explosion in acreage planted with these crops. Volumes of corn produced in the USA had more than doubled by the year 2000. World production of soya oil has quadrupled in the same period, thanks also in part to Latin American countries increasing production. About 70 per cent of the value of the US soya bean today comes from the US government.

There has also been a six-fold increase in the production of palm oil which is subsidized by the main producing country, Malaysia. The EU, thanks to its sugar support mechanisms, now produces one and a half times as much sugar as it can consume and has kept world prices low (see Chapter 6). The USA also subsidizes sugar heavily. If you want to understand why your processed food labels contain such long lists of apparently obscure ingredients, you need look no further than this.

Concentrations of power in this part of agribusiness mirror those elsewhere in the food chain. Bill Vorley's *Food Inc.* notes that four big soya traders/processors, Bunge, ADM, Cargill and Dreyfus, control about 75 per cent of the US and European soya market. Cargill also controls 42 per cent of all US corn exports. Four international trading companies, Cargill and Dreyfus among them, collected $1.4 billion in export subsidies from the US government between 1985 and 1989. Three sugar trading/refining companies dominate sugar, Cargill, Dreyfus and Tate & Lyle. The EU paid sugar exporters 1.5 billion euros in export refunds for sugar in 2001.

Needless to say, these corporations represent powerful political lobbies. When the World Health Organization prepared its global strategy on diet, physical activity and health, and with the consensus of experts from around the world proposed that no more than 10 per cent of calories consumed should come from processed sugars, the American Sugar Association, which gives generously to political parties, lobbied the Bush administration for changes. A special assistant at the US Department of Health drafted a thirty-page critique, questioning the WHO science, and the Secretary of State for Health, Tommy Thompson, flew to Geneva with representatives from the Grocery Manufacturers' Association to try to force the WHO to back down.

To turn these products of highly subsidized agriculture, the cheap fats, sugars and starches, into acceptable foods, you need additives.

Around $20 billion is spent each year by the food industry on chemical additives to change the colour, texture, flavour and shelf-life of our food. Over $1 billion a year is spent on food colourings alone, to deceive our senses. Manufacturers wanting to create the impression of fruit or vegetables or other expensive ingredients without the bother of paying for the real thing have 4,500 different flavouring compounds at their disposal.

Salt is one way of providing flavour where it is lacking, which is why it is added in such hefty doses. (About 75 per cent of salt in our diets comes from processed foods such as ready meals and snacks, according to the FSA, which has been pressurizing industry to cut down on the quantities used, since high salt consumption is linked to high blood pressure and cardiovascular disease.)

Other flavourings and colourings replace the natural flavours and colours that are either absent because of the lack of real ingredients or because they have been lost in processing; emulsifiers and stabilizers bind water and fat together and stop them separating out again.

Some additives are necessary to help the ingredients survive the factory process. In cheap yoghurt manufacture, for example, high-speed machinery pumps the yoghurt along miles of pipes. This breaks its delicate structure, which traditionally comes from the natural thickening associated with the incubation of bacteria. So gums are added at the beginning of the process to make the product 'bullet-proof', as one manufacturer described it. (More expensive yoghurts are not pumped to such an extent, and have their fruit added by hand to preserve the structure, but that adds to labour costs.)

Erik Millstone, Reader in Science Policy at Sussex University, has studied the additives industry for many years. He points out in *The Atlas of Food* that consumers in industrialized countries now eat 13–15lb (6–7kg) of food additives a year.

There are 540 food additives ruled as safe by regulatory bodies, but according to Millstone, critics of the testing system have raised doubts about many of them. Uncertainty surrounds the safety of about 150 compounds, he says. Some may cause allergies or adverse reaction in a few people, but about thirty additives presently in use could cause significant long term harm to any consumers. Flavourings are not tested for safety and currently do not have to be declared individually on the label.

The food industry often defends the use of additives by saying that they protect consumers from food poisoning, but additives used as preservatives or to stop fat going rancid account for less than 1 per cent by weight of all the additives used. About 90 per cent of additives in processed food are cosmetic. The vast majority are used to make cheap fat, constipating starch and subsidized sugars look and taste like natural food.

Food manufacturers have always cut corners and substituted cheap alternatives for expensive ingredients. In 1429, the Guild of Pepperers battled to stop people mixing gravel and twigs with pepper. But the first mass adulterations came with the Industrial Revolution, and as with labour conditions, the historic parallels are instructive. Feeding cities with their newly urbanized populations required new supply systems. Whereas previously most people would have grown their own food or bought from their immediate neighbours, city dwellers were dependent on much longer chains and soon became ignorant of how their food was made. With no legal obstacles and fierce competition, adulteration became commonplace. Whereas before, an unscrupulous butcher or baker might have been restrained by the knowledge that any shortcuts he chose could poison his neighbours and friends, now he could hide in the anonymity of distance and the city.

Analytical chemistry was still in its infancy in the eighteenth and early nineteenth centuries, and there was little fear of detection until Frederick Accum developed methods to examine food. His work, *There is Death in the Pot*, as it was popularly known, or more properly, *A Treatise on Adulterations of Food and Culinary Poisons*, was a bestseller when it was published in 1820. Its subtitle was 'exhibiting the fraudulent sophistications of bread, beer, wine, spiritous liquors, tea, coffee, cream, confectionery, vinegar, mustard, pepper, cheese, olive oil, pickles and other articles employed in domestic economy, and methods of detecting them'. Accum fled the country after a minor scandal but the cause was taken up by Dr Arthur Hassall who first used the microscope to show that coffee was being routinely adulterated with roasted chicory, peas and wheat. Thomas Wakley, owner and editor of the medical journal the *Lancet*, told Hassall that he would never achieve anything until he defied the libel lawyers and named and shamed the perpetrators of the adulterations. With government apparently uninterested in action, the two men agreed to work on a series of articles analysing samples of food and drink bought from shops around London and exposing the fraud, together with the names and addresses of the shops involved.

Their work revealed a scandal of immense proportions as Hassall reported fortnightly in the *Lancet* on samples of coffee, sugar, water, bread, milk and a whole range of other foods and found lead, water, dyes, alum and flour all being used to debase food. The scandal eventually led to the 1875 Sale of Food and Drugs Act which made it an offence to sell adulterated food. Early food branding emerged as a response to the anxiety that surrounded the adulterations. Before then, most food was sold loose. Brands were the customer's guarantee of the quality and provenance of the ingredients.

With each generation the adulterations have changed but

the elements have followed a pattern: ignorance among the consuming public, an assumption among the producers that what they are doing is entirely acceptable, the lure of large profits, and weak law or weak enforcement.

In her 1931 book, *The Suffragette Movement*, Sylvia Pankhurst gave as an example of sweated labour the work of women whose job it was to rub pieces of wood into seed shapes so they could be added to raspberry jam made without the aid of raspberries. Outraged, she helped open a factory making jam from real fruit at affordable prices to create jobs for pacifist women during the First World War.

After the Second World War, fruit squashes entirely devoid of real fruit were made with sugar, citric acid and flavourings. Starch was added to give the impression of cloudiness created by fruit, cellulose imitated pith, and tiny bits of wood were made to look like pips.

The adulteration of twenty-first century food adheres to the pattern. The difference, however, is that today it is being practised by some of the world's largest manufacturers entirely within the law. Adulteration now takes place on an unprecedented scale and is of unparalleled sophistication. The food industry's response in the early nineteenth century has a familiar ring to it. It claimed then that people wanted cheap food, and that the added ingredients were not adulterants but made food look and taste better. It argued that the poor couldn't afford anything else and therefore richer people's interventions were misguided. It said that if people didn't like what was being sold they wouldn't buy it.

Real food does cost more. Legal adulteration trades on this, but the evidence is that when people do understand what is happening they are in fact very concerned indeed.

In 1983 new European legislation required manufacturers to list additives in food by E numbers for the first time. As they started to see how their processed food was made, consumers become increasingly suspicious about these additives. Then, as if by a miracle, E numbers started to disappear. The E numbers were still there in the food of course but manufacturers stopped using them on labels. The pork sausage bit of my lamb casserole, for instance, contains E262, E221, either E450 or 544 or 545, E300 and E331, but there's not an E number in sight. Listing the additives in full might seem helpful, but actually I end up knowing less. Which polyphosphate is it? Is it the one that may prevent the absorption of vital nutrients such as iron, or the one associated with bowel disorders, or neither? Polyphosphates are used to make meat absorb water, saving manufacturers' costs, so why is it there anyway? E221, incidentally, is one of the sulphite group of preservatives which act ultimately as sulphur dioxide. They destroy vitamin B_1, have been shown in animal studies to increase the incidence of tumours and are commonly associated with adverse or allergic reactions. Sulphites are permitted in high concentrations in many foods and are therefore easy to consume in worrying amounts.

While some additives started declaring themselves by another name, others simply went underground. Food legislation helps manufacturers here. Additives used as 'processing aids' do not have to be declared. Nor do the individual ingredients of all 'compound ingredients' have to be declared on the label. At the moment, manufacturers do not have to list the ingredients of compound ingredients that are less than 25 per cent of the total weight of the product. For example, the label on a fruit yoghurt might say '15 per cent fruit conserve', but the producer does not have to say how that fruit conserve is made. It could actually be made up of just 1 per cent strawberry and 99 per cent other ingredients such as added sugars and flavourings and colourings. The law is in the process of being changed in an effort to curb the widespread abuse of the rule and to protect the growing numbers of people suffering from allergies caused by food additives and other allergens in factory foods. By the end of 2005, manufacturers will have to list what is in compound ingredients unless they make up less than 2 per cent by weight of the total product. Although this is a step forward, whether the new rules will stamp out abuse entirely is debatable, since in weight terms only a small quantity of additives may be needed to achieve the desired results. So, for example, if I want to make a drink for children without having to mention preservatives on the label, I can buy some 'natural lemon flavouring' (which incidentally does not mean that the flavouring is natural, merely that if it has been chemically synthesized, it is 'nature-identical') and make sure the natural flavouring has a hefty dose of preservative added to it. The preservative, which will be surplus to the flavouring's requirements, will also have a preservative effect on the whole product.

For a glimpse behind the façade of the food industry today, there is no better place than Paris, the culinary capital of the world. Every second year, the food industry gathers here for a trade fair to which members of the public are not invited. Le Salon International de l'Alimentation (SIAL) is where manufacturers and processers, retail buyers and new product development managers, catering suppliers and exporters from some 100 countries gather to do deals. Spread over six vast exhibition halls on the outskirts of the city are displays of the latest innovations in our convenience-meal existence.

I went to the fair with an undercover team from *Panorama* when we were investigating the scandal of Dutch chicken adulterated with beef waste, for this is where the agents for chicken pumped full of water and additives take orders from takeaway restaurants and ready-meal manufacturers around the world. While the BBC reporters were being told by Dutch exporters how they could turn water into money, I visited other alchemists' stalls. Everywhere there was evidence of a vast and wondrous scientific effort to turn base materials into lucre.

Endless display fridges showed the possibilities: frozen meat ready-chopped and flavoured for convenient ready-meal manufacture, Chinese spice, tikka- or chargrilled-style; Mediterranean vegetables premarked with even black grill lines for that instant barbecue feel; frozen prawns with added water and polyphosphates to keep it in, or not, depending on the price; ready-frozen industrial sauce pellets; puréed cubes of sugared, coloured and flavoured frozen kiwi, mango and raspberry for desserts. One giant banner advertised 'industrial cheese'; another boasted a miracle soft cheese that is 'always fully ripe'.

A section on new trends gave its assessment of the super-markets' efforts to create their own upmarket added-value brands, an assessment which would certainly be disputed by the retailers: 'All supermarkets have introduced premium brands . . . on average these are 75 per cent more expensive for the same quality . . . this sector is showing strong growth . . .'

I wandered off into a stand that resembled a Victorian perfume shop. Its olde worlde wooden shelves were full of silver vials that looked like exquisite aromatherapy bottles. An assistant offered me a sprayer and invited me to sample the essences. I gave one a quick squirt and the stand was immediately filled with the delicious smell of wild mushroom. These 'natural extracts' were being marketed to restaurants for chefs to spray on to dishes as they left the kitchen, effortlessly conjuring up the intensity of basil or truffle with only a metal canister for a prop.

I decided to join the lecture tour on additives titled 'Additives are everywhere. Discover them'. I learned that consumers are becoming 'more sophisticated', they want cleaner labels, they want things to 'nourish their intellects' as well as their tastebuds, and they are preoccupied with 'nomadism'. The tour took in several new neutraceutical products. This is where the drugs industry meets the food industry and where many believe the money of the future is, with vitamins and minerals added to highly processed foods so that they can be sold as healthy. Then we visited a company that has devised a way to distil oak smoke into a liquid to add to wine. Is that legal, I asked. 'Everyone accepts the taste very happily, but legislation is a problem.' On another stand, scientists were explaining how they hydrolyze fish flavour from crab shells for ready meals.

*

It was while I was at the SIAL exhibition, that I had picked up my copy of *Innovative Food Ingredients* magazine. As well as the illuminating piece on uses of cornstarch, it contained an article covering the use of flavours to mask bitterness from other additives and to disguise chemical burn from preservatives. There was a discussion on the use of colours to simulate good-quality ingredients; and another on the unfortunate laxative effect of bulk sweeteners, added to confectionery and baked goods to provide, yes, bulk.

All this would be serious enough if we were just being ripped off, but debasement of our food is having a profound effect on our health. The fresh foods which provide vital nutrients, the vitamins, minerals and essential fatty acids we need for health, are being replaced by large quantities of hardened fats, sugars and salt. Our industrialized diet is now known to be a major contributor to disease. We are being fed junk and it is making us sick.

The WHO summarized the situation in its 2000 report. It found that 60 per cent of deaths around the world are 'clearly related to changes in dietary patterns and increased consumption of fatty, salty, and sugary foods'. Cardiovascular disease (CVD), diabetes and cancer now account for about 30 per cent of the burden of ill health. Conservative estimates suggest that around one third of the risk of CVD is related to 'unbalanced nutrition' and 30–40 per cent of cancers could be prevented through better diet, the report concluded.

As Western diets high in fats, sugars and salt are adopted in developing countries, the same Western patterns of disease emerge. The dramatic rise in consumption of fats and sugars in China and India that has crept in with industrialization and urbanization, for example, is mirrored by an equally dramatic and alarming rise in cardiovascular disease, obesity and diabetes in those countries.

Professor Philip James, who produced the blueprint for the British FSA at the personal invitation of Tony Blair, and is chair of the International Obesity Taskforce, estimates that half of all middle-aged British adults are suffering from a 'clinically evident nutritional problem', in other words one that impairs their current health or requires treating with medicine. Diet is in fact now roughly on a par with tobacco as a cause of illness.

Nutrition is still a poorly understood science. But as the state of knowledge grows, consistent messages are becoming clearer. Industrialized diets encourage the consumption of too much of the wrong sorts of energy-dense food, saturated and processed fats, highly refined carbohydrates and sugars which load us with calories without providing nutrients. These energy-dense foods have replaced the unrefined ones that we need to provide the essential vitamins, minerals and fats vital for health – fresh fruit and vegetables, fish, nuts and seeds, and unrefined carbohydrates. It is hard to get fat on unrefined foods, because their natural bulk fills us up. When we eat highly processed energy-dense foods, however, our bodies may fail to realize when we have had enough. And a product like high-fructose corn syrup may even be metabolized in a different way to other foods. It appears not to need to be broken down in the way that other sugars are, but to be delivered straight to the liver and turned into fat.

The most visible evidence of the impact of our industrialized diet on health is the obesity pandemic. While half the world starves, the other half is afflicted by the diseases of excess. With uncomfortable symmetry, the numbers on each side are now almost perfectly balanced. Some 1.2 billion people in the world still have too little to eat; the same number today suffer from being overweight.

The International Obesity Taskforce has described obesity as 'the most critical public health issue of the twenty-first century'. For the first time in 100 years, medical experts are predicting, life expectancy in developed countries will fall. Thanks to obesity, our children face the prospect of dying younger than us.

The figures make disturbing reading. The National Audit Office report in 2001, *Tackling Obesity*, found that the incidence of obesity in the UK had trebled between 1980 and 1998 to 21 per cent of women and 17 per cent of men. 'Most evidence suggests that the main reason for the rising prevalence is a combination of less active lifestyles and changes in eating patterns.' According to a more recent survey commissioned by the government from the National Centre for Social Research, more than one in five men and women now are obese. Almost one third of all children are either obese or overweight, a rise of 50 per cent since 1990.

There is also a clear link between poverty and obesity. Some 30 per cent of girls and 36 per cent of young women are obese or overweight in the most deprived areas of the country, compared to 23 per cent of girls and 27 per cent of young women in the most affluent areas. The government's Health Development Agency has talked of a 'timebomb'. The president of the International Diabetes Federation, Professor Sir George Alberti, who is closely involved in government health policy, has warned of 'one of the biggest health catastrophes the world has ever seen'.

The reason these eminent and normally restrained experts are talking in such apocalyptic terms is that obesity goes hand in hand with other diseases. Type 2 diabetes, which used to be called adult-onset diabetes and is caused by poor diet, is now being found in children in the UK for the first time. Being diagnosed with diabetes is the equivalent of having had your first heart attack. It reduces your life expectancy by several years. Diabetes is not only linked to heart disease, but also affects the eyes, kidneys and circulation. More than 300 million people around the world are believed already to have impaired glucose tolerance, the precursor to diabetes. Diabesity, as the Americans call it, could undo the progress made in health in Europe since the war.

Obesity is the disease that has finally pushed the panic button over diet and health, although there have been plenty of reasons to activate it before now. The relationship between industrialized diets and the largest causes of premature death and morbidity in the UK, heart disease, strokes and cancer, is compelling and has been generally agreed for much longer. The British government has at last woken up to the costs of diet-related diseases. The Wanless report on the National Health Service, commissioned by the Treasury, estimated that diet-related diseases cost the NHS £6.2 billion a year. But because the aetiology of these diseases is complicated, it has been easier for the food industry to dispute the connections.

Coronary heart disease is the biggest killer in the UK, and 40 per cent of premature deaths in men – that is, men dying before the age of retirement – are caused by heart disease and stroke. The rates of death have in fact fallen dramatically since the 1970s as treatments have improved, but the numbers suffering heart disease have not. The UK still has one of the highest rates of heart disease in the world. Immigrant populations soon show the same patterns of diet-related disease as they adopt Western lifestyles.

The same processes that are causing furring up of the coronary arteries appear to be going on in the circulatory system in the brain. There is increasing evidence that dementia is linked to diet.

Although there has been much dispute over the years on the relationship between diet and cancer, the UK Department of Health and the World Cancer Research Fund have both concluded that diets which include large amounts of fruit and vegetables will cut cancer rates. And conversely, a diet which is high in saturated fats but poor in antioxidant vitamins, particularly A, C and E, puts you at greater risk. Yet few people in the UK eat the amount of fresh fruit and vegetables recommended. Children do particularly badly. On average, they eat only two portions of fruit and vegetables each day. One in five children never eats fruit in an average week, and more than half never eat green leafy vegetables.

But it doesn't end there. The part played by some nutrients in good health is still being uncovered. Some of the most interesting new work at the moment is being done on the role of essential fatty acids. The brain, vascular system and to a lesser extent every cell in the body relies on essential fats for its construction.

Professor Michael Crawford, who in the 1960s and 1970s worked on essential fats and their role in Western degenerative diseases, points out that one of the most dramatic changes in the composition of food that has taken place in the last fifty years as it has become industrialized is the shift in the balance of fatty acids in the diet. He explained the role of essential fatty acids in his 1972 book, *What We Eat Today*.

Mammals cannot make essential fatty acids but must find them in their food. In plants there are two kinds of essential fatty acids, alpha-linolenic (found mostly in leaves, but also in the seed of some leguminous plants), and linoleic (found in seeds). These are polyunsaturated and when animals eat them they build on them, making longer-chain fatty acids, which are used in brain construction. Alpha-linolenic acid is converted into the omega-3 family of essential fatty acids, including EPA and DHA. Linoleic is converted by the body into the omega-6 family of essential fatty acids, particularly arachidonic acid. Crawford showed in 1972 that both arachidonic and DHA acids were specifically used in the brain. The DHA is particularly concentrated in the synaptic junctions and signalling systems of the brain and retina. The requirement of the brain for DHA has since been confirmed by many research papers. The richest source of DHA and EPA is fish.

Polyunsaturated compounds such as these are unstable and susceptible to oxidation, but luckily in nature they are present in plants together with antioxidants such as vitamin E, which acts as a natural preservative. Flavones, responsible for the bright colour in fruits such as tomatoes, are also antioxidants.

When seed oils are processed, any alpha-linolenic acid is generally selectively removed because it is unstable. When rice is polished or when wheat is processed into white flour, the germ of the seed and its essential fats are removed. When corn is made into breakfast cereal, the essential fats are also purified out. Palm oil, meanwhile, has almost no essential fats.

The essential fatty acids are vital for reproduction, for neural, vascular and immune system function, for food metabolism, and for the regulation of cell growth and regeneration. The body's inflammatory response, created to deal with injury or microbial attack, is regulated by omega-3s. The reduction of omega-3s in the diet leads to chronic inflammation and plays a significant part in degenerative diseases.

The omega-3 family of fatty acids plays a particularly important role in brain structure and function. About 60 per cent of the brain by dry weight is fat.

Whereas our ancestors would have eaten wild game, green leaves, nuts, seeds and fish which are all high in omega-3 fatty acids, we now consume much more omega-6. And whereas in the past, our diets would have provided a roughly equal balance of omega-3 and omega-6, now manufacturers who are looking for long shelf-life use mostly processed soy, corn, palm and cotton seed oil which provide high amounts of omega-6 fatty acids and very little omega-3. Hydrogenating oil also wipes out polyunsaturated omega-3.

The ratio of omega-6 to omega-3, instead of being 1:1, as in the brain, is now thought to be between 10:1 and 20:1 in the American diet. The annual consumption of soy oil in the USA has increased a thousand-fold in less than 100 years, with the average American knocking back 11kg of soy oil in various forms a year. In the UK today we probably eat sixteen times as much omega-6 as omega-3, whereas a century ago we would have been getting amounts much closer to 1:1. Intensive farming has played a part in the changes too. The meat of cows fed grass has omega-3 in it but intensively reared grain-fed cattle have higher levels of saturated fats and little omega-3. Wild fish are high in omega-3 essential fatty acids, but in farmed fish omega-3s are displaced by omega-6s. Moreover, some of the vital trace elements and vitamins needed to metabolize essential fatty acids and other foods are being depleted.

Soils fed only with artificial fertilizers containing nitrogen, phosphate and potash (NPK) gradually lose their vital trace elements. Anne-Marie Mayer of Cornell University has charted the reduction in the vitamin and mineral content of food grown in Britain between the late 1930s and the 1990s. She found significant falls in the levels of calcium, magnesium and copper in vegetables and in magnesium, iron, copper and potassium in fruit. Her findings have been replicated by the geologist David Thomas, who analysed data from the bible of nutrition, *The Composition of Foods*, and found a huge dip in mineral content over the last sixty years. In just a few decades, the zinc content of seven common foods fell by nearly 60 per cent. Between the beginning of the Second World War and the early 1990s, the mineral content of vegetables dropped by 27 per cent in iron, and 24 per cent in magnesium, for example. Overall, levels of minerals have declined between a quarter and three quarters in fruit and vegetables. Scientific understanding of some of these nutrients and their biochemistry is very new. Selenium, for instance, was only recognized in 1957 but it is needed to metabolize essential fatty acids, and deficiency is now known to be linked to heart disease and other illnesses.

A whole range of studies is now being conducted into the effects of essential fatty acid deficiency on mental health, behaviour, and developmental problems. It is too early to say with certainty what the links are between dietary imbalance and these other disorders that appear to be rising dramatically in industrialized countries, but increasing numbers of scientists believe there is a connection. Joseph Hibbeln, a biochemist and psychiatrist from the National Institutes of Health, Washington, DC, has looked at the links between essential fats and depression to see if there could be a nutritional factor behind the soaring rates of depression in affluent countries. In the USA, people born after the Second World War are twice as likely to develop depression as their parents, and the age at which it first strikes is falling. In the UK the number of prescriptions for antidepressants has risen by one third in just ten years.

Hibbeln explained the mechanisms to *New Scientist* magazine. All chemical and electrical signals must pass through the outside wall of the brain. This membrane is composed almost entirely of fats. Neural cell membranes are in fact 20 per cent essential fatty acids. If their composition and therefore their shape changes, their function is impaired. Fatty acids have also been linked to the neurotransmitter serotonin. Hibbeln has found that people with little omega-3 in their spinal fluid seem to have low levels of serotonin (some antidepressant drugs work by boosting serotonin levels).

Cross-cultural studies show a strong link between national consumption of essential fatty acids and levels of depression. As a Western diet full of processed foods and animal fats infiltrates a culture, the rate of depression rises accordingly. Other studies have found that some patients with manic depression respond to supplements of fish oils.

In the UK, scientists have been exploring the link between essential fatty acid deficiency or imbalance and developmental conditions. There is mounting evidence that deficiencies are involved in dyslexia, dyspraxia, attention deficit and hyperactivity disorder and autistic spectrum disorders, and that children suffering from these problems respond to supplements of essential fats with antioxidant vitamins. The incidence of these disorders has risen dramatically in recent decades.

Even more startling are the implications of a randomized, double-blind placebo-controlled trial conducted by Bernard Gesch, senior research scientist in the Department of Physiology at Oxford University, and his colleagues. During the study, which took place in one of Britain's maximum security prisons, where inmates reported some of the highest levels of prison violence in the country, prisoners were randomly assigned a placebo or a course of supplements containing essential fatty acids and key vitamins and minerals necessary to metabolize them. The number of serious offences including violence committed by the prisoners fell by nearly 40 per cent in those taking the supplements but not at all in those not taking them.★

Gesch began his work when he was a probation officer in Northampton working with juvenile offenders. He was seeing young girls and boys who were committing strings of burglaries or violent offences. 'They'd turn up with bags of sweets, or junk, and they looked so unhealthy.' Nutritionists were asked to look at the children's diets and by improving them managed to reduce reoffending. The local court started using diet as a component of its sentencing, but critics said the improvements in clients could be explained by other factors. The attraction of conducting a properly scientific trial in a prison was that in such a controlled environment, exact intakes could be measured and other potentially confounding factors removed to see if there was a link. To Gesch, the case is 'just bleeding obvious'.

The brain is a metabolic powerhouse, which despite being only 2 per cent of our body mass, consumes around 20 per cent of available energy. To metabolize this energy requires a range of nutrients, vitamins, minerals and essential fatty acids. These are essential for the normal functioning of the brain, which means there may be consequences if we don't get enough of them from our diet.

The trial has yet to be replicated, and Gesch is certainly not suggesting that nutrition is the only cause of antisocial behaviour. He also admits he is entering the realms of speculation when he points out that the dramatic rise in notifiable criminal offences

★ The idea that nutrition might be a key factor in anti-social behaviour is not new. Dr Hugh Sinclair persuaded the wartime British government to supplement the diet of all pregnant mothers with cod liver oil and orange juice because he had found blood levels low in many vitamins and essential fatty acids in much of the population and speculated that this could cause illness and bad behaviour.

in the UK from 1,100 per 100,000 people in 1950 to 9,400 per 100,000 people in 1996 coincides with dramatic changes in diet post-war. It may just be coincidence that the greatest levels of criminal behaviour are seen in male youths in late adolescence, just at the point when their accelerated growth puts their brains in competition with their bodies for nutrients. But for Gesch, one of the most powerful drivers to finding out more was the response from the prison inmates whose behaviour appeared to have improved. He starting receiving little thank-you notes from some of the country's most feared and violent offenders.

There is a long way to go before we fully understand the links between diet and mental processes, but one of the reasons all these lines of research are so appealing is that they are intuitive and suggest cheap, non-invasive remedies. They confirm what many parents and teachers now experience, that children fed a diet of junk are often unmanageable. Growing children, who need the best food, nowadays nearly always eat the worst. A study by the Consumers' Association (CA) showed the scale of the problem we are building for the future. Researchers asked 246 primary and secondary school children to keep food diaries in an effort to draw a picture of the average diet of today's children.

Zoë, aged fifteen, started day one with a slice of white toast and butter and a mug of tea. During mid-morning break at school, she had a bag of Walker's salt and vinegar crisps. School lunch was a plate of chips and gravy with two small sausages. At mid-afternoon break at school she had a Chupa Chups 'orange flavour' lollypop. After school she had more crisps, Golden Wonder crispy bacon flavour, a bar of Terry's chocolate orange, a packet of sweets and a bottle of 'toothkind' Ribena with blackcurrant flavour. Tea-time at home provided home-made shepherd's pie with baked beans and a glass of sugar-free lemon-ade. During the evening Zoë consumed a small packet of wine gums and six chocolate sweets. Before bed she had a glass of skimmed milk. Day two was similar, except that the white toast and tea for breakfast was supplemented with a small tin of macaroni cheese on toast and more Ribena. Mid-morning snack was crisps again with a small bottle of diet lemonade. Lunch was chips and gravy again, this time accompanying a turkey twizzler. The afternoon lollipop and after-school crisps were followed by supper at home of chips, gravy and chicken nuggets, with a small portion of mushy peas and lemonade. During the evening Zoë consumed two Aero chocolate bars, before a bedtime glass of orange juice. And so on through the week.

Lynne, aged eleven, had even less variety in her diet, eating the same sweetened processed cereal with milk each morning for breakfast, having the same packed lunch of peanut butter sandwiches, crisps and flavoured yoghurt, and cheese and tomato pizza for tea each day, either with cola or water to drink, and the same cake during the course of each evening. She regularly ate four bags of crisps in the course of a day, having them at both school break-times, at lunch-time and after school.

The contents of the typical cheap chicken nugget were revealed in Chapter 1. On average, schools spend just 35p on the ingredients of each meal. Inevitably, they end up buying the poorest quality. A well-made pizza, with a dough of flour, yeast, olive oil and salt, is both healthy and delicious. But cheap ones get up to 2 per cent sugar added, along with modified starch, corn syrup and flavourings. The same goes for the tomato sauce: the wholesome ones are made with tomatoes, oil, garlic and not much else; the cheap ones are made with sugar, modified starch and flavourings to disguise a light touch on the tomatoes. Cheese can be good cheese or industrial cheese analogue made with vegetable oil, proteins, starch and flavourings. And sausages have always provided a licence to adulterate. Here's a recipe for a school sausage given to me by a manufacturer who preferred to remain anonymous. It is for what he described as a 'pork product' made 'down to a price' to win a local authority contract. The sausage contents: 50 per cent meat, of which 30 per cent is pork fat with a bit of jowl, and 20 per cent mechanically recovered chicken meat,* 17 per cent water, 30 per cent rusk and soya, soya concentrate, hydrolyzed protein, modified flour, dried onion, sugar, dextrose, phosphates, preservative E221 sodium sulphite, flavour enhancer, spices, garlic, flavouring, antioxidant E300 (ascorbic acid), colouring E128 (red 2G) and casings made from collagen from cow hide.

Sadly, children's packed lunches are often little better. Favourite ingredients include ham sandwiches made with white sliced bread, packets of crisps, sweet drinks and sugary cereal bars. Even the ham is often not what it seems. Most of what we buy these days is sold pre-sliced and packed. It is nearly all either 'formed ham' or 'reformed ham'.

Formed ham is made by dissecting the muscle meat from the leg bone of a pig and roughly chopping it. Then it is either passed under rows of needles on hydraulic arms which inject it with a solution of water, sugars, preservatives, flavourings and other additives or put into a giant cement-mixer-like machine to be tumbled or massaged with a similar solution. The machinery is the same as that used to adulterate chicken. Both technologies enable the processors to pump large quantities of water into the meat. Many hams contain up to 20 per cent added water.

The tumbling process dissolves an amino acid called myosin in the meat which becomes very sticky, so that when the pork is next put into D-shaped or ham-shaped moulds and cooked, it comes out looking like a whole piece of meat. If the ham is to be presented sliced as a traditional cut, a layer of fat is stuck round the edge of the mould to make it look as though it has just been cut off a whole leg. Ham made this way is uniformly wet. It must be labelled 'formed from cuts of legs'. It should be made from muscle meat but does not have to have been made from cuts from the same animal.

Moving down a grade, 'reformed' ham is made from chopped-

---

* Mechanically recovered meat is a sludge extruded from bones, tissue and sinew left over once prime cuts have been removed from a carcass.

up or emulsified meat which is not necessarily all muscle meat. During the process of making 'formed' ham, a gunge of scraps gathers at the bottom of the machines and this may be used in making 'reformed ham', as can mechanically recovered or mechanically deboned meat. The process is the same as that for 'formed ham' but the ingredients of 'reformed ham' are even cheaper.

Few of the 246 children's diaries in the CA study mentioned fresh fruit and vegetables; most described diets high in fat, sugars and salt and lacking many vital nutrients. The nutritionist who analysed them found many were low in iron, zinc, folate, vitamins A and C and calcium. The school meals, which were for many children the main meal of the day, read like fast food menus, with pizza, chicken nuggets and fishcakes being the most popular main courses, and chips, cakes and biscuits coming with everything.

Children today also consume thirty times the amount of soft drinks and twenty-five times the amount of confectionery they did in 1950. Overall consumption of soft drinks has doubled in the last twelve years, the period between the most recent official National Diet and Nutrition Surveys.

The food industry argues that parents decide what their children eat and are responsible for their diets. It says that if they are not providing balanced ones, it is a question of education.

But the children in the CA survey are not peculiar, nor are their parents negligent. For most parents it has become a struggle to make sure their children eat well. Although our food in the West is more plentiful and varied than ever before, anxiety about what we eat has probably never been higher.

How did we become so removed from good food? Why, if the experts' advice is now so clear, have governments done so little to ensure that we eat what we need for health?

Part of the explanation is certainly cultural. Since the war, working hours have lengthened, more women have gone out to work, and family structures have changed. As societies in the West have become more affluent, the proportion of income spent on what we eat has declined. We have chosen to spend our new wealth not on better-quality food but on other pleasures. The time we give to food has also declined dramatically. In the 1930s we spent over three hours preparing food each day. By the 1970s that had dropped to one hour. Today we spend on average less than fifteen minutes a day cooking. As individual gratification has taken over from the communal, the home-cooked family meal has become an endangered species.

Our choice of food is also powerfully influenced by advertising. The food industry spends over £450 million a year advertising in the UK, and about three quarters of that is spent on marketing to children. Coca-Cola spent £23 million, Walker's crisps £16.5 million and Müller pot desserts £13.5 million on advertising in this country in 2001–2.

The big four categories of food advertised are sugary breakfast cereals, confectionery, soft drinks, and savoury snacks such as crisps. Advertising of fast-food brands comes in fifth but is catching up. The figures are hard to come by, but *The Atlas of Food* records that the world's biggest food advertisers in 1999 were Nestlé, Coca-Cola, McDonald's, Mars, Pepsi, Danone and Kellogg's.

The foods advertised are not exactly the sum of what is recommended for a healthy diet. Exposure to this manipulation of our appetites starts young; the techniques used have become increasingly sophisticated.

TV Dinners, a survey by Sustain in 2001, found that more than half of the adverts shown during children's television are for food and drinks products, and of these 99 per cent are for what is described as junk food, that is, processed food high in fat and/or sugar.

Marketing experts have worked out ways to engage with children from a very early age using psychological techniques. Studies have shown that children do not discriminate between television programmes and adverts until sometime between the ages of four and seven. They don't recognize bias until the age of eight. But jingles, graphic symbols and repetition are used to catch their attention.

Animated characters children recognize are used to endorse products; sporting heroes are used to associate products with social acceptance; and repeat purchases are encouraged with collectable free toys. A psychologist who has led several public health education campaigns for the Department of Health, Dr Aric Sigman, has explored how marketing is designed to exploit children's basic needs. He identifies four 'vulnerabilities that advertisers aim for': the need for peer group acceptance, the need for stimulation, the need for role models and the need for nurture and protection. He says that advertising disrupts the normal process of child-rearing, subverting a child's needs when they are most vulnerable and pliable. Many advertisements make appeals to pester power, that phenomenon that is most subversive of parental control.

In its report on the role of food advertising, *Broadcasting Bad Health*, the independent campaign group the Food Commission has charted how soft drinks companies focus their attention on the teenage market. It highlights methods of reaching children that slip under the radar of parents – the internet and text messaging. They sponsor music and pay for links with the most popular pop singers, sports celebrities and film stars.

The brilliance of the techniques is not in any doubt. The team that marketed the launch of Kellogg's Real Fruit Winders described some of them in detail in their submission to the Institute of Practitioners in Advertising's Advertising Effectiveness Awards in 2002. 'Communications worked by getting on to kids' radars . . . by creating the desired sense of "cool" . . . we went to toy fairs, we studied the success of Pokemon . . . we would have to give kids ownership of the brand and not let Mum in on the act . . .' To do this, the advertisers created the world of the Chewchat gang, whose pranks centred round winding up terrified fruit and squishing it into Real Fruit Winders. They invented a language to 'spread the word about the brand virally' and placed it on websites children use to get music news and celebrity gossip. Measured by acceptance among young people, and volume of sales, the campaign was a huge success. Mothers were also impressed by the 'fruit' message, seeing these products as healthier treats than sweets.

When children are receiving this sort of subliminal education, it can be very hard for parents to counter it. Schools are also being used increasingly to win endorsement for products. Vending machines and tuck shops selling snacks, sweets and sugary drinks have become a source of much-needed income.

Cadbury's was severely criticized in 2003 for its marketing campaign aimed at children in schools. (Walker's crisps had been there before it with a school scheme to swap crisp packets for books.) Like most of the food industry, Cadbury's argues that the crisis of obesity is more to do with the fact that children today are less active than they used to be than with what they eat. It launched a £9 million marketing drive to get children to exchange chocolate wrappers for free school sports equipment and persuaded the UK Sports Minister, Richard Caborn, to give his endorsement to the scheme, which it said would help tackle obesity.

But the Food Commission calculated that to earn one netball worth about £5, primary schoolchildren would have to spend nearly £40 on chocolate and consume more than 20,000 calories. A ten-year-old child eating enough chocolate to earn a basketball through the scheme would need to play basketball for ninety hours to burn off the calories consumed. A junior basketball team would have to play twenty-seven full-length games to burn off the calories. Cadbury's defended the promotion, which it said was 'a genuine attempt . . . to encourage greater physical activity among young people', inactivity being 'the greatest cause of obesity among young people'. The FSA subsequently said that it had not been consulted about the Sports Minister's endorsement of the scheme, but had it been, it would have advised against what it deemed to be conflicting messages.

Growing pressure to ban or at least control much more tightly food advertising to children is being fiercely resisted by the industry. It argues that advertising encourages brand loyalty, not consumption in itself. To settle the issue, the FSA commissioned a comprehensive review of research on the effects of advertising food to children from Professor Gerard Hastings of the University of Strathclyde. His team found that not only did advertising influence what food children choose but also what they feel about it. 'The debate should now shift to what action is needed,' Professor Hastings concluded.

The big guns from the manufacturers in these sectors were summoned before the House of Commons health select committee inquiry on obesity to account for themselves at the end of 2003. Top executives from McDonald's, PepsiCo (which owns the Walker's brand as well as Pepsi), Kellogg's and Cadbury Schweppes were grilled by MPs in a room packed with journalists, campaigners and industry representatives.

It was hard to ignore the parallels with the tobacco industry. The committee's chairman, David Hinchliffe MP, had been a leading political figure in the fight to ban cigarette advertising. On the other side, the food industry was marshalling many of the sort of arguments used by the tobacco lobby. Obesity would not be tackled by restricting freedom of choice. Its advertising did not increase sales which were really 'pretty flat' but simply encouraged brand loyalty. The scientific evidence was unclear. Education about good diet and greater physical activity – calories in, calories out – were more important than controls on the industry. Tim Mobsby, President of Kellogg's Europe, told the committee for example that he had not seen anything that clearly demonstrated that there is a link between sugar and obesity and that he would be quite happy if children ate his Coco Pops most days of the week. There are no such things as bad foods, only bad diets, the companies agreed.

But Andrew Cosslett, the managing director of confectionery for Cadbury Schweppes in Europe, the Middle East and Africa, unintentionally made the campaigners' own point while trying to defend his chocolate. He had bought a low-fat yoghurt thinking it would be healthy, he said, and had taken it home, only to find to his amazement, when he examined the label, that it contained more calories than a large Crunchie bar. 'Yoghurt, you would assume, has a certain health profile and when you see a low-fat yoghurt with a clear statement drawing attention to the fact that it is low-fat, you would be doubly convinced and it would reinforce your instinct that this is a good food product. It is only when you get it home and examine the calories that you find it has two hundred-plus calories in it, which was a surprise to me and I have been in the food industry for a long time.' In fact, Mr Cosslett went so far as to say, there are people being deluded on a daily basis about what they are buying.

To be fair, in a free market, and in the absence of tighter controls, the advertising and manufacturing industries are only doing what industries do, selling themselves as hard and effectively as possible. The debate about the advertising really needs to address the role of the public realm.

Just as the emergence of oligopolies and dominant powers in retailing and manufacturing calls into question what sort of institutions we want to regulate them and how far, so action to improve the quality of our food needs to redefine political boundaries.

But government today is paralysed by fear of being accused of nanny statism. Professor James traces much of the problem today back to the late 1970s. Until then the food standards of many foods were tightly regulated. But many of the standards were outdated – specifying, for example, that ice cream had to contain a certain percentage of fat. Power blocs built around the old farming lobbies maintained them. The new mood of consumerism that swept in with Mrs Thatcher demanded they should be abolished and replaced by free choice. So food standards were deregulated. Manufacturers were allowed to make what they liked so long as it was microbiologically safe and so long as it was labelled so that consumers could make that choice. 'Choice', the

Conservative mantra of the 1980s and 1990s, is still the prevailing philosophy in food.

The trouble with this notion is that choice is so often illusory. Children bombarded with advertising and left with a vending machine do not make informed choices. Nor do adults who practically need a PhD to decipher food labels.

Lacking a vision of how public health might look in a global free market, government is left with divided responsibilities. The Department of Culture, Media and Sport must decide whether food advertising should be restricted; the Department of Health is supposed to take care of nutrition but has until recent stirrings been focused more on sickness than health; the Department of Environment, Food and Rural Affairs is supposed to look after the food supply chain and negotiate reform of subsidy regimes.

The FSA was set up in 2000 after the BSE crisis, in recognition of the need for an independent body to protect public interest in food. Its objectives are to 'reduce foodborne illness, help people eat more healthily, promote honest and informative labelling, promote best practice within the food industry, and improve enforcement of food law'. An analysis of its accounts for 2003 by Professor Tim Lang shows that it spent about 60 per cent of its budget on food safety and less than 1 per cent on nutrition and the quality of diet. The political ideology is stuck on consumer choice and labelling, and not surprisingly, the FSA line has tended to be the same (see Chapter 1). A new European FSA is being set up, but an outline of its responsibilities by consumer protection commissioner David Byrne made clear that safety, hygiene, labelling and new technologies are the priorities.

Who will concern themselves with whether we are sold junk? We must look to ourselves. It will take a coalition of interests in which the public, as in previous centuries, takes the lead. Change will come when ordinary people, realizing that our current food system is environmentally, ethically and even biologically unsustainable, exert their buying power and finally say, 'Enough is enough.'

Afterword

So much of the current food system needs the sort of reform only political action can address that it is easy to feel helpless as individuals. But governments are more likely to act if they face pressure, and pressure for change is growing. An immediate shopping-list for governments has broader support than ever before from a whole range of interest groups covering health, environment, development and both consumer and labour rights. What is in that first shopping-list?

Changes to subsidy regimes to stop supporting the sort of food that is bad for us, and to stop undermining farmers in developing countries at taxpayers' expense. Proper enforcement of labour regulations and registration of gangmasters so that cut-price wages and exploitation are brought under control. Tighter competition policy at local, national, European and international level, which recognizes and deals with the adverse effects of concentrations of power. A ban on predatory pricing. Statutory codes of practice to prevent the abuse of buying power. A tax on air fuel to end the hidden subsidy on this most polluting form of freight. Tighter planning policies that really enforce the aims already laid down by government: preserving the vitality of town centres where they survive, or regenerating them where they are under threat. Curbs on advertising to children and on the infiltration of market forces into schools.

It is possible to send powerful signals to government, manufacturers and retailers by changing the way we shop. Thousands of small rebellions by consumers in revolt can force change.

That consumer power can make a difference became clear when supermarkets agreed a moratorium on the use of genetically modified foods in the products they sold. Despite industry pres-

sure to introduce GMOs, most ordinary people remained unconvinced that any benefits, which would largely accrue to the
companies that owned the patents and produced the pesticides,
outweighed the potential risks. True, by early 2004 the industry
and government were planning a new assault to wear down
public opposition. But with a clear lack of public demand,
retailers had not only said they would not stock the products but
had also invested thousands of pounds in keeping supply streams
separate. Such clear messages from consumers can and do have
an impact.

I first started writing about food because I love cooking and I
love eating. I have probably always spent more than the average
as a proportion of my income on food. But now I also shop very
differently to the way I did even a couple of years ago. It requires
time and a change of habits, and it is not without its surreal
moments, but I also enjoy it.

It has involved making choices: choices about how important
food is to me and therefore how much of my time and money I
am prepared to devote to it rather than to other things. As we
have become more affluent as a society overall, the average
proportion of money we spend on food has fallen dramatically
from about one third of our income to just 10 per cent, and the
amount of time we spend cooking it and sitting down together
to enjoy eating it has reduced almost to vanishing point. So for
many of us these are choices, albeit unconscious ones.

I am acutely conscious that not everyone has the luxury of
choice. When people who care about the quality of our diet
discuss what needs to change, they frequently get in a tangle over
cheap food. The reason is that the poorest fifth of the population
already spends a much higher proportion of its income, about a
third, on food than the more affluent. What right has anyone to
suggest that food should be more expensive for them? The answer
to this is twofold. First, it is precisely those on low incomes that
the current 'cheap food' policy hits hardest: it is the low-paid
who lose their jobs when global 'just-in-time' sourcing finds

cheaper labour elsewhere; it is the poorest who suffer the most from diet-related diseases; it is the least affluent who have least access to good shops; it is the recipients of gangmasters' semi-slave wages who are most marginalized and go hungry; and it is the smaller farmers who are struggling most to earn a living. Secondly, if what we are really saying is that people on low incomes cannot afford good food, the answer is not that food needs to be cheaper but that political action is necessary to make sure they can afford it.

But I also question how much improving the quality of our food is dependent on higher prices. Paying more for the raw materials of a good diet does not necessarily mean that the food we eat at the end of the chain needs to be more expensive. It is how the money is distributed within that chain that can make so much difference.

One of the people I met on my trip to Highgrove was Jeanette Orrey, a dinner lady at a village school in Nottinghamshire. She has since become something of a celebrity, although she always says she doesn't quite know what the fuss is about, since she's just following common sense. Unlike most contracted caterers who allocate 35p or less to ingredients for a school lunch, Jeanette spends half as much again but still manages to charge her pupils the same price. The secret, she says, involves two things: cutting out the middle men who were taking so much of the money, and using her buying power to source good-quality food from local producers. Rather than dishing up the centrally prepared and generally highly processed foods she was required to serve when school meals were deregulated and put out to tender, she now cooks fresh food herself from scratch and knows exactly where it comes from.

Hundreds of small producers, markets and independent shops elsewhere are already leading a revival in good food. Some of them are popping up in the most unlikely places, such as the Tebay motorway service station on the M6, where local farmers and bakers supply delicious, well-made fast food for travellers.

Apart from making time to cook and eat regularly with family and friends, what can you do to make a difference? One of my aims in this book has been to show that all the different concerns about food connect. The things that turn out to be best for sustainable development in poor countries turn out to be the best things to protect the environment. The things that best look after other people's rights turn out to be the best for our own health. As it happens, they actually taste better too. If only we can move beyond the oversimplistic definitions of cheap food, we can change the current system.

In practical terms, what this means is shifting shopping patterns to follow three main principles: local, seasonal and direct. How you exercise your buying power will depend on how and where you live. Urban commuters will be short of time but will generally have access to a range of specialist delicatessens or ethnic shops selling fresh food outside the network of mainstream supermarket distribution. Those in rural areas may be within reach of more producers from whom they can buy direct. My choices are adjusted to my personal circumstances – I have three young children and at various periods am a full-time and part-time worker who alternates the cooking and shopping with a partner. I describe how I have changed my shopping habits as an example only. The Appendix (page 237) lists some of the directories that tell you where to find independent shops and markets near you, and how to join the co-ops and other food projects that serve areas which have become food deserts.

As well as going for local, seasonal and direct, I try to buy organic where possible, though not exclusively. This is partly because, despite the sceptics, I believe that as our knowledge grows, organic farming will be shown to be better for our health. It is also because, from my experience, those who farm organically are more concerned with a whole raft of other things – from looking after wildlife to keeping rural economies alive to bothering about the conditions in which people work. When the gangmaster Zad Padda (see Chapter 2) took me to a packhouse to explain his system of checks and training for labour, it was an organic packhouse. To win certification for manufactured food from the organic farmers' organization, the Soil Association, you must avoid hydrogenated fat and modified starch. As new concerns about the way we process food gain prominence, it usually turns out that organic standards have already addressed them. I say organic farmers *on the whole* are more concerned with these issues, because as supermarkets have joined the organic bandwagon, part of this market is also becoming industrialized, with organic food being transported vast distances or produced alongside conventional intensive crops as a mere exercise in 'added value'.

Therefore, I buy most of my organic fresh food not from the supermarkets but through a weekly box scheme, with direct links to farmers. The scheme guarantees that half the price of the food goes back to the producer, and that none of its fruit and vegetables are air-freighted. Nearly three quarters of its fresh produce is British. I can either have a box delivered to my house when the company is in my area or pick up a bag of seasonal fruit and vegetables from my local school, which acts as a delivery point (other box schemes use delivery points such as local shops for those who are out at work all day). In return, the company, Abel and Cole, donates a percentage of the profits – about a quarter of the retail value – to the Parent-Teacher Association. It is now working with over thirty schools in London in this way, many of them in deprived areas.

The hair-shirt element of organic box schemes – muddy, tired vegetables; lack of choice; erratic deliveries – is now largely a thing of the past. Avoiding air-freight does not mean you cannot import anything – bananas, mangoes and avocados, for example, are shipped, a much less environmentally damaging form of transport. And of course we can continue to enjoy fruits and vegetables from Europe, although we might want to ask a few more questions about how they are produced. We are not in any case talking about prohibition here, but about tilting the balance back to what is sustainable. If I want to buy the cheapest, which is considerably less than what it would cost at the supermarket, I let the company choose the mix in my box from the best value in season; but if I want something specific, I can order it online or by phone. Yes, it's still muddy and needs washing, but then it arrives conveniently on the doorstep without me having to go out to shop, which saves time.

When I see cosmetic perfection, it sets alarm bells ringing. How many chemicals or how much waste was needed to achieve it? Who was paid how little to wash and grade for me? How much extra am I paying for the dubious advantage of uniformity? Without current levels of grade-outs, our food would be cheaper. Highgrove, for example, has just started a scheme to sell its organic grade-outs, the undersized carrots rejected by the supermarkets even though they happen to be the sweetest, to local schools at the same price as conventionally farmed vegetables. It also runs a box delivery scheme to those who are lucky enough to live nearby. If I'm honest, my children, although entertained by misshapen produce, are not convinced of the beauty of blemishes. But changing our attitudes to appearance, so recently acquired, will make a huge difference.

I also follow the seasons more. This means there are lean periods: not, as I had imagined, in the winter, when there are dozens of different root vegetables to enjoy, but in May, when local winter crops are finished and stores have declined but spring and summer crops are not ready. It was a revelation to discover that local carrots can be available either from the ground or from store from September until May, and that English apples are available from September until early April.

A bigger surprise was realizing how narrow our diet had become since we started to shop mainly at supermarkets. Despite the huge range on offer and all our interest in food, we had fallen into fixed patterns built around what the children would eat. It feels no loss to forgo tasteless out-of-season strawberries flown halfway round the world, but green beans are harder to do without, so we still buy those from the shops. We now find ways of using vegetables we had almost stopped buying – cabbage, celeriac, artichokes, chard, beets. We eat a lot of soup. And we wash our own lettuce.

There are times when I have chosen local over organic – buying local apples delivered to local shops in Herefordshire, for example – since if there is no local agriculture left because we have failed to support it, there is no prospect of switching to ways of farming that are sustainable in the long term. There are many farmers around the country who still farm in an extensive as opposed to intensive way, on mixed farms that care for the land but have not managed to attain organic status. Keeping alive alternative systems of distribution is one of the most important things individuals can do in the face of ever-growing retail concentration. That, and ensuring farmers get a fairer share from our shopping so they can survive.

Making use of local independent shops is also a priority. Living in inner London, this is relatively easy (although there was a period when our local high street appeared to be in terminal decline) and I live within walking distance of an excellent butcher. Buying good meat from a reputable butcher is more expensive than from the supermarket, but I'd rather eat well-reared meat occasionally than cheap, factory-farmed livestock regularly. I have adjusted the way I think of meat and eat it less frequently. (And to those who argue that we must have genetically modified crops to feed the world's poor, it is worth pointing out that there is enough grain to feed the world if we don't feed a large proportion of it to animals first.)

While the organic movement has been vital in raising awareness of our meat's provenance, there are farmers producing outstanding meat without organic certification – perhaps their local organically certified abattoir has closed down, or they may have trouble getting enough organically certified feed. I happily choose grass-fed, extensively reared beef and lamb from producers the butcher knows.

As well as using the local butcher, I order direct from an organic farm, clubbing together with others nearby to spread the cost of delivery. Sheepdrove Farm, on the Berkshire downs, has its own abattoir, so animals are not transported long distances. Its chickens are allowed to forage and are reared for nearly twice as long as intensively fed ones: they actually taste of something; they are a luxury. I also like my meat to be properly hung so that its flavour develops along with its texture, rather than have it zapped with thousands of volts of electricity to tenderize it instantly, as happens in red-meat factories. But long hanging takes time and costs money, so if I want cheap meat I buy the cuts that have become just a memory to those dependent on supermarkets' meat shelves – Sheepdrove's mutton mince, for example. Most of Britain's mutton – that is, meat from ewes once they have finished lambing – goes to the French and Italians, who love to import our inexpensive rejects, but Sheepdrove is helping to revive it locally. These cheap cuts need long slow cooking and so they take time, though once you have done the initial cooking they can be left alone in the oven for several hours. I buy organic dairy products and eggs too, because organic producers' standards of animal welfare are high and I know these farmers will not have needed routine antibiotics.

The quality of my staples has become very important to me. The Lighthouse Bakery (Chapter 4) is my nearest proper bread shop. The bread is not certified organic but its flour is the best, coming from Shipton Mill. Not everyone is lucky enough to have such a good baker on hand, but the explosion in sales of breadmaking machines in the last couple of years suggests that people are finding other ways to make their small rebellions.

The Lighthouse Bakery is in the middle of a street market that nearly died a few years ago but was kept going by a few local campaigners. After shopping there I top up with other produce from the market: an Italian family runs a fish stall several times a week, driving up early in the morning from Cornwall with the day's local catch.

Fish represents a dilemma that I have not been able to cover here. I love it and it is fantastically good for you. But with many species under threat because of overfishing, the Marine Conservation Society (MCS) has compiled a list of twenty species to avoid. Fish farming, meanwhile, has been responsible for serious environmental degradation. Some of the British fish-farming industry has tried to clean up its act recently, but you cannot get round the basic problem that it takes 3–4kg of wild fish to make 1kg of farmed fish. However, the MCS has also published a list of twenty-five species you can eat with a clearer conscience (see page 238). Again, nothing beats a good independent fishmonger to tell you where your fish comes from and how it was caught. Some of the fishing communities in Cornwall are leading a movement in sustainable fishing, using lines and nets that conserve stocks, and landing their catch each day rather than freezing their fish during long trawls at sea. This is what our market stall offers, and indeed it is often the stallholders in old markets that keep such local traditions alive and can advise on how best to cook what is on offer. *The Good Fish Guide* published by the MCS provides excellent practical information.

I buy Fairtrade products where I can because they guarantee a decent income to the farmers who grow the raw materials. They may, as the coffee exporter in Uganda said, be a drop on a hot stone, but that is a reason to buy more, not less: radical social movements often have small beginnings. But I resent the fact that supermarkets see Fairtrade products as a way of increasing their margins and take a higher proportion of the higher price they command than they do from other goods. So whenever I can I buy my Fairtrade from alternative sources, such as specialist shops, and from the supermarket only when I can't. Garstang, in Lancashire, has taken it much further, and has declared itself a Fairtrade town, as John Vidal reported in the *Guardian*. Its schools, local council, churches, garage, hairdressers, and ninety of its 100 businesses all sell, use or actively promote Fairtrade products. More than eighty other towns and cities have applied to become Fairtrade communities too.

How often do I shop at supermarkets? I am not anti-supermarket, just against the consequences of their overweaning dominance. But it is also true that I buy less and less of my fresh food at the supermarket. Instead, I shop more often than I used to, and more often on foot than before. Some of the things I buy are much more expensive than previously, but some are cheaper and I waste less. Overall, I spend what I have always spent.

What about processed foods? You don't have to be puritanical about this. Nobody is suggesting that occasional fast food or a highly processed meal is going to kill you, or that you should never use processed foods. It's just that when you understand more about how these things are produced and the consequences of their production, they lose their attraction. The Food Commission also provides a useful rule of thumb: the more highly processed a food, the poorer its nutrition is likely to be. If there are things on the label you don't recognize, put it back on the shelf. But again, it involves making choices about how much time you are prepared to give food.

Whenever I want to be reminded of the pleasure of good food, I pop out to the tiny North Street Deli that opened recently near my house. Madalena Bonino, the Italian chef who runs it, will give me a new cheese to try – a meltingly ripe yet fresh soft cheese like the Lo Straccino I'd never heard of, perhaps – or her prize salami, a finocchio made of pork and fennel by a small producer in Tuscany. Like most Italians, she is passionate about what she sells and we can talk for hours. If I'm in a rush and need to provide an instant meal, I'll buy a pot of her fresh neapolitan tomato sauce, which is the same price as the own-brand stuff from the big retailers. Madalena makes hers in her own kitchen with nothing but tomatoes, carrots, celery, onions, garlic, olive oil and seasoning, using the ingredients I would use if I had time but with rather more skill and a better blender. My children, who refuse to eat celery, wolf it down unaware that anything green has been slipped past their guard. Nathan Middlemass, her partner, is a former maître d' and has a miraculous memory for names and faces, so that all their customers get to know each other. This is where people come in on their way home for really handmade ready meals.

The North Street Deli is making a decent profit but, as Madalena points out, most of the money she spends goes into the food. The shop's reputation is growing by word of mouth, not as the result of expensive marketing. Many of its suppliers are local, like the baker who is tucked away on a grim industrial estate nearby but makes his artisan sourdough from a mother culture that he has kept going for three years; others are farmers Madalena knows in Italy who supply the shop direct, so I am not paying for any vast distribution and packaging systems, just for their hard work and the producers' costs. It's a small shop in an unlikely place. If you weren't looking, you might not notice it. However, there are still such places around the country and good directories to help you find them (see Appendix, page 237).

The Italians have their own, very characteristic, grassroots rebellion – the slow food movement, which has been anything but slow to spread. It was founded by Carlo Petrini as a backlash against fast food and the destruction of local economies. It has caught on because it is not about denial but about celebrating food. But as Petrini says, you have to slow down enough to realize. While we need governments to take action, we also have to make this cultural shift ourselves. Food is one of life's great pleasures. Shopping for it, preparing it and eating it has bound people together for centuries. It is in eating together that we are socialized. In the end, it's about what kind of society we want.

Appendix: Where to Find Out More

If you want to find out more about local shops and alternative distribution systems in your area, there are some excellent books that provide directories. But it is also worth remembering that there will be places and organizations near you that do not make it into national guides. They may be too small to cope with large orders. They often defy categorization – which is what makes them attractive. Their presence is often spread by word of mouth. There are also probably nearly as many ways of running food co-ops as there are food co-ops. Some may consist of just a small group of friends who place the orders together. You need to ask around and seek out the most vibrant sources of good food near you. The list below makes no pretence to be anything other than a starting point.

The *Guardian*'s food series, The Way We Eat Now, published in May 2003, included a guide to the best places to find information about good organic box schemes, plus lists of bakers, butchers and other independent shops; food co-ops; and a list of British fruits and vegetables in season. Some of it is archived at www.guardian.co.uk/food/focus/part3.

The Soil Association, Bristol House, 40–56 Victoria Street, Bristol BS1 6BY, 0117 929 0661, www.soilassociation.org, provides information on organic producers and delivery schemes.

Lynda Brown's *New Shopper's Guide to Organic Food* (Fourth Estate, 2002) is a comprehensive and authoritative guide to organic producers, shops and delivery services.

The Organic Directory, edited by Clive Litchfield (Green Books with the Soil Association, 2003), is another useful source of listings.

Henrietta Green's *Food Lovers' Guide to Britain* is now sadly out of print, but lives on at her website www.foodloversbritain.com and in her food lovers' fairs around the country, which bring together many of the best craft producers and small farmers. See also Henrietta Green's *Farmers' Market Cookbook* (Kyle Cathie, 2001).

Rick Stein's *Food Heroes* (BBC Books, 2002) has an embryonic directory of good shops and producers.

Food from Britain publishes a guide to over 2,000 regional food and drink producers at www.regionalfoodanddrink.co.uk.

Most local tourist boards produce leaflets and guides to local farmers, markets and producers in their areas.

The National Farmers' Union keeps a directory of farmers' markets around the country (www.nfu.org.uk), or you can send an s.a.e. to the National Association of Farmers' Markets, South Vaults, Green Park Station, Green Park Road, Bath, BA1 1JS (www.farmers markets.net).

www.organicbutchers.co.uk produces a directory of organic meat producers and butchers around the country.

The Good Fish Guide published by the Marine Conservation Society lists species of fish which are endangered and so are best avoided, together with a list of ones that you can eat with a clearer conscience. www.mcsuk.org.

www.fairtradeonline.com is the online shop set up by Oxfam with Traidcraft and Yahoo! to sell a large range of Fairtrade foods direct, with nationwide delivery.

To find a co-op near you, try Sustain's *Food Poverty Project*, which lists nearly 300 organizations in its database, www.sustainweb.org (tel.: 0207 837 1228). The Soil Association, see above, has a website with information on co-ops (www.localfoodworks.org). Most towns and counties have Co-operative Development Agencies, which can help you set up a food co-op or find one that already works in your area. Ask at your local library.

Food Magazine, published by the Food Commission, provides wonderful insights into the politics and adulteration of food (www.food comm.org.uk).

RECOMMENDED READING

Detailed bibliographical notes for sources I have quoted are found in the Notes and References section (pages 241–65), so the following list of recommended reading is more an eclectic selection of books for the general reader who wants to find out more.

Rachel Carson, *Silent Spring* (Penguin, 1965); the classic critique of modern industrial farming and its effects.

Greg Critser, *Fat Land* (Penguin, 2003); the political and economic forces that shaped America's obesity crisis.

Elizabeth David, *English Bread and Yeast Cookery* (Penguin, 1977); the original polemic against factory bread.

Felipe Fernandez-Armesto, *Food: A History* (Macmillan, 2001); an erudite and witty account of the cultural significance of food.

Dorothy Hartley, *Food in England* (McDonald and Co., 1954); a classic history of English cooking and domestic life.

Graham Harvey, *The Killing of the Countryside* (Vintage, 1998); a lyrical description of the devastation of the British countryside caused by misguided subsidies.

Patrick Herman and Richard Kuper, *Food for Thought* (Pluto Press, 2002); the radical French farmers' union, the Confédération Paysanne, and their take on agribusiness.

Matthew Hilton, *Consumerism in Twentieth-century Britain* (Cambridge University Press, 2003); a history of consumerism as a social and political movement.

Miriam Jacobs and Barbara Dinham, *Silent Invaders* (Zed Books, 2003); an account of the impact of pesticides on women's livelihoods and health.

Joy Larkcom, *Grow Your Own Vegetables* (Frances Lincoln, 2002); a practical guide to growing vegetables in even the smallest garden from one of the gardening greats.

Mark Lynas, *Hide Tide: News from a Warming World* (Flamingo, 2004).

Erik Millstone, *Food Additives* (Penguin, 1986); an authoritative academic guide to food additives and adulteration.

Erik Millstone and Tim Lang, *The Atlas of Food* (Earthscan, 2003); a sourcebook of global food and health with full-colour graphics.

George Monbiot, *Captive State* (Macmillan, 2000); leading Green on the corporate takeover of Britain.

Marion Nestle, *Food Politics* (University of California Press, 2002) and *Safe Food* (University of California Press, 2003); devastating accounts from a leading American academic of the food industry's attempts to corrupt public health policy in the USA.

Andrew O'Hagan, *The End of British Farming* (Profile/London Review of Books, 2001); a novelist's update on William Cobbett.

Craig Sams, *The Little Food Book* (Alastair Sawday Publishing, 2003); a pithy critique of all that's wrong with the food system.

Eric Schlosser, *Fast Food Nation* (Penguin, 2003); the best-selling exposé of the impact of American fast food on the world.

Amartya Sen, *Development as Freedom* (Oxford University Press, 1999); the classic on development issues.

Joseph Stiglitz, *Globalization and its Discontents* (Penguin, 2003); the former chief economist at the World Bank explains what's wrong with World Bank policy.

Geoff Tansey and Tony Worsley, *The Food System* (Earthscan, 1995); a brilliant overview of the modern food system.

Colin Tudge, *So Shall We Reap* (Allen Lane, 2003); a scientist's philosophical plea for enlightened agriculture that could feed the world.

Bill Vorley, *Food Inc.* (UK Food Group, 2003); a detailed account of corporate concentration from farm to consumer.

Caroline Walker and Geoffrey Cannon, *The Food Scandal* (Century, 1984); an early warning on what was wrong with the British diet and food industry attempts to block government action.

Notes and References

CHAPTER 1: CHICKEN

The work for much of this chapter was carried out in my role as a special correspondent for the *Guardian*. I am grateful to the editors and legal team at the paper who gave me great support, in particular Ian Katz, Harriet Sherwood and Siobhain Butterworth. David Leigh guided me during the investigation at Lloyd Maunder, which was published on 6 December 2001. Rob Evans helped gain disclosures under the European open government code.

At *Panorama*, I should like to thank Betsan Powys, Howard Bradburn and Andy Bell.

Several sources acted as whistleblowers at considerable personal risk. Their number grew as my investigations went on and I would like to thank them anonymously. Names of workers have been changed to protect them.

Several people gave me the benefit of their detailed knowledge: John Sandford of Hull Trading Standards on the water in chicken scandal; Richard Young on antibiotic use in farming; Sue Sonnex, Lewis Coates and Steve Haslam on the recycling of condemned meat; Peter Bradnock of the British Poultry Council and Peter King of the National Farmers' Union on the chicken industry.

p. 2   *Half of the chicken on sale in UK supermarkets is contaminated with campylobacter*: Food Standards Agency, UK-wide survey of salmonella and campylobacter contamination of fresh and frozen chicken on retail sale, February 2003 (www.foodstandards.gov.uk).

p. 11   *The owner of Denby Poultry, Peter Roberts: Guardian*, 30 August 2003.

p. 11   *Meat from the companies involved in the recycling*: FSA food hazard warning, 11 April 2001, and statement, 24 April 2001.

p. 14   *When Leicester Trading Standards received a complaint*: Leicestershire County Council Trading Standards, Chicken nuggets complaint prompts investigation, January 2002.

p. 16   *The FSA announced the results of the tests*: FSA, press release, Survey uncovers added water in restaurant and takeaway chicken, 11 December 2001.

p. 18   *The baton had passed to Ireland*: Food Safety Authority (Ireland), press release, Food Safety Authority finds some imported chicken fillets in breach of food labelling laws, 21 May 2002.

p. 19   *The English FSA's public response*: FSA, letter to the *Guardian*, 10 July 2002, from David Statham, director of enforcement.

p. 19   *They caught a Dutch additive supplier and a German protein manufacturer*: BBC *Panorama*, The Chicken Run, 22 May 2003.

p. 20   *At first the FSA maintained the line that it was a labelling issue*: FSA water in chicken update, 21 May 2003; F. Lawrence, Move to halt tainted chicken, the *Guardian*, 20 June 2003.

p. 20   *A chicken farmer, who may also have invested £1 million or more in chicken units*: personal communications with the National Farmers' Union and chicken processors.

p. 21   *The modern broiler chicken*: Sustain, *Food Facts*, No. 9: Fowl Deeds, 1999 (www.sustainweb.org); RSPCA, Behind closed doors – the truth about chicken bred for meat, 2002 (www.rspca.org.uk); Compassion in World Farming, *Chicken, How Come It's So Cheap?* and *The Detrimental Impacts of Industrial Animal Agriculture* (www.ciwf.co.uk); Farm Animal Welfare Council, *Interim Report on the Animal Welfare Implications of Farm Assurance Schemes* (Defra, 2001).

p. 22   *In fact a survey conducted by Compassion in World Farming*: CIWF, *Supermarkets and Farm Animal Welfare*, 2001.

p. 23   *A study in 1992 by the University of Bristol*: S. Kestin *et al.*, Prevalence of leg weaknesses in broiler chickens and its relationship with genotype, *Veterinary Record* (1992, 131, 190–9).

p. 24   *A 1996* Which? *survey of chicken on sale in leading supermarkets*: How safe is chicken?, *Which?*, October 1996.

p. 24   *In 1999 the government's Advisory Committee on the Microbiological Safety of Food (ACMSF) said*: ACMSF, *Report on Microbial Antibiotic*

Resistance in Relation to Food Safety (The Stationery Office, 1999); R. Young *et al.*, *The Use and Misuse of Antibiotics in UK Agriculture* (The Soil Association, 1999).

p. 25   *But by 2003 it had become clear that one in five producers*: J. Meikle, the *Guardian*, 27 May and 6 June 2003.

p. 27   *The UK poultry industry escaped*: World Health Organization, press release, 23 January 2004; Avian influenza, the threat looms, the *Lancet* (24 January 2004, 363, pp. 257ff).

CHAPTER 2: SALAD

The information in this chapter has come from dozens of interviews with individual workers, with government and police officers, and with employers, most of whom cannot be identified. Some fear for their contracts or jobs, others for their safety. Most names have been changed. I am grateful for the many hours these people gave to explaining the system to me.

For information about the UK, I am able to thank publicly: Don Pollard of the T&G union; David Jackson and other officials from Operation Gangmaster; and Nuno Guerreiro of the Portuguese Workers' Association.

For explanation of the issues surrounding pesticides, I am grateful to David Buffin and Barbara Dinham of the Pesticides Action Network UK, Sandra Bell of Friends of the Earth, and Dr Vyvyan Howard of the University of Liverpool.

I am also indebted to many people who helped me on my trip in Spain, some of whom cannot be identified.

Hector Gravina of Amicos de la Terra gave me the benefit of his extensive knowledge and facilitated introductions. Viktor Gonzalves and SEAE, the Spanish ecological society, welcomed me to their conference; Jorge Pajares Miravalles acted as translator in conversations with Manuel Ariza. Nicholas Bell of the European Civic Form provided background studies on migrant labour. Thanks also to Pedro and Cello Garcia of ANSE.

I am particularly grateful to the members of SOC, the Spanish rural workers' union, who introduced me to workers in Almeria and helped with translations: Mari Garcia Bueno, from the head office, and Abel Cader, Gabriel Ataya and Mustafa Ait-Korhci from the Almeria office.

p. 29   *The value of the UK salad vegetable market*: *UK Salad Market Report 2003* (The Greenery Information Service, London W1T 6BT).

p. 29   *Modified-atmosphere packaging (MAP) can now increase the shelf life*: Li Xiong, *Modified Atmosphere Packaging, A Fact Book* (Department of Food Science, Pennsylvania State University, 1999); A. B. Smyth *et al.*, Modified atmosphere packaged cut iceberg lettuce: effect of temperature and CO_2 partial pressure on respiration and quality, A. B. Smyth *et al.*, *Journal of Agricultural Food Chemistry* (1998; 46, 4556–62).

p. 29   *this new invention to prolong shelf life*: M. Serafini *et al.*, Effect of acute ingestion of fresh and stored lettuce on plasma total antioxidant capacity and antioxidant levels in human subjects, *British Journal of Nutrition* (2002; 88, 615–23).

p. 30   *When the results of this trial*: Packing is OK, but not the water: letter from Jon Fielder, Waterwise Technology, to the *Grocer*, 29 March 2003.

'With a chlorine rinse, there is also a long-term possible risk associated with carcinogens'. Mary Ellen Camire, Head of Food Science, University of Maine, USA, quoted in *Progressive Grocer*, May 1998 (www.progressivegrocer.com/news/0511998).

p. 30   *There appears to be good reason for supermarkets selling prewashed salads to worry*: S. K. Sagoo *et al.*, Microbiological study of ready-to-eat salad vegetables from retail establishments uncovers a national outbreak of Salmonellosis, *Journal of Food Protection* (col. 66, no. 3 (2003), 403–9).

S. O'Brien *et al.*, The microbiological status of ready-to-eat fruit and vegetables, discussion paper, ACM/510 of the Advisory Committee on the Microbiological Safety of Food, 2001 (www.good. gov.uk/multimedia/pdfs/acm510.42m.pdf).

PHLS 2000, Outbreaks of Salmonella typhimurium DT 204b infection in England and Wales and elsewhere in Europe, *Communicable Disease Report Weekly* (10:349); and PHLS 2000, Case control study links salad vegetables to national increase in multi-resistant Salmonella typhimurium DT104, *Communicable Disease Report Weekly* (10:333, 336).

p. 34 *Labourers are often needed at very short notice*: Gangmasters, House of Commons, Environment, Food and Rural Affairs Committee, 14th report of session 2002/3 (Stationery Office, tel. 0870 600 5522; http://tso.co.uk/bookshop).

p. 34 *The exceptionally hot weather*: Personal communication, salad growers.

p. 36 *Don Pollard, who did extensive research for the T&G union*: D. Pollard, report of UK survey on gangmaster labour, Rural Agricultural Workers' Trade Group, T&GWU, between 1998 and 2000.

p. 37 *Operation Shark, a pilot investigation into illegal labour*: First reported in the *Guardian*, Food: The Way We Eat Now series: F. Lawrence, The New Landless Labourers, 17 May 2003.

p. 41 *Both supermarkets' representatives and the farmers' union deny*: Gangmasters, House of Commons, Efra committee, as above.

p. 42 *If you want evidence of the impact of supermarkets' price wars on wages*: Is Wal-Mart too powerful? *Business Week*, 6 October 2003 (www.businessweekeurope.com).

New York Times, leader, 15 November, 2003: 'Wal-Mart's prices are about 14 per cent lower because the company is aggressive about squeezing costs, including labour . . .'

p. 51 *Citizens' Advice Bureaux (CABs) around the country*: Memorandum submitted to Efra committee, 25 April 2003.

p. 52 *Although the housing conditions frequently and blatantly flout UK regulations*: Memorandum submitted by Cambridge Housing and Environmental Consultants to Efra committee, 3 June 2003.

p. 52 *One of the local doctors . . .* : Personal communication with Dr Giles Smith, Thetford, and letter to Efra committee, 3 April 2003.

p. 57 *The nitrate problem is not confined to Spain*: J. N. Pretty *et al.*, An assessment of the total external costs of UK agriculture, *Agricultural Systems* (65 (2), 113–36).

p. 57 *Some 55 per cent of the country has recently been designated as 'nitrate vulnerable zones'*: the figure would have been much higher but for intense lobbying from the National Farmers' Union. Water companies estimate that over the next five years UK customers will have to pay £25 a year on their water bills to cover the cost of removing nitrates from drinking water. In the past the utilities have diluted drinking water with high concentrations of nitrates with water that has lower levels to meet safety limits, but now they are finding it increasingly difficult to find uncontaminated supplies. Personal communication, the Environment Agency.

P. Brown, Nitrate pollution raises water bills, the *Guardian*, 11 August 2003.

p. 60   *Lettuce appears on the 'persistent offenders list'*: Avoiding pesticide residues, *Which?* magazine, September 2003 (www.which.co.uk/which). See also The List of Lists, PAN UK catalogue of particularly harmful pesticides (www.pan-uk.org).

p. 61,n.   *The agrochemical industry has seen rapid concentration*: Agrochemical sales worldwide and market share, compiled from *Agrow's Top 20*, 2003 edition, Richmond UK, 2003, by Barbara Dinham, Pesticides Action Network, UK (www.pan-uk.org).

p. 61   *The government's Central Science Laboratory records*: Central Science Laboratory Pesticide Usage Survey, reports 163 and 164, 1999 (www.csl.gov.uk).

p. 62   *The most recent Pesticide Residues Committee monitoring report*: Pesticide Residues Committee, pesticide residues monitoring report, January–March 2002 (www.pesticides.gov.uk/citizen/residues/enforcement/UK Lettuces enforcement 200 1 2.htm).

F. Lawrence, Pest sprays exceed safety levels, the *Guardian*, 17 September 2002.

p. 63   *The FSA's advice is*: FSA, *Pesticides, Your Questions Answered* (www.foodstandards.gov.uk/safereating/pesticides/).

p. 63   *the so-called 'cocktail effect'*: WiGRAMP, Risk Assessment of Mixtures of Pesticides and Similar Substances, Committee on the Toxicity of Chemicals in Food, Consumer Products and the Environment (COT) September 2003 (www.food.gov.uk/multimedia.pdfs/report(indexed)pdf).

Royal Society Working Group report on endocrine-disrupting

chemicals, chair Professor Patrick Bateson, June 2000 (www.royal soc.ac.uk/files/startfiles/document_111.pdf).

Vyvyan Howard *et al.*, *Endocrine Disrupters: Environmental Health and Policies* (Environmental Science and Technology Library, Kluwer Academic Publishers, June 2001).

J. Blythman, Bite the dust, in the *Guardian*, Food: The Way We Eat Now series, 10 May 2003.

p. 64   *The problem for the supermarkets is*: Friends of the Earth press release, 17 September 2003 (www.foe.co.uk).

'A briefing paper for Defra on the Spanish Horticulture industry', Horticulture study tour to southern Spain, March 2000 (www.adas. co.uk/horticulture/govreports/spain00.htm).

See also Sustain, Salad Days, *Food Facts*, 8, 1999 (www:http:// users.charity.vfree.com/s/sustain/).

CHAPTER 3: BEANS

Dr Andy Jones, formerly of the Stockholm Environment Institute at the University of York, and MEP Caroline Lucas have both done copious work on food distribution and its impact, and I am indebted to both of them.

Tara Garnett, of Transport 2000 Trust, also provided expert research papers and statistics.

The Food Miles debate was started in 1992 by Tim Lang and the SAFE Alliance with its 1994 report on the environmental and social implications of the rapid escalation in the distance the food was travelling. SAFE became Sustain, the alliance for better food and farming, which has published a series of inspiring *Food Facts* booklets. Vicki Hird and Jeannette Longfield of Sustain have both helped with many of my investigations.

Nicola Ellen, Dave Timpson, Peter Ferguson, and Roy Attree of Safeway generously gave several hours to explaining distribution systems to me on my trips to Aylesford. Kevin Hawkins of Safeway facilitated the trips and has remained good-humouredly open, even when he knows my views are opposed to his. I am also grateful to the press office of Tesco for organizing a trip to its distribution centre at

Chepstow, and to Martin Tate and Bob, and to the Asda press office, for facilitating the lorry trip.

The Austrian Consumers' Association provided data on the impact of transport on the nutritional content of food.

Additional statistics came from the Institute of Grocery Distribution, Retail Logistics; Department of Transport, *Transport Statistics, Great Britain*; Achieving the UK's Climate Change Commitments, e3 Consulting, 2002, quoted in T. Garnett, *Wise Moves*, Transport 2000 Trust, 2003.

For sources on oil reserves, see Daniel Yergin, *The Prize: The Epic Quest for Oil, Money and Power* (Simon and Schuster, 1991), and *Commanding Heights: The Battle for the World Economy* (Simon and Schuster, 1999).

On Global Warming, see: *Climate Change. The UK programme, Defra; First Assessment Report*, Intergovernmental Panel on Climate Change, Geneva, 1990; IPCC special report, *Aviation and the Global Environment*, Geneva, 1999.

p. 78   *Tesco lorries belt up and down our motorways*: Institute of Grocery Distribution, *UK Retail Logistics Overview*, January 2003 (www.igd.com).

p. 78   *Between 35 and 40 per cent of lorries on UK roads today*: A. Jones, *Eating Oil* (Sustain, 2001); Department of Transport, *Transport Statistics: Great Britain, 2002*.

p. 78   *The supermarkets Asda, Marks and Spencer, Tesco and Nisa-Today*: the *Grocer*, 4 January 2003.

p. 86   *International trade in food has almost trebled*: C. Lucas, *Stopping the Great Food Swap* (The Greens/European Free Alliance, European Parliament, 2001).

p. 86   *Live animals are not spared*: CIWF, *Live Exports*, 2000.

p. 86   *A ready-made lasagne can contain around twenty different ingredients*: T. Garnett, *Wise Moves* (Transport 2000 Trust, 2003).

p. 88   *Packaging in fact now makes up about a quarter of household waste*: A. Jones, *Eating Oil*, as above. According to the Environment Agency,

7–8 million tonnes of food waste is sent to landfill each year in addition to food packaging.

p. 90   *I have on previous occasions, without trying too hard, filled a supermarket shopping basket*: The way we eat now, the *Guardian*, 10 May 2003. Dr Andy Jones helped calculate the mileage of my basket.

p. 90   *Over 80 per cent of organic food now comes from abroad*: The Soil Association, 2001.

p. 91   *Ironically, the baby potatoes are quite likely to have been in store*: personal communication with potato buyer.

p. 91   *our self-sufficiency in fruit and vegetables has fallen dramatically*: Policy Commission on the Future of Farming and Food, January 2002, from the Cabinet Office (www.cabinet-office.gov.uk/ farming).

p. 92   *The FSA advised recently that frozen broccoli*: BBC News, 31 March 2003.

p. 92   *Their comments followed research by the Austrian Consumers' Association*: VKI, April 2003 (www.konsument.at).

p. 93   *Dr Andy Jones, author of the groundbreaking report*: A. Jones, *Eating Oil*, as above.

p. 93   *The government's report on Climate Change*: Climate Change: The UK Programme (Defra, 2000).

p. 93   *The Intergovernmental Panel on Climate Change (IPCC)*: IPCC, Geneva, 1990.

p. 93   *Since the Industrial Revolution*: For figures on atmospheric carbon dioxide, Sir David King, chief scientific adviser, Climate change science: adapt, mitigate or ignore? *Science* magazine, 9 January 2004; for figures on global warming, The Hadley Centre, *Climate Change, Observations and Predictions* (The Met Office/Defra, December 2003).

p. 94   *Mark Lynas*: M. Lynas, *Hide Tide: News from a Warming World* (Flamingo, extracted in *Granta*, vol 83 (Autumn 2003), www.granta.com).

p. 94   *That we are facing a catastrophic loss*: C. Thomas *et al.*, Extinction risk from climate change, *Nature*, 8 January 2004.

p. 96   *There was particular irony in UK farmers*: personal communications with salad growers.

p. 98　　*David Ingram, the head of logistics for Unilever Frozen Foods, described the experience*: The *Grocer*, Supply Chain supplement, 14 June 2003.

p. 99　　*Dr Colin Campbell is the leading exponent of this view*: Dr C. Campbell, *The Coming Oil Crisis* (Petroconsultants–Multi-Science Publishing, 1997), and subsequent lectures.

p. 99　　*As Richard Hardman, vice-president for exploration*: BBC News, 23 October 2001.

p. 99　　*Recently Matthew Simmons*: M. Ruppert, Peak oil blues, 15 September 2003 (www.GNN.com).

p. 100　　*Since the September 11 terrorist attacks*: Aegis Consultancy, *Implications of Terrorism* report, 2003.

p. 100　　*The government was caught on the hop*: V. Elliott, *The Times*, 14 September 2000.

p. 101　　*In the end it was not a question of days*: personal communications with John White, Federation of Bakers, and anonymous sources.

CHAPTER 4: BREAD

Elizabeth Weisberg and Rachel Duffield of the Lighthouse Bakery, 64 Northcote Road, London SW11, instructed me in the art of real breadmaking in the course of many visits. John White of the Federation of Bakers was generous with his knowledge and kindly organized my visit to the bread factory. Elizabeth David's *English Bread and Yeast Cookery* (Penguin Books, 1979) has said it all before, and is particularly eloquent on the ills of factory bread. I am also indebted to the work of Geoff Tansey and the Agricapital Group of the British Society for Social Responsibility in Science, which produced the report *Our Daily Bread*, sadly no longer in print; however, Tansey's book *The Food System*, co-authored with Tony Worlsey (Earthscan, 2000), is in print. The New Economics Foundation provided detailed analysis of the crisis facing independent grocery shops. The Food Standards Agency helped with information on legislation. On food poverty, see E. Dowler and S. Turner with B. Dobson, *Poverty Bites: Food, Health and Poor Families* (Child Poverty Action Group, London 2001), and Sustain, *Hunger from the Inside: The Experience of Food Poverty in the UK*.

p. 104 *Like much of food manufacturing today, the bread sector has become highly concentrated*: Figures from the Federation of Bakers (www.bakers federation.org.uk). See also Keynote report, *Bread and Bakery Products*, March 2003.

p. 106 *Then in the early 1960s a method evolved*: Information on the Chorleywood Bread Process from Campden and Chorleywood Food Research Association, *The Master Bakers' Book of Breadmaking*, published by the National Association of Master Bakers, 21 Baldock Street, Ware, Herts, SG12 9DH, and the Federation of Bakers.

p. 107 *The ingredients manufacturers still advertise 'pumpable fats'*: For ingredients catalogues, see for example Bakels Products (www.british bakels.co.uk).

p. 107 *'where trans fats are an issue'*: see Aarhus Oils (www.aarhus united.com).

p. 107 *The alternative is generally 'fractionated fat'*: personal communication, Campden and Chorleywood Food Research Association (CCFRA).

p. 108 *Its hardness is double-edged*: Malaysian Palm Oil Board, *Health and Nutritional Aspects of Palm Stearin, Perceptions and Facts* (www.mpob.gov.my/article/nut_stearin.htm).

p. 108 *The most commonly used group of emulsifiers*: personal communication, CCFRA.

p. 108 *Double the amount of yeast*: *The Master Bakers' Book of Breadmaking*, as above.

p. 108 *Salt goes into bread to add flavour*: salt levels in factory bread have been reduced by an average of 21 per cent since 1998 but remain high by Food Standards Agency guidelines. Food Standards Agency (FSA) healthier-eating series (www.foodstandards.gov.uk); FSA, *Determination of sodium content of bread*, 29 November 2001.

p. 108 *It took from 1927*: *Our Daily Bread*, British Society for Social Responsibility in Science, 1978; Bread and Flour regulations 1998; D. J. Jukes, *Food Legislation of the UK* (4th edition, Butterworth-Heinemann, 1997); Food Law pages maintained by David Jukes at the University of Reading (www.fst.rdg.ac.uk/foodlaw).

p. 109 *Since the 1980s, however, companies have been using genetic modifi-*

cation: J. Elkington & J. Hailes, *The New Foods Guide* (Gollancz, 1999); European Food Information Council, *Applications of Food Biotechnology: Enzymes* (www.eufic.org/gb/tech/); personal communication, CCFRA.

p. 109   *A report in the technical journal* New Food: T. Sharp, CCFRA, *Baking*, Issue 4, 2001. See also the technical news on the bakery industry website (www.bod.bakery.co.uk/bodpages.nsf/ Enzymes in Baking).

p. 109   *Getting water into the dough*: *The Master Bakers' Book of Breadmaking* notes: 'The extra water needed in [CBP] is usually about 3.5 per cent more on flour weight than used in a three-hour bulk fermentation process.' For the increase in percentage water added to bread, see the London Food Commission, *Food Adulteration: Water in Food* (Unwin Hyman, 1988).

p. 114   *The diet*: R. Atkins, *Dr Atkins New Diet Revolution* (Vermilion, 2003).

p. 115   *The GI takes glucose as the benchmark*: for a full list of GI values, see K. Foster-Powell *et al.*, International Table of Glycemic Index and Glycemic Load Values, *American Journal of Clinical Nutrition*, (2002; 76, 5–56).

p. 116   *During the milling of white flour*: Food Standards Agency, *McCance and Widdowson's, the Composition of Foods* (6th edition, 2002, Cambridge: Royal Society of Chemistry).

p. 116   *When Lord (then plain Mr) Boothby rose to his feet*: *Our Daily Bread*, as above.

p. 117   *The government now requires millers*: CCFRA, as above.

p. 118   *That's why stone-ground wholemeal tastes different*: The big millers admitted that the proportion of germ and bran varied in wholemeal when they told a government advisory committee in the early 1980s that they could not give precise figures for the amount of dietary fibre in bread; see C. Walker and G. Cannon, *The Food Scandal* (Century, 1984).

p. 119   *An inquiry by the UK's Competition Commission*: The Stationery Office, *Supermarkets*, Competition Commission report, October 2000 (www.ukstate.com).

p. 119   *Professor Paul Dobson of Loughborough University*: P. Dobson, *The Economic Effects of Constant Below-Cost Selling Practices by Grocery Retailers* (Loughborough University/Federation of Bakers, July 2002).

p. 119   *Sainsbury's told the Competition Commission*: Competition Commission, *Supermarkets*, as above.

p. 120   *In July 2003 the cheapest white sliced bread on sale*: Figures from P. Dobson, as above, and Federation of Bakers.

p. 122   *Independent retailing in the UK is reaching a crisis point*: Centre for Food Policy Research, Thames Valley University, *The Crisis in UK Local Food Retailing*, July 2000; New Economics Foundation, *Ghost Town Britain*, 2002.

p. 124   *Food deserts*: BRC press release, Food Deserts a Mirage, 21 November 2002.

p. 126   *The co-op scheme was started here by Eric Samuel*: For details see New Deal for Communities West Ham and Plaistow, *NDC News*, Summer 2003.

CHAPTER 5: APPLES AND BANANAS

Tim Lang, currently professor of food policy at City University, London, has shared much of his academic research on supermarkets for this chapter. His latest book is *Food Wars* (Earthscan, with co-author Michael Heasman). I am also grateful to Bill Vorley of the International Institute of Environment and Development in London for his insights into concentrations of power in the food and agriculture sectors.

Joanna Blythman has been a source of support and inspiration. Sandra Bell of Friends of the Earth provided information from FoE surveys.

I am grateful to Patrick Holden of the Soil Association, who, as well as taking me to Highgrove, has explained many aspects of the food system; and to David Wilson, farm manager of Highgrove for all his help. John Breach, chairman of the British Independent Fruit Growers' Association provided expert practical knowledge. John Vidal of the *Guardian* enlightened me on some of the environmental impacts of intensive farming.

The *Grocer* magazine is the source of some of the details about trade investment and manufacturers' attitudes to supermarkets. Thanks to editor Julian Hunt.

I have also talked to many farmers, packers, manufacturers and their trade associations, and occasional supermarket buyers, to understand how supermarket buying works. Most fear that if they were identified their ability to continue to do business or their jobs would be compromised. Some names have been changed.

p. 131   *A Dutch company provides the packhouses with the machines*: www.greefa.nl.

p. 137   *Figures from the Department of Environment, Food and Rural Affairs*: see *Food and Farming: A Sustainable Future*, report by the Policy Commission on the Future of Farming and Food, chaired by Sir Don Curry, January 2002, available from http://www.cabinet-office.gov.uk.

p. 138   *We have lost nearly two thirds of our apple orchards*: Safe Alliance, *How Green are Our Apples?* (London, 1999).

p. 138   *Supermarkets increasingly buy their apples abroad*: Friends of the Earth, *Survey of Apples and Pears in UK retailers*, November 2001 (www.foe.co.uk/campaigns/real_food).

p. 139   *Each cow may produce twice as many litres of milk a year*: Figures on loss of wildlife from J. Vidal, in the *Guardian*'s The Way We Eat Now series, 17 May 2003.

p. 140   *But in his report on agribusiness*: B. Vorley, *Food Inc.: Corporate Concentration from Farm to Consumer* (UK Food Group/IIED, London, 2004, www.iied.org).

p. 140   *The crisis is not unique to Britain*: Figures from *Food Inc.*, as above.

p. 141   *The battle of the bananas*: personal communication, Bernard Cornibert, Windward Bananas; F. Lawrence, Unfair Trade Winds, the *Guardian*, 17 May 2003; Banana Link (www.bananalink.org.uk); *Food Inc.*, as above.

p. 143   *The stranglehold that supermarket buyers now have*: J. Grievink, *The Supply Chain Funnel in Europe* (Cap Gemini/OECD 2003, lecture at the OECD conference on Changing Dimension of the Food Economy, The Hague, February 2003.

p. 143   *The concentration of retail power*: see M&M Planet Retail (www.planetretail.net) for figures on supermarket market share. For concentration in Europe, see also P. Dobson, *Retailer Buyer Power in European Markets* (Loughborough University Business School, research series paper 2002: 1).

p. 143 *Wal-Mart is not just the world's largest retailer*: Is Wal-Mart too Powerful, *Business Week* magazine, 6 October 2003 (www.business weekeurope.com).

p. 145 *When New Labour came to power*: See, for example, the speech by Stephen Byers, Labour Party Conference, 29 September 1999.

p. 145 *That same spring, the chief executive of Wal-Mart visited England*: *BBC News*, Blair aims for enterprise economy, 6 July 1999.

p. 145 *When the Competition Commission published the results of its inquiry*: *Supermarkets*, a report on the supply of groceries from multiple stores in the UK, by the Competition Commission, October 2000; and *Safeway Merger Inquiries: Remedies Statement*, by the Competition Commission, June 2003 (the Stationery Office, PO Box 29, Norwich NR3 1GN, www.competition-commission.org.uk).

p. 146 *'We all want cheaper food'*: *BBC News*, 2 March 2001.

p. 150 *The chairman and chief executive of Nestlé UK*: the *Grocer*, 4 October 2003.

p. 151 *Writing in the trade magazine the* Grocer, *the sales director of Unilever Bestfoods UK*: 4 October 2003.

p. 151 *Almost half the manufacturers*: the *Grocer*, 15 October 2003.

p. 152 *Asda does not announce its profits separately*: H. Tomlinson, the *Guardian*, 1 December 2003.

p. 152 *Studies in Australia*: www.pag.com.au/articles/strat.htm, quoted in *Food Inc.*, as above.

p. 152 *In Europe 10,000 new food products are launched every year*: T. Lang, the *Guardian*'s The Way We Eat Now series, 17 May 2003.

p. 153 *The concentration of power is narrowing our choice*: the *Grocer*, 1 November 2003.

p. 153 *The recent takeover of Express Dairies*: the *Grocer*, 18 October 2003.

p. 154 *the company's commercial director for non-food, Richard Brasher*: the *Grocer*, 1 November 2003.

p. 156 *In February 2003 the Organization for Economic Co-operation*

and Development: http://webdomino1.oecd.org/comnet/agr/food
eco.nsf/view/html/index/$file/confdoc.htm.

p. 157   *Called* State of the Art in Food: Cap Gemini, Ernst & Young/
Reed Elsevier, *State of the Art in Food, The Changing Face of the
Worldwide Food Industry*, 2003.

p. 158   *Professor John Connor*: J. Connor, *The Changing Structure of
Global Food Markets: Dimensions, Effects, and Policy Implications* (paper
given to the OECD conference on Changing Dimensions of the
Food Economy, The Hague, February 2003, by John M. Connor,
Professor of Industrial Economics, Purdue University, West Lafay-
ette, Indiana, USA). See also *Competition Policy and Food*, a lecture
given to a conference at City University, 24 September, 2003, by
Professor John Cubbin, Economics Department, City University,
available on UK Food Group website.

p. 158   *This time at the UN's Food and Agriculture Organization*:
FAO Urbanization Working Party, Globalization of Food Systems
workshop, 8–10 October 2003 (www.fao.org/es/ESN/nutrition/
national_urbanization_en.stm).

p. 160   *Governments in middle-income countries*: For details of grocery
market shares, see the *Grocer*, 22 March 2003; *Food Inc.*, as above;
M&M Planet Retail, as above.

CHAPTER 6: COFFEE AND PRAWNS

I am grateful to all the staff of Oxfam in the Kampala office who helped
organize my trip to the coffee areas of Uganda. Monica Asekenye was
a knowledgeable and companionable guide, and many of her colleagues
were generous with their time. In the UK, Lys Holdoway also helped
facilitate my trip.

Oxfam's 2002 report on the coffee crisis, *Mugged: Poverty in Your
Coffee Cup* by Charis Gresser and Sophia Tickell, is the source of much
of the detailed analysis, and I am grateful to them for permission to use
it here. Updates are available on Oxfam's websites: www.maketrade
fair.com and www.oxfam.org.uk.

Thanks also to ActionAid for their studies on the impacts of subsidies and WTO investment agreements on development: *Farmgate* and *Unlimited Companies* (www.actionaid.org).

Food Inc. by Bill Vorley (UK Food Group/IIED, London, 2003, www.iied.org) has detailed analysis of concentrations in commodity trading and manufacturing.

The investigation into prawns was originally written for the *Guardian* and published on 19 June 2003. I am indebted to the Environmental Justice Foundation for background analysis and introductions. Thanks in particular to Coralie Thornton and Steve Trent. Thanks are also due to Dr Cecilia Luttrell of the Overseas Development Institute, Hannah Crabtree of ActionAid, and Alex Renton of Oxfam in Bangkok. In Vietnam, I would like to thank Dr Tran Triet of the Vietnam National University in Ho Chi Minh City, who allowed me to join his study tour of the mangroves. Bao Hoa acted as guide and translator. In Thailand I am also indebted to Lek Yimprasert.

p. 161   *'Martin Luther used to wonder'*: Deutsche Bank AG, *Soluble Coffee: A Pot of Gold?*, analyst report by J. Parker and A. Erskine, 2 May 2000, quoted in Oxfam coffee report, *Mugged*, as above.

p. 161   *Nestlé's Nescafé is one of those global A-brands*: Figures on global brands and global food manufacturers from Leatherhead Food International, *Global Food Markets*, and OC&C Strategy Consultants, *Global Giants Index*.

p. 161   *This is where you can see the other half of the picture*: Cap Gemini, Ernst & Young/Reed Elsevier, *State of the Art in Food: The Changing Face of the Worldwide Food Industry*, 2002.

p. 161   *In 2000, Nestlé, the world's largest food manufacturer*: Oxfam, *Mugged*, as above.

p. 162   *three companies – Cadbury Schweppes, Nestlé Rowntree and Mars*: B. Vorley, *Food Inc.*, as above.

p. 163   *Fifty years ago, 50–60p of every £1 spent on food and drink*: T. Lang, the *Guardian*'s The Way We Eat Now series, 17 May 2003.

p. 163   *The significance to developing countries of fluctuations*: Oxfam, *Mugged*, as above.

p. 164   *Kraft, which buys heavily from Vietnam*: Kraft Foods, *Sustainable Coffee* statement (www.kraft.com/corpresp.html).

p. 165   *Its authoritarian leader, Yoweri Museveni*: see, for example, J. Stiglitz, *Globalization and Its Discontents* (Allen Lane, 2002); FT World Report, *Uganda* (FT.com, 15 April 2003).

p. 166   *It was rewarded by being made the first country to qualify for debt relief*: personal communication, DIFD.

p. 166   *In 1994/5 when the price of coffee was high*: Figures from Uganda Coffee Trade Federation, *The Coffee Yearbook, 2000–2001*.

p. 169   *Nestlé says that it is not in favour of low coffee prices*: Nestlé position paper, 18 September 2002, and personal communications.

p. 172   *The road this side of the country runs past the Coca-Cola factory*: *East African Weekly*, 4 March 2002.

p. 175   *When coffee is made into instant*: personal communication, Food Standards Agency.

p. 176   *From 1947 to 1994 the General Agreement on Tariffs and Trade*: For an introduction to international trade rules, see G. Tansey and T. Worsley, *The Food System* (Earthscan, 2000); the Consumers' Association, *Unwrapping the WTO* (2 Marylebone Road, London NW1 4DF); Save the Children Fund briefing papers on WTO and the International Monetary Fund (www.savethechildren.org.uk); and the Bretton Woods Project (www.brettonwoodsproject.org).

p. 176   *The EU's common agricultural policy*: Consumers' Association, *Setting aside the CAP* (2 Marylebone Road, London NW1 4DF).

p. 176   *President Bush's controversial Farm Bill*: BBC News, 10 May 2002.

p. 176   *These subsidies have a devastating effect*: Oxfam, *Rigged Rules and Double Standards*, 2002; ActionAid, *Farmgate: The Developmental Impact of Agricultural Subsidies*, 2002.

p. 177   *Thailand deregulated and liberalized its economy*: For details of export-led growth and its impact in Thailand, see Oxfam, *Thailand: Growth Development and Poverty* (paper presented at the launch of *Rigged Rules and Double Standards* (as above), Bangkok, 2001); Food and Agriculture Organisation/International Food Policy Research Institute, *Livestock to 2020: The Next Food Revolution* (1999); D. Burch et al., *Regulation and Restructuring of Agri-Foods in Post-Crisis Asia* (paper to International Rural Sociological Association Congress, Brazil, 2000); D. Hoffman, *Asian Livestock to Year 2000 and Beyond* (FAO, 1999); L. Garces, *The Detrimental Impacts of Industrial Animal Agriculture* (Compassion in World Farming, 2002).

p. 178   *The effect of moving to food for export*: F. Lawrence, the *Guardian*'s The Way We Eat Now series, 10 May 2003.

p. 180   *Aid agencies, including Save the Children Fund and Oxfam*: see E. Delap and R. Lugg, *Not Small Fry: Children's Work in Bangladesh's Shrimp Industry* (SCFUK, 1999); A. Renton, *Risking It All for Prawns* (Oxfam, August 2001, www.oxfamgb.org/eastasia/vietnam).

p. 180   *The pattern of events accompanying the arrival of large-scale prawn farming*: See Environmental Justice Foundation reports, *Risky Business: Vietnamese Shrimp Aquaculture* (2003) and *Smash and Grab: Conflict, Corruption and Human Rights Abuses in the Shrimp Farming Industry* (2003) (www.ejfoundation.org); and C. Luttrell, *Embracing and Resisting the Global Shrimp Boom* (IASCP, 2002).

p. 183   *About 50 per cent of prawn ponds in Thailand*: A. Quarto, *The Rise and Fall of the Blue Revolution* (www.earthisland.org).

p. 185   *When the UK Food Standards Agency (FSA) began testing*: FSA, 14 and 22 March 2002.

p. 185   *And although the World Bank has encouraged the trade*: Tariff figures from Renton, *Risking It All for Prawns*, as above.

p. 186   *Oxfam's influential study*: *Rigged Rules and Double Standards*, as above.

p. 186   *Powerful voices have joined the call for reform*: Stiglitz, *Globalization and Its Discontents*, as above.

p. 186   *But there are still plenty of economists*: See, for example, E. Graham, *Fighting the Wrong Enemy* (Institute for International Economics, 2000); J. Bhagwati, *Free Trade Today* (Princeton, 2003) and 'The Poor's Best Hope', in the *Economist*, 22 June 2002; D. Henderson, *Anti-liberalism* (Institute of Economic Affairs, 2000); D. Dollar and A. Kray, World Bank Development Research Group, *Spreading the Wealth* (Foreign Affairs, February 2002).

p. 187   *He agreed to write two pieces for the Guardian*: S. Byers, 19 May 2003, and The Way We Eat Now series, 21 May 2003.

p. 188   *I asked him what had led him to this new view*: F. Lawrence, the
Guardian, 19 May 2003.

p. 189   *The EU sugar regime*: personal communications, Defra, and
ActionAid.

p. 189   *The inevitable response from the incumbent negotiators*: V. Amos
and P. Hewitt, letter to the *Guardian*, 21 May 2003.

p. 190   *They have grubbed up their unprofitable coffee bushes*: Oxfam, *Crisis
in Coffee* update, 2003 (www.oxfam.org.uk); M. Thomson, Ethiopia
Swaps Coffee for Drugs, BBC *Today* programme, 10 December
2003.

CHAPTER 7: THE READY MEAL

Caroline Walker, who died in 1988, first explained the relationship
between modern adulterations of food and ill-health to me. I am indebted
to her pioneering spirit. Craig Sams first opened my eyes to the relationship between subsidies and cheap ingredients for processed foods. Tim
Lobstein and Kath Dalmeny of the Food Commission have shared their
research over the years. David Walker of Shropshire County Council has
acted as a walking dictionary of food adulteration and meat processing.
Marks & Spencer have helped with detailed inquiries. Thanks also to
the press office of the Food Standards Agency for details on legislation.

p. 191   *Britain is in fact the largest consumer in Europe of ready meals*:
Mintel, February 2001; www.readymealsinfo.com.

p. 193   *The maximum recommended salt intake*: Food Standards Agency,
Ready Meals Salt Levels Revealed, 10 June 2003.

p. 193   *Frozen food manufacturers point out*: the *Grocer*, 21 June 2003.

p. 194   *In fact, a quarter of all processed foods*: US Corn Refiners' Association (www.corn.org); Economic Research Service, US Department
of Agriculture, briefing room: corn (www.usda.gov); Institute of
Food Research, Norwich, *Soya* briefing paper (www.ifr.ac.uk).

p. 194   *As the US Corn Refiners' Association explains*: www.corn.org/
web/tapping.htm.

p. 195   *In an article in* Innovative Food Ingredients *magazine*: S. F.
Shoesmith, Innovative Uses of Corn Starch in Food, *Innovative Food*

Ingredients (business briefing, World Markets Research Centre, 2002, www.wmrc.com).

p. 195 *In October 2003, Shropshire trading standards officers*: Shropshire County Council Trading Standards Service, *Chicken Survey*, 17 October 2003.

p. 196 *A strawberry-flavoured yoghurt has had a briefer encounter with the fruit*: F. Lawrence (ed.), *Additives* (Century, 1986); J. Meek, the *Guardian*'s The Way We Eat Now series, 17 May 2003.

p. 196 *Greg Critser describes the effect*: G. Critser, *Fat Land* (Penguin, 2003).

p. 197 *Soya oil is the commonest in processed foods*: US Department of Agriculture ERS, briefing: soybeans and oil crops; USDA/PG/Agra, *Soyabeans and Derivatives*, 1999; Sustain, *Fat of the Land*, 2000. Latin American soya production has also expanded rapidly in the last few years.

p. 197 *Hydrogenation was developed in the 1920s*: Sustain, *Fat of the land*, 2000; C. Sams, *The Little Food Book* (Alastair Sawday Publishing, 2003).

p. 198 *It is now generally accepted that it is safest to avoid hydrogenated fats*: US Food and Drug Administration, *Revealing Trans Fats*, September–October 2003; FSA, *Healthier Eating, Ask an Expert, Hydrogenated and Trans Fats* (www.foodstandards.gov.uk).

p. 199 *A new system of direct payments to American farmers*: M. Pollan, The (Agri)Cultural Contradictions of Obesity, *New York Times*, 12 October 2003; Critser, *Fat Land*, as above; USDA.

p. 199 *There has also been a six-fold increase in the production of palm oil*: Sustain, *Fat of the Land* (2000); Malaysian Palm Oil Board.

p. 199 *Concentrations of power in this part of agribusiness*: B. Vorley, *Food Inc.* (UK Food Group/IIED, London, 2004).

p. 199 *Needless to say, these corporations represent powerful political lobbies*: For a detailed account of the sugar lobby's efforts to control US government dietary advice, see M. Nestle, *Food Politics: How the Food Industry Influences Nutrition and Health* (University of California Press, 2002); and G. Cannon, *The Politics of Food* (Century, 1988).

p. 199 *When the World Health Organization prepared its global strategy*:

S. Bosely, US accused of sabotaging obesity strategy, the *Guardian*, 16 January 2004.

p. 200   *Around $20 billion is spent each year by the food industry on chemical additives*: *Innovative Food Ingredients*, as above; T. Lang & E. Millstone, *The Atlas of Food* (Earthscan, 2003).

p. 201   *Erik Millstone*: see *Atlas of Food*, as above; also, E. Millstone, *Food Additives* (Penguin, 1986) and *Additives: A Guide for Everyone* (Penguin, 1988).

p. 201   *Food manufacturers have always cut corners*: E. P. Thompson, The Moral Economy of the English Crowd in the Eighteenth Century, *Past and Present*, 50, 1971; T. Smollett, *Humphry Clinker* (Penguin, 1967); C. Walker and G. Cannon, *The Food Scandal* (Century, 1984).

p. 202   *His work,* There is Death in the Pot: F. Accum, *A Treatise on Adulterations of Food and Culinary Poisons*, 1820 (Longman, Hurst, Peel, Orme and Brown).

p. 202   *Thomas Wakley*: F. Bing, Frederick Accum: A Biographical Sketch, *Journal of Nutrition*, 89, 1966; E. Gray, *By Candlelight: The Life of Dr Arthur Hill Hassall* (Robert Hale, 1983); A. Amos, *Pure Food and Pure Food Legislation* (Butterworths, 1960).

p. 204   *The pork sausage bit of my lamb casserole*: F. Lawrence (ed.), *Additives* (Century, 1986).

p. 204   *Nor do the individual ingredients of all 'compound ingredients'*: Personal communication, Food Standards Agency; Directive 2003/89/EC of the European Parliament and of the Council, 10 November 2003; C. Sams, *The Little Food Book*, as above.

p. 205   *Le Salon International de l'Alimentation*: SIAL (Paris, 2002, www.sial.fr).

p. 207   *The WHO summarized the situation*: WHO, *The Impact of Food and Nutrition on Public Health* (Regional Office for Europe, Copenhagen, 2000), and WHO/FAO, *Report of the Joint Expert Consultation on Diet, Nutrition and the Prevention of Chronic Diseases*, 916 (Rome, 2003).

p. 207   *As Western diets high in fats, sugars and salt*: WHO/FAO, 916, as above.

p. 207   *Professor Philip James*: P. James, *Nutrition and the Future* (Lecture given to the Caroline Walker Trust, 1997).

p. 208   *When we eat highly processed, energy-dense foods*: A. M. Prentice, S. A. Jebb, Fast foods, energy density and obesity: a possible mechanistic link, *Obesity Reviews*, 28 October 2003 (as announced at www.mrc.ac.uk/txt/public-22_october_2003); see also Dr Jebb on supermarket ready meals in the same link.

p. 208   *And a product like high-fructose corn syrup*: Evidence presented to the House of Commons Health Committee inquiry into obesity, 27 November 2003; Critser, *Fat Land*, as above.

p. 208   *The International Obesity Taskforce*: press briefing, London, 11 November 2003.

p. 208   *The National Audit Office report*: NAO, *Tackling Obesity in England* 2001.

p. 209   *According to a more recent survey*: Department of Health/National Centre for Social Research/Department of Epidemiology, Royal Free, December 2003.

p. 209   *There is also a clear link between poverty and obesity*: DoH/NCSR/Royal Free, as above.

p. 209   *Type 2 diabetes, which used to be called adult-onset diabetes*: S. Bosely, Diabetes creating world catastrophe, warns leading doctor, the *Guardian*, 25 August 2003; see also International Diabetes Federation.

p. 210   *The Wanless report on the National Health Service*: HM Treasury, *Wanless Review: Securing Our Future Health*, April 2002.

p. 210   *Coronary heart disease is the biggest killer*: British Heart Foundation statistics (www.heartstats.org).

p. 210   *Although there has been much dispute over the years*: Department of Health, *Nutritional Aspects of the Development of Cancer*, 1998; World Cancer Research Fund, *Food, Nutrition, and the Prevention of Cancer: a Global Perspective*, 1997.

p. 210   *Children do particularly badly*: Report of the Policy Commission on the Future of Farming and Food (Cabinet Office, January 2002).

p. 211   *Professor Michael Crawford*: M. & S. Crawford, *What We Eat Today* (Neville Spearman, 1972).

p. 212 *The ratio of omega-6 to omega-3*: M. Small, The Happy Fat, *New Scientist*, 175, 24 August 2002.

p. 213 *Soils fed only with artificial fertilizers*: A.-M. Mayer, Historical Changes in Mineral Content of Fruits and Vegetables, *Agricultural Production and Nutrition* (Tufts University School of Nutrition Science and Policy, May 1997); replicated by D. Thomas, *The Loss of Minerals in Our Food between 1940 and 1991* (Cleave Lecture, delivered to the McCarrison Society, 20 November 2003).

p. 213 *Joseph Hibbeln*: Small, The Happy Fat, as above; D. Horrobin, Omega-3 Fatty Acid for Schizophrenia, *American Journal of Psychiatry* (2003; 160: 188–9).

p. 214 *There is mounting evidence that deficiencies are involved*: See, for example, A. J. Richardson, B. K. Puri, A randomized, double-blind, placebo-controlled study of the effects of supplementation with highly unsaturated fatty acids on ADHD-related symptoms in children with specific learning disabilities, *Prog Neuropsychopharm Biol Psychiat* (2002; 26 (2) 233–9); A. J. Richardson, Fatty Acids in Dyslexia, Dyspraxia, ADHD and the Autistic Spectrum, *Nutrition Practitioner* (2001; 2(3), 18–24); and www.durhamtrial.org.

p. 214 *During the study, which took place in one of Britain's maximum security prisons*: B. Gesch *et al.*, Influence of Supplementary Vitamins, Minerals and Essential Fatty Acids on the Anti-Social Behaviour of Young Adult Prisoners, *British Journal of Psychiatry* (2002; 181, 22–8).

p. 216 *A study by the Consumers' Association*: School Dinners, *Which?* magazine, March 2003.

p. 219 *Children today also consume thirty times the amount of soft drinks*: School Dinners, *Which?* magazine, as above.

p. 220 *The time we give to food*: Figures from Unilever.

p. 220 *The food industry spends over £450 million a year*: C. Parry, End of the Party, *Marketing Week*, 20 November 2003.

p. 220 *The big four categories of food advertised*: Food Standards agency, *Review of Research on the Effects of Food Promotion to Children*, by Professor Gerard Hastings *et al.* (University of Strathclyde, September 2003).

p. 220 TV Dinners: Sustain, *TC Dinners*, 2001.

p. 220   *Marketing experts have worked out ways*: M. K. Lewis and A. J. Hill, Food Advertising on British Children's Television, *International Journal of Obesity* (1998; 2, 206–14).

p. 221   *Dr Aric Sigman*: *Blackmail*, Co-op inquiry into the Ethics of Food and Drink Advertising to Children (The Co-op, July 2000).

p. 221   *the independent campaign group the Food Commission*: K. Dalmeny, E. Hanna, T. Lobstein, *Broadcasting Bad Health* (International Association of Consumer Food Organizations, July 2003).

p. 221   *The brilliance of the techniques*: Advertising Effectiveness Awards, Institute of Practitioners in Advertising, 2002.

p. 222   *Cadbury's was severely criticized*: The Food Commission, press release, 29 April 2003.

p. 223   *The big guns from the manufacturers*: Oral evidence presented to the House of Commons Health Committee inquiry into obesity, 27 November 2003.

p. 224   *Professor James traces much of the problem*: James, *Nutrition and the Future*, as above.

p. 225   *An analysis of its accounts for 2003*: FSA, 2003 Department Report (www.food.gov.uk/multimedia/pdfs/departmental_report03.pdf), quoted in T. Lang lecture in ESRC Cultures of Consumption series at Royal Society, London, 17 November 2003.

Index